Betrayal in th[illegible]

Vol

By Dan Moorhouse

Also by Dan Moorhouse

On This Day Series:

On this day in the Wars of the Roses

On this day in the Hundred Years War

Educational Publications:

Medicine and Health Through Time: People and Places

Medicine and Health Through Time: Review and Revise

GCSE Modern World History Dynamic Learning

GCSE History Germany 1918-1945 Dynamic Learning

Dan Moorhouse dan@schoolshistory.org.uk

www.thewarsoftheroses.co.uk

facebook.com/thewarsoftheroses

Dedication

This book is dedicated to the memory of

Andy Maltas

A very good friend who passed away as I was writing this book.

Acknowledgements

Thanks are due to the people and organisations who have offered assistance or support during the writing of this book. In particular: the Battlefields Trust, Graham Evans, David Grummitt, Su Harrison, Kathy Jones, the Northamptonshire Battlefields Society, Richard III Society, and Tim Upton for their advice and thoughts. Finally, I owe a great deal to the people who have supported me whilst I was working on this book, in particular to Zenta Brice, Sherri Oates and Victoria Scott. Cover design by Corinne M Knight.

Contents

Wars of the Roses: Chronology

31 August 1422	Death of King Henry V.
14 January 1423	The opening of Henry Vis first Parliament.
30 July 1447	Richard 3rd Duke of York appointed Lieutenant of Ireland.
2 May 1450	Murder of William de la Pole Duke of Suffolk.
3 July 1450	Jack Cade crosses London Bridge and declares himself Mayor.
7 September 1450	Richard Duke of York returns from Ireland.
3 March 1452	Standoff at Dartford.
17 July 1453	Battle of Castillon (Last battle of the Hundred Years War).
10 August 1453	Henry VI suffered mental breakdown.
1453-54	First Protectorate of Richard 3rd Duke of York.
25 December 1454	Henry VI regained his senses.
22 May 1455	First Battle of St. Albans.

1455-1456	Second Protectorate of Richard 3rd Duke of York.
13 January 1456	Resignation of Richard Duke of York as Protector.
20 April 1456	The Earl of Warwick appointed Captain of Calais.
24 March 1458	Loveday Parade at St. Pauls Cathedral.
23 September 1459	Battle of Blore Heath.
12 October 1459	Battle of Ludford.
20 November 1459	Parliament of Devils opens.
15 January 1460	Raid on Sandwich.
10 July 1460	Battle of Northampton.
25 October 1460	Act of Accord.
30 December 1460	Battle of Wakefield.
2 February 1461	Battle of Mortimer's Cross.
17 February 1461	Second Battle of St. Albans.
29 March 1461	Battle of Towton.
28 June 1461	Coronation of Edward IV.
25 April 1464	Battle of Hedgeley Moor.

1 May 1464	Secret marriage of Edward IV and Elizabeth Woodville.
15 May 1464	Battle of Hexham.
24 July 1465	Henry VI captured by Yorkists.
24 July 1469	Battle of Edgcote.
12 March 1470	Battle of Losecote Field.
22 July 1470	Angers Agreement.
14 April 1471	Battle of Barnet.
4 May 1471	Battle of Tewkesbury.
21 May 1471	Death of King Henry VI.
29 August 1475	Treaty of Picquigny.
18 February 1478	The trial of the Duke of Clarence.
9 April 1483	Death of King Edward IV.
26 June 1483	Richard III accedes to the throne.
7 August 1485	Henry Tudor lands at Milford Haven.
22 August 1485	Battle of Bosworth.
18 January 1486	Marriage of King Henry VII to Elizabeth of York.
16 June 1487	Battle of Stoke Field.

4

Chapter One. Introduction: kinship, patronage, and loyalty in the late medieval period

Betrayal, or perceptions of it, lay at the heart of many of the key moments in the era of the Wars of the Roses. It was an era dominated politically by assertions of the betrayal of the laws of nature and inheritance. It triggered a dynastic clash that raises questions as to whether oaths of allegiance could legitimately be replaced with claiming of the crown.

From this argument of dynastic right and betrayal stemmed a series of wars that led to the crown changing hands in 1461, 1470, 1471, 1483, and 1485. These changes often resulted from actions that were perceived by some contemporary chroniclers, and the people involved in the events, as being caused by treachery. At the outset of these wars were accusations of political duplicity, contributing to the emergence of factions. Throughout the 1450s charges of treason were levelled at many of the key players in what would become known as the Wars of the Roses. It led to underhand dealings and manipulation of political systems to undermine rivals. Loyalties were tested, often changed, as men of power sought to enhance their positions, often through underhand methods.

Turncoats abound in the history of the Wars of the Roses. In the middle of the conflicts Richard Neville, 16th Earl of Warwick masterminded rebellions and then formed an alliance with Margaret of Anjou, whom he previously clashed with. George, Duke of Clarence raised forces against and for his brother, King

Edward IV. The events of 1483 included executions of Earls and Lords on charges of treason. The Duke of Buckingham who had played a pivotal role in the accession of Richard III soon rose in revolt against the very man he had been politically close to just months earlier. At Bosworth Field there was the infamous decision of Sir William Stanley to commit to the side of Henry Tudor at a crucial moment.

These are merely a snapshot of some of the better-known examples of deeds that are often considered to be betrayals. The reality is that there were many more acts that were clear breaches of trust, perhaps non less so than the location of King Henry VI being given away in 1465. Other examples include the defection, mid battle, of Lord Grey of Ruthin at Northampton in 1460 and the possibility of Yorkist plans being handed to the Lancastrians by a defector as the Second Battle of St. Albans broke out. So too are there more obvious acts of treason that are a violation of the laws of the land and responsibilities of a subject. Within the context of a civil war, the definition of what constituted treason was often arbitrary with summary judgement. An act of betrayal could be as simple in the context of the day as having fought for or backed the losing side.

In the medieval mindset the idea of betraying somebody was frequently couched in terms of something being unnatural, a great treason, against god's will. A most succinct definition of how a medieval mind worked in relation to the concept of betrayal can be found in one line from the 1485 proclamation made by Richard III against Henry Tudor.

"...contrary to the pleasure of God and against all truth, honour and nature[1]"

Whilst that proclamation was a rallying cry and a denunciation of a claim, it acts as a useful starting point for a study of the topic of betrayal. The reality is that acts that the modern mind would find virtually unforgiveable were viewed differently in the 1400s. Changing allegiance during the Wars of the Roses did not necessarily result in someone being viewed in a negative light for very long. Within this book there are several examples of men who did exactly that, in some cases more than once, often with little or no consequence.

Betrayal was not restricted to the great and the good of the day. The power of civic bodies was growing, and if the Earl of Warwick was a Kingmaker, so too can that term be applied to the City of London, or to Calais. This was evident at a relatively early stage in the Wars of the Roses. In an example that shows how easily a town or city can change its mind, or allegiance, the City of London in 1460:

"...decided to resist the entry of the Yorkists and ordered measures to be taken to defend the city; within two days, however, they were less confident or less loyal, and a deputation was sent...[2]"

Betrayal during this conflict needs to be set against the values of the day. Monarchs had a great number of rights but equally they had numerous responsibilities. Kings were expected to rule effectively. This related to the priority areas of military matters;

maintaining law and order; effective and efficient economic policies; diplomatic successes; and ensuring that the church could effectively provide for the spiritual wellbeing of the nation.

The nobility in turn had a responsibility to the gentry and commons to administer this type of good lordship in the lands they held from the king. They were also expected to aid the crown as required, through good lordship, efficient collection of taxes, and with military support in times of threat. At each level of society there was the two-way flow of rights and responsibilities. These extended into the church and towns. Within towns the mayor, aldermen, guilds and in the unique case of Calais the garrison and Company of Staplers expected good governance from the crown. In return, they were expected to fulfil a variety of functions on behalf of the state.

A key question in a study of this period is what happens when this system breaks down? If somebody, or an institution, fails to deliver on its responsibilities, what is the consequence? On a simple level the offender can be dealt with through the justice system. The mechanisms for justice are top down though. What happens when the responsibilities that an Earl, Duke, or King, are not being fulfilled?

If council, or the king himself, is failing to deliver on things that are their areas of responsibility are they betraying the people? How can a king or his closest advisors be held to account? By the council, who is appointed by the crown? By the lords, who hold lands and grants from the king and his parliament?

Mechanisms for combatting poor governance are hard to implement. If government is dominated by people who are perceived by some to be failing, it is unlikely that they would tolerate being held to account.

And this is very evident. 1450 saw revolts in Kent led by Jack Cade. It saw William de la Pole, Duke of Suffolk murdered after having been exiled by parliament. In just these examples we see that the system could work, the Duke of Suffolk was held to account by parliament. It also shows that when good lordship and governance is not in place, the commons may feel that their only option is to take up arms to force change.

Good governance and fair application of justice was a problematic issue in the 1440s and 1450s. There was a break down in the effective management of disputes over awarded positions, inheritance, and rights to land. The system for dealing with such matters was one of arbitration. However, in this period the mechanisms for dealing with disagreements broke down. And it did so in cases where very powerful men were making counter claims against each other.

When the nobility made alternative claims on land the matter ought to be settled through hearings held by a more senior magnate, by the collective lords of the land, or by the king. The structure is in place to enable a disagreement at any level to be dealt with through judgement at an appropriate level, with recourse to take the matter further. England in the 1440s and 1450s saw this process challenged and, in many cases, broken.

Disputes happened across the country. In the south west the Courtenay Earls of Devon had been involved in wranglings over land with the Bonville family since the mid-14th century. In the 15th century this feud had developed. Both families held the stewardship of the Duchy of Cornwall at various points. It was highly lucrative, and both families were eager to retain the position at the expense of the other.

The families had clashed over these rights in the 1440s with attacks on property increasing to a level that Thomas Courtenay and William Bonville were summoned to appear at Council for arbitration and a final settlement of the dispute. In cases of strong government and an expectation that the decisions made would be final, this would be the end of the matter as the consequences of not adhering to the council's decisions would be clear. By 1449, that was not the case. Thomas Courtenay, Earl of Devon lay siege to a Bonville castle at Taunton for a year. That an Earl could besiege another noble's castle for a year without intervention from the Council or King is indicative of how fractured the systems for enforcing law and order were in places.

Similar disputes were taking place elsewhere. Most famously in the north east, where several disputes broke out in the 1440s. In common with the feuds in the south west, these centred around land and roles. Two branches of the Neville family, the Percy family, and the Prince-Bishop of Durham became embroiled in quarrels over rights to important positions, and rights to land and castles. These disputes also saw arbitration, some of which worked. However, by the early 1450s the disagreements between the Neville's of Middleham and the Percy family turned violent. A skirmish at Heworth Moor in 1453 was followed by attempts by the crown to arbitrate and bring about a peaceful solution to the conflict. It failed as both families engaged in attacks on property. Later another skirmish took place, at Stamford Bridge near York.

These feuds made it clear that the king was failing to maintain law and order. They also led to the adversaries in each of the regional conflicts seeking assistance from other nobles. In turn this led to factionalism at court becoming entrenched as men enjoying the patronage of senior nobles formed close alliances around those dominant peers[3].

Whilst these alliances in themselves are not acts of betrayal, they formed in part since the nobles involved felt that their rights had not been upheld, or to protect what they believed was theirs by right. In some cases, this implied that the responsibilities of the crown had not been fulfilled. At times withing the build up to the conflict and during it, some nobles felt as though they had been betrayed by the system, or persons within it. From this arises suspicion, anger, and war.

The implications of poor governance were recognised at the time. *An English Chronicle* noted it in 1459:

"The Evils of Misgovernment

In this same time the realm of England was out of all good governance, as it had been many days before, for the King was simple and led by covetous counsel, and owed more than he was worth. His debts increased daily, but payment there was none; all the possessions and lordships that pertained to the Crown the King had given away, some to lords and some to other simple persons, so that he had almost nought to live on. And such impositions as were put to the people, as taxes, tallages and quinzimes (fifteenths), all that came from them were spent in vain, for he held no household nor maintained no wars. For these misgovernances, and for many other, the hearts of the people were turned away from them that had the land in governance, and their blessing was turned into cursing.[4]"

These issues of good governance, rights, and fairness are recurrent themes in the arguments presented by the belligerents in the Wars of the Roses as they justify their cause. *The Kentish Memorial*, a 1460 Yorkist statement of their grievances and demands reiterates the manifesto issued by Jack Cade in 1450 and makes the case for good governance at the highest level to be fair and just:

"They say, that our Sovereign Lord is above law, and that the law was made but to his pleasure; and that he may make and break it as often as him list, without any distinction. The contrary is true. And also, that he should not have been sworn, in his coronation to keep it, which we conceive for the highest point of treason that any subject may do against his prince, to make him reign in perjury[5]".

It was an argument that was used again in the period 1469-71 as rebellions and the alliance of the Earl of Warwick and Margaret of Anjou sought to gain support. As such, the contemporary argument presented, by opponents of the crown, was that the crown had a duty and that breaking that duty, as noted in the *Kentish Memorial*, can be classed as an act of treason. By this logic, opposing or turning on a king or magnate who is not fulfilling his duty, is not an act of betrayal. Conversely the people who turn against the crown have sworn oaths of allegiance. Such oaths were taken incredibly seriously in the late medieval era. At every level from kingship to mayors' oaths were taken. They legitimised authority and affirmed the responsibility to fulfil their role according to law and customary practice[6].

Similarly, the granting of lands, grants, roles, and titles was expected to be conducted in a fair manner. Some roles were hereditary, others customary, and many changed hands because of attainders and land redistribution during conflicts such as the Wars of the Roses. Any such role or land grant that was awarded due to a noble's contribution to the cause of the king was highly prized. The example of Richard, Duke of Gloucester, being granted Neville lands in 1471 shows how well a senior member of the king's close council could benefit. With much wealth and prestige being attached to such grants the assumption was that they would be for life, or for as long as the awarding monarch remained in power. When changes in the distribution of lands and titles were made, was that a betrayal on the part of the king? In 1471 John Neville certainly believed it was the case. He had been rewarded for his significant role in the north east with the Earldom of Northumberland. It strengthened Neville hegemony in the region and John, as Earl of Northumberland, gained much prestige through the roles along the Scottish Marches associated with the Earldom. Following the uprisings of 1469 Edward IV decided that it would be a better option to restore the Percy family to the Earldom. John Neville was compensated with an elevation to the rank of Marquis and granted lands elsewhere. However, the prestige of Northumberland and its military roles were the prize that the Marquis of Montagu had wanted. It led to him declaring for King Henry VI and presenting an immediate threat to King Edward IV.

"the said Marquis Montague hated the King, and purposed to have taken him; and when he was within a mile of King Edward, he declared to the people, that were there gathered with him, how King Edward had first given to him the Earldom of Northumberland, and how he took it from him, and gave it (to) Harry Percy[7]"

Over the period 1455 to 1487 the cry of 'treason' was heard or written numerous times. Indeed, at some point every crowned king of the second half of the century had been attainted by parliament. By legal definition at some stage all these men had been considered traitors. The same is true of many of the nobility. Senior dukes were also attainted, including Richard, 3rd Duke of York, George, Duke of Clarence, and Richard, Duke of Gloucester. Many nobles met their end at the hands of an executioner. Others changed sides on a regular basis, with some finding longstanding notoriety as being perpetual turncoats and battle avoiders.

The aim of this book is to assess what the contemporary view of Betrayal was. A selection of people, and places, have been chosen to represent a broad spectrum. With so many examples of perceived betrayal to select from, some difficult decisions as to who to include, or omit, were made. To include all the most famous examples would have resulted in a narrow view of the roles of Kings, Dukes, and the most powerful of the Earls. Instead, a selection has been made that covers some of the more famous, or infamous, examples of perceived betrayal. Alongside these are examples of men who changed sides, of towns who influenced national affairs, and of people who made decisions based upon their choice of whom to be loyal to. Additional examples of perceived betrayal will be explored in volumes two and three of this series.

Chapter Two. George, Duke of Clarence

Described by Shakespeare as *'false, fleeting, perjured, Clarence,*[1]*'* George Plantagenet is most often remembered for his demise. Arrested on his brother's orders, tried, sentenced to death, and reputedly executed by being drowned in a barrel of Malmsey Wine. On the face of it, George, Duke of Clarence is the textbook example of a man who betrayed those to whom he owed loyalty. His adherence to rules of kinship, patronage, and ducal rights and responsibilities seems to have been severely lacking. Yet George, only eleven at the time his brother seized the crown and was an active magnate for a decade. It was a time of war, political intrigue, manipulation, deception, double bluff, and military strategy. Had he been so disloyal to those to whom he owed so much; would he have been allowed to hold rank for so long? Would a King, or council, have enabled his growth in stature as a landed magnate, facilitated his maintenance of a large household, or accepted ongoing abuses of diplomatic, legal, and traditional systems and networks? George Plantagenet, Duke of Clarence, was many things. In a volatile society in the middle of a series of civil wars, he is perhaps the most enigmatic of any of those at the heart of events. His is a story of betrayals, but also one of flawed systems and the failures of others.

How did George's loyalties come to be viewed in such different ways in a relatively short period of time?

Born in Ireland in 1449, George was the fifth son, third to survive infancy, of Richard, 3rd Duke of York, and Cecily Neville. His father returned to England from his Lieutenancy of Ireland whilst George was an infant. For most of his childhood George was raised by his mother. In these early years of George's life there was not an expectation that he would inherit the highest of titles.

The events of 1459-61 saw George elevated from a noble but relatively unimportant third surviving son to being the heir of his elder brother, the newly crowned Edward IV. In quick succession George was knighted, created Duke of Clarence, elected as a Knight of the Bath, and granted many estates and administrative roles. George was still a minor whilst these appointments were made. His affairs were managed by a household appointed on his behalf, and he lived in Greenwich Palace under his mother's care.

George gave homage as a magnate to his brother on 10 July 1466. Upon taking up his position as Duke he had a range of rights and responsibilities. The Duke's lands were centred around Tutbury Castle in Staffordshire. He made the castle his home and set about the duties of a landed magnate. This included responsibility for justice within his lands, acquisition, and patronage of retainers and attendance at parliament.

The power, authority, and wealth that George had bestowed upon him in 1466 were all provided for him by his brother, through parliamentary grants. He was a beneficiary of patronage and grants far more than that which was required to maintain the household, lifestyle, and offices of a Duke. This is demonstrated at the first parliamentary opportunity that there was to take the Duke's majority into account. The King himself handed in bills relating to the Duke's claims under the proposed Act of Resumption. That Act then provided:

"...lordships, manors, lands, tenements and possessions which shall be given or granted, or confirmed by us to our said brother to make up the said annual sums or sum of 5,600 marks in possession and 1,000 marks in reversion,[2]"

The patronage and grants offered by Edward IV to his brother were roughly three times more than the minimum amount required for a Dukedom. This is quite a remarkable amount, almost matching the income of his father which was in the region of £4,000 a year[3]. George was therefore being provided for handsomely by his brother. This was extended through Edward IV's plans for George to marry for diplomatic reasons. This would bring a dower, and potentially lands in the future.

As a young, wealthy, and powerful magnate George was at the heart of government and his brother's political thinking. He owed this to kinship and patronage that was publicly celebrated. George's ducal title was a nod to the House of York's hereditary claim to the throne. His estates and income reflected his affinity to King Edward IV, his position at the time as heir to the throne, and to his importance in the future as an ally. Roles that were assigned to the Duke were also symbolic.

The Lieutenancy of Ireland had been his father's position when George was born, in Ireland. There too were the roles as a justice of the peace and administrator which reflect the responsibilities that go hand in hand with the patronage bestowed upon a noble of his rank. George, in short, owed everything to the successes of his father and brother in firstly staking the claim to the throne, and then securing it.

Despite the seemingly lavish settlement rested on the Duke of Clarence through the Act of Resumption, it was not enough to cover the expenditure of George. He set about improving Tutbury Castle, adding new buildings, and setting out an ordinance for his household. His intended household was proposed in an ordinance in 1468. It was vast. At an annual cost of £4500 with 399 staff the ordinance drawn up by George was more than the income he derived from the Act of Resumption. Had it ever been implemented; it would have been the largest household of any noble in Medieval English history[4]. Lavish expenditure of this kind is not unheard of but until George is generating significant revenues from his estates, the financial burden ought, perhaps, to tie him more closely to the crown and its patronage.

King Edward IV now wanted to utilise this elevated position for diplomatic purposes. On 22 March 1466 powers were granted to commissioners to treat with the Duke of Burgundy with regards a series of diplomatic matters[5]. One was the repeal of restrictions on Anglo-Burgundian trade, the second a marriage union between the King Edward and George's sister, Margaret of York, to the Duke of Burgundy. The third strand of negotiations was to be for a marriage to be agreed between the Duke of Clarence and Mary, daughter of the Duke of Burgundy and sole heiress to the Burgundian empire.

The proposed duo of marriages would be diplomatically significant. It would bind two of the economic powerhouses of Western Europe together. It would see Margaret as the Duchess of Burgundy and George would almost certainly become Duke of Burgundy by right of his wife should the proposals come to fruition. This would be of benefit to England in terms of trading links into the Low Countries and cement military ties with the Burgundians which would minimise the risks of any recurrence of war with France. The Burgundians, however, were only interested in negotiating a match between Margaret of York and their Duke.

The failure of negotiations with Burgundy came as George was planning for his ducal and administrative roles. Soon he found that the future that he had envisaged was met with obstacles. Whilst parliament was passing the Act of Resumption that settled a large amount of money on the Duke, Edward was also busy firming up arrangements for the governance of his domain. This included Ireland, of which George had been appointed Lord Lieutenant. Edward, however, appointed the Earl of Worcester as a deputy and sent him to Ireland to govern, denying his brother the opportunity to rule over the domain. George's estates also became the subject of disputes. Less than a year after he had come of age, he was involved in arguments with nobles including his own deputy in Ireland, the Earl of Worcester, and other notables such as Lord Hastings[6]. The Duke of Clarence found out at an early stage that his position did not guarantee success, losing parts of his estates in the process.

George was now in a position where he had seen his sister negotiated a high-status marriage whilst he had been spurned. He had acquired significant wealth from the Act of Resumption but proposed expenses beyond the limits of the grant's generosity. His right to govern as his father had in Ireland had also been removed. His disputes had opened divisions in court with men who the king regarded very highly and the benefits of patronage that he had expected to enjoy were not as he had assumed.

George was not the only senior magnate to feel somewhat aggrieved. His cousin, the Earl of Warwick, was also frustrated. As the chances of a high-status foreign marriage diminished, George made it clear that his preference was to wed Isabel Neville. This was a problematic proposal. Isabel was George's cousin once removed. Such a union would usually be prohibited on grounds on consanguinity. A marriage would therefore require Papal dispensation, a decision that was as much a political a decision as it would be based on theological argument. Additionally, George had to obtain his brother's consent for a marriage, and Edward would not countenance a marriage of George and Isabel.

Regardless of Edward's opposition to the idea of George and Isabel marrying, the Duke chose to proceed with gaining the approval of the Pope. At first George, aided by the Earl of Warwick, attempted to gain Papal Dispensation through the Archbishop of York, George Neville, and his links to the Papal Legate. This failed but a further attempt was more successful. Negotiations with the Vatican resulted in Papal Dispensation being granted on 14 March 1469. George and Isabel sailed to Calais where they married on 11 July 1469 in a service presided over by the Archbishop of York.

At first glance the issue of a marriage may not seem all that significant. The context in which the negotiations took place do, however, raise questions. The attempts to gain Papal dispensation began shortly after King Edward IV had formalised a treaty with Burgundy. The Duke of Clarence and Earl of Warwick were aggrieved by the outcome. The same period saw accusations levelled at the Earl of Warwick of meeting agents of Margaret of Anjou[7]. The widening gap between the duke and his brother also took place as there was a rise in civil unrest and Lancastrian backed plots. These included the siege of Caister Castle, Norfolk, between the Duke of Norfolk and the Paston Family which George unsuccessfully attempted to settle through arbitration. Elsewhere there were disturbances in the South West, London, North Wales, and further insurrections in

East Anglia. The Duke of Clarence was presenting unwanted political problems for the crown at a time when his responsibility as a senior magnate was to attend to matters such as keeping the peace. Whilst he did arbitrate at Caister, his pursuit of a marriage that had been dismissed by the King is a dereliction of his ducal responsibilities. Eventually the marriage was approved by Cardinal Bourchier and attended by members of court.

The marriage of George and Isabel in Calais on 11 July 1469 was clearly a politically sensitive matter. It was also designed to mask the involvement of George and his allies in insurrection planned to coincide with their time in Calais. Whilst the party were overseas an uprising was instigated in the north. It was large enough to draw King Edward away from London and was followed by a second revolt almost as soon as the first had been suppressed. It was the beginning of a series of events that rapidly changed the political landscape in England.

The timing of the revolt and the decision to distance themselves from the revolt, and the King, was realised by chroniclers. John Hardyng noted the uprisings in his Chronicle:

"that this sedicion migh bee the soner begonne, where with all Englad was sore troubled a greate tyme, he had apoincted that sone after he was gone to Caleis his brother th archebishop & th lord marques should, make an insurreccion in Yorke, wher by the battaill might bee begonne Vhile he was so farre frome theim[8]".

Hardyng briefly alludes to a series of uprisings that occurred in quick succession. The issuing of the Papal Dispensation in March 1469 was followed in April and May of 1469 by the Robin of Redesdale and Robin of Holderness Revolts. John Warkworth attributes the Robin of Redesdale revolt to the lords who were absent in Calais:

"And anone aftere that, by ther [Clarence and Warwick] assig[n]ment, there was a a grete insurreccyon in Yorkeschyre, of dyvers knyghtes, squyres, and comeners, to the nowmbere of XX^{ti} M^{1}.; and Sere William Conyers knyghte was there capteyne, which called hym self Robyne of Riddlesdale.[9]"

The uprisings, which were claimed to be firstly in protest about taxation and secondly calling for the restoration of Henry Percy to the Earldom of Northumberland, were of great concern to the King. Edward appears to have had no intelligence to suggest that either his brother or cousin, the Earl of Warwick, were involved in the planning and execution of either revolt. So much so that the King wrote to the Duke of Clarence, Earl of Warwick, and Archbishop of York requesting their attendance.

"To our Brother of Clarence.

BRODIR, we pray you to yeve feight [faith] and credence to our welbeloved Sir Thomas Montgomery and Morice Berkly, in that on our behalf thei shal declare to you. And we truste ye wole dispose you accordyng to our pleser and comaundement. And ye shal be to us right welcome. At Notyngham the ix. day of Jull.[10]"

Dated 9 July 1469 the letter shows that King Edward IV was in Nottingham because of the ongoing unrest. George was married in Calais on 11 July 1469. The day after, knowing full well that the King had travelled north, the three senior nobles in Calais issued a manifesto of their grievances about the way England was being governed. The manifesto was addressed to the common weal of England and dispatched across the Straights of Dover to be distributed throughout the south east and within London.

Manifesto of the Duke of Clarence, the Archbishop of York, and the Earl of Warwick, issued 12 July 1469:

"...certain seditious persons... their mischievous rule opinion and assent, which have caused our said sovereign Lord, and his said realm, to fall in great poverty of misery, disturbing the 'ministration of the laws, only attending to their own promotion and enriching...[11]"

The manifesto and accompanying documents issued by the northern rebels are reminiscent of the arguments put forward from Calais by the Earl of Warwick in 1459[12] and 1460. The King was surrounded by counsellors who only had their own gain in mind. Government was malfunctioning as a result. For the good of the people, the Duke of Clarence, Earl of Warwick, and Archbishop of York would be tackling the matter head on:

"...wherefore we...for the honour and profit of our said Sovereign Lord, and the common weal of his realm, fully purposed with

other lords to show the same to his good grace, desiring and pray you to dispose and array yourselves, to accompany us thither, with as many persons defensibly arrayed as ye can make... at Canterbury upon Sunday next coming...[13]"

Edward's Kingship is called into question along with explanations of the greed and corruption of some of his chosen counsellors. The lords issuing the manifesto oppose the influence of the Queen's family and are dismayed by major policies, the alliance with Burgundy being one such example.

The coordination of uprisings in the north, the marriage, the manifesto, and the call to arms was a major undertaking. The extent to which this was a betrayal of the King by his brother and the Earl of Warwick can be judged based on the contents of their manifesto, the deeds undertaken at their bidding, and the response that King Edward IV made to the series of events.

The manifesto itself comprises a list of complaints which are summarised as follows:

1) The listed people[14] had used sedition and malicious means to separate the King from the good advice offered by the Council of nobles and blood relatives. The inference being that the kid was listening to the Queen's family over his own.
2) Crown revenues should be secured to limit the need for taxation to extraordinary situations.

3) Duties raised from Tonnage and Poundage should be reserved for expenditure on the Keeping of the Seas.
4) Law and order should be maintained, with the laws being those set out in the reign of King Edward III, for the good of all the people.

These four grievances call for good governance, law and order, and a fair system of taxation. The first item is a demand for the return to grace of the Duke of Clarence, Earl of Warwick, and those aligned with them. That is politically charged but not in itself treasonable or a betrayal. Where there is a problem with the letters and manifesto is the way they were disseminated, from Calais to the South East, whilst the King was away from London. Furthermore, the introduction to the manifesto had called for, *"as many persons defensibly arrayed as ye can make... at Canterbury upon Sunday next coming"*. At best the lords expect to have their point of view challenged.

As is made clear from events that happened in the north and midlands, the intention was for the duke and earl to force the issue. Is this a betrayal? In many respects, yes, it is encouraging the raising of arms against his brother, the King. But in the context of the day, there were precedents that had been set. In 1452 the Duke of York had attempted to use a show of force to shift policy. It had very nearly worked, only the Queen's intervention turning those events in favour of the Duke of Somerset. It was an embarrassment for the Duke of York but had not resulted in any major punitive measures against him. In

1460, Edward as Earl of March was one of the Yorkist nobles who had entered London claiming to be loyal to Henry VI but demanding changes.

The uprisings in the north of England included many of the Earl of Warwick's retainers[15]. There was no coincidence in the timing of the unrest alongside the marriage of George in Calais. How much of the plan George was involved in, or knew about, at the outset is difficult to determine and so that aspect is discussed in more depth in the chapter on the Earl of Warwick. As a signatory to the above manifesto, George was fully aware of the intentions in the south.

George, the Earl of Warwick, and Archbishop of York returned to England as stated in their manifesto. They made their way towards Northampton, where they intended to meet with the rebels from the north. King Edward was based at Nottingham. He had called for reinforcements from Wales and the South West. The Royal reinforcements and Northern rebels came close together near Banbury. Alert to the fact that the Duke of Clarence and Earl of Warwick were marching in support of the rebels, the force loyal to Edward IV chose to try and tackle the northern rebels before the arrival of the Duke and Earl. They failed, the Earl of Warwick's men coming into view as the brief Battle of Edgcote was fought on 24 July 1469[16].

The major consequence of the Battle of Edgcote was that in the days following the rebel victory they captured King Edward, Earl of Devon, Earl of Pembroke, and Pembroke's brother, Sir

Richard Herbert. The follow up operations then resulted in the Queen's father, Earl Rivers, and her brother John Woodville, being taken prisoner at Chepstow.

The stated objective of the campaign was to reform Edward's government. Edward himself was taken to Middleham Castle, the Earl's stronghold in Wensleydale, and George and the Earl of Warwick attempted to rule in his name.

"...they will make an end as they mean to be the rulers at all costs... from what they say the King is not at liberty to go where he wishes... they wish to arrange for a parliament to meet and in that they will arrange the government of this realm.[17]" 16 August 1469, Luchino Dallaghiexia to Galeazzo Maria Sforza, Duke of Milan.

Within weeks of this assessment by the Milanese, all the Earls who had been captured, along with John Woodville, were executed. As the Milanese suggested, the Duke of Clarence and Earl of Warwick set out to govern. However, Edward was soon able to gain his freedom and re-establish himself.

George had been party to a usurpation of power limited only by not seizing the crown and the inability of the rebels to govern successfully. A series of non-judicially sanctioned executions had taken place, including Richard Woodville, Earl Rivers who at the time of his death was Constable of England and Lord Treasurer.

To revolt, detain the King, govern in his name, execute holders of offices of state without a trial and marry without the consent of the King is surely a betrayal on the part of George, Duke of Clarence. Yet, Edward, when free in late September of 1469, did not treat his brother as a traitor. Instead, Edward...

"made a proclamacyone at the Kynge's Benche in Westmynstere, and in the cyte of Londone, and in alle England, a generalle pardone tylle alle manner of men, for all manere [of] insurreccyons and trespasses[18]".

In usual circumstances such a series of actions would be considered treason and be met with swift and lethal justice. Why then did King Edward IV choose not to pursue this response? Simple pragmatism is one explanation. Whilst the attempt of his brother and the Earl of Warwick to rule in his name had failed, the pair remained powerful. To act against them may not be popular with other nobles, and the pair retained much military support. Edward, uncertain as to who was truly loyal to him, was simply better served by gradually reasserting his authority.

The *Croyland Chronicle* offers a second reason for the King's response. It says that in conference the Duke and Earl had...

"...fairly stated to him their intentions to remain firm in their allegiance, and had resolutely exposed the treachery of those who had adhered to him, he became more calm, and received them more freely into his favour and good will.[19]"

Thirdly, the situation had changed. In executing Earl Rivers, and the Earls of Devon and Pembroke, the aims of the manifestos published in Calais, and that of the northern rebels, had been achieved. The poor counsel to which the King had been subjected had been eliminated. Unrest, however, remained an issue. Attempts to tackle the unrest had been unsuccessful. The Duke of Norfolk had rebuffed the Council's attempts at arbitration over Caister Castle. A Lancastrian uprising had taken hold in the north. The Duke of Clarence and Earl of Warwick faced an escalation of the unrest if the King were to be overthrown. The course of action taken was to negotiate with King Edward[20]. In doing so, the Duke and Earl could maintain the argument that they had remained loyal.

The resolution was a practical solution that was not entirely satisfactory to any party. That the King had been betrayed is noted in several chronicle accounts. The *Great Chronicle of London* notes that the Duke and Earl...

"...after [executing Earl Rivers] did many other feats contrary to the King's pleasure...[21]'

The *Croyland Chronicle* comments on the King's views:

"...a great council of all the lords of the realm where the peace was made and the abandonment of all disagreements resolved upon. There probably remained, however, a sense of outraged majesty, deep in the heart, on the one side and, on the other, a guilty mind conscious of an over daring deed...[22]"

George, Duke of Clarence had set out with the Earl of Warwick to affect change. The method chosen in large parts replicated that which had been used by the Yorkist lords a decade earlier: use of force to gain control of Council, the removal of the King's favourites, and the manipulation of public opinion to garner support for their cause. Throughout the episode George had maintained that he was a true liegeman of his brother. Loyalty mattered, if only in terms of the justification for actions.

George claimed to have been loyal to his brother, albeit in a rather unwanted manner, in 1469. The actions of early 1470 were altogether different.

"...the Lorde Willowby, the Lorde Welles his sonne, Thomas Delalond knyght, and Sere Thomas Dymmoke knight... [rose against a loyal knight]...toke alle his goodes and cataylle... and thei gaderid alle the comons of the schyre... and cryed "Kynge Harry' and refused Kynge Edwarde. And the Duke of Clarence and the Erle of Warwyke causede alle this[23]".

The Lincolnshire Rebellion of early 1470 was a large uprising that again forced the King to raise a large army to attempt to suppress the insurrection. This uprising had some very notable figures at its heart. The Dymock family were the hereditary champions of the monarchy, it was they who issued the traditional challenge at coronation banquets. Lord Willoughby and Lord Welles were from a staunchly Lancastrian family of considerable note. The men who had been convinced to join in this revolt were from a range of backgrounds, and they commanded a large force. *The Chronicle of the Rebellion in Lincolnshire* is clear in its statement as to the motives of this uprising, though it must be born in mind that the Chronicle was sympathetic towards King Edward IV:

"[Sir Robert Welles] confessed the Duke and earl to be partners and chief provokers of all their treasons. And this plainly, their purpose was to destroy the King, and to have made the Duke King...[24]"

Later adding:

"My lord of Clarence's servant came to us at Lincoln exhorted and urged our host many times and many places that, when the matter should come near the point of battle, they should call upon my lord of Clarence to be King...[25]"

The capture of Sir Robert Welles enabled the King to extract information about the nature of the revolt and the extent to which his brother and the Earl of Warwick were implicated. The capture of Sir Robert also allowed the King to press the rebels into dispersing, resulting in the rout at Losecote Field. Items found within the baggage train added to the weight of evidence that George was at the heart of the plans against the King. However, as the *Chronicle of the Rebellion in Lincolnshire* was sympathetic to the views of Edward's government it is possible that events have been exaggerated or embellished for political purposes.

Edward IV's response to the events of March 1470 illustrates the types of belief that were held at the time about the importance of family and loyalties based on kinship. They also show the way in which the responsibilities of the King and senior nobles lend themselves to seeking a non-violent end to disputes. On the matter of blood ties, Edward wrote:

"...yet nevertheless our Sovereign Lord, considering the nearness of blood to him and the tender love he aforetime bore them, being loth to lose them if they would submit to his grace and give surety for their demeaning hereafter...[26]"

Loyalty was clearly of importance to the King. Despite the clear breaches of trust and the treasons that were evident, he had provided the Duke of Clarence and Earl of Warwick with a demand to submit to him.

"...which if they had done and declared them not guilty he would have been right glad and would have shown them favour and pity...[27]"

It is only when George and the Earl of Warwick failed to attend the King and submit to him that Edward felt obliged to condemn them. This was stated as being on the grounds that they intended the 'King's destruction and the subversion of the realm[28]' and Edward asserts that this was affirmed by the blessed sacraments.

It is possible therefore to establish the way in which a betrayal of great magnitude could be undertaken with knowledge that the risk of failure is to an extent softened by the monarch's own responsibilities. In this scenario the King is attempting to prevent further uprisings whilst also attempting to offer his kin an opportunity for forgiveness. Decision making on these types of issue were difficult, taking into consideration the wider socio-political ramifications of all options, whilst also recognising a simple familial attachment and loyalty. This is made clear in Edward's letters following the flight of his brother and Earl of Warwick to the west. In correspondence to Thomas Stonor, Edward notes the importance of the realm, faith, and allegiance:

"...without failling as ye love and tendre the wele of us and of owre said Realme, and uppon the feith and liegeaunce that ye owe unto us.[29]*"*

In late March of 1470 George and the Earl of Warwick's facade of their loyalty to King Edward had evaporated. The King marched on them, and the duke and earl chose to sail from Dartmouth for the safety of the continent as the royal army drew closer. France would offer an opportunity to regroup and make plans that would maximise the vast but scattered resources upon which they could draw. In the King of France, they had a continental ally who had cause to back them. So too did they have the more unlikely ally of Margaret of Anjou. In the spring and summer of 1470, George was involved in the plotting with Louis XI of France, the Lancastrians in exile, and with his retainers and allies in the midlands and north of England.

Things may not have been as straightforward as appears. Yes, George's name had been cited by rebels. So too had he been declared a traitor by his brother. And yes, he had fled to France. But there is evidence to suggest that whilst in France, the Duke of Clarence was double crossing the Earl of Warwick.

Phillipe de Commines was a diplomat who served first the Duke of Burgundy and then the King of France. He was well connected and was party to news, and gossip, from all sides in the conflicts in England. His memoir suggests that whilst in France, George was approached by a lady who had travelled with messages for the Duchess of Clarence. Her task was to persuade the Duke:

"...not to contribute to the subversion of his own family, by endeavouring to restore the house of Lancaster; that he would remember their old insolences, and the hereditary hatred that was between them...[30]"

If Commines' suggestions are true, the Earl of Warwick and his men in Calais were as assuming of George's loyalties as his brother had been. Lord Wenlock, charged with the defence of Calais which would include vetting persons to ensure that there was no subterfuge, was outwitted.

"Wenlock was a cunning man, and shrewd enough; yet this lady was too hard for him, wheedled him, and carried on her intrigues till she had affected the ruin of the Earl of Warwick and all his faction[31]".

If the intention was to lure the Earl of Warwick into a trap from which he could not escape, it was a high-risk strategy. In August 1470 Sir John Paston wrote to John Paston that,

"There may be many folks up in the north, so that Percy is not able to resist them... Courtenay's be landed in Devonshire, and there rule; Lords Clarence and Warwick will assay to land in England any day, as folks fear.[32]*"*

Whether George had determined to betray the Earl of Warwick at this point is debatable. Commines had the benefit of hindsight when writing his memoir. What is clear is that the various elements required for the invasion of England were being put into place. The Duke of Clarence had significant influence in the south west, where the Courtenay's are cited by Sir John Paston as having landed in advance of the invasion. Is this a necessary ruse for the Duke to maintain the impression that he is committed to what is now a Lancastrian cause?

The Angers Agreement provided George with a position close to throne, compensation for lands which he agreed to surrender to their pre-Towton Lancastrian lords and, according to the *Warkworth Chronicle*[33], a place in the line of succession to the throne should King Henry VI's heirs not survive him.

George played a full and active role in the readeption of King Henry VI. He sailed with the Earl of Warwick. His retainers and allies were active in raising forces. King Edward, Richard Duke of Gloucester, and other Yorkist nobles were forced to flee.

Nothing had been done by George to prevent this, or to aid them. Was this through choice, or lack of opportunity? The coordinated uprisings and landing of forces were virtually unopposed by King Edward. If George was intending to deceive the Earl of Warwick, September of 1470 was not the time to do so.

From the readeption of King Henry through to late February 1471 George held a significant position in Government. Yet he stood to lose lands through the clauses of the Angers Agreement that were ratified by Henry VI's parliament, and upon the arrival of Prince Edward in England he would likely be an increasingly peripheral influence on Council. The *Arrivall* notes two issues of relevance at this time. First, George was not in a position of real power within the Readeption government:

"And, in especiall, he considred well, that hymselfe was had in great suspicion, despite, disdeigne, and hatered, with all the lordes, noblemen, and othar, that were adherents and full partakers with Henry, the Usurpar[34]".

The Duke of Clarence was now party to an agreement and system that nominally had himself as next in line to the throne after Prince Edward and any heirs who may result from his union with Anne Neville. He had been heir to his brother until the birth in Sanctuary of Edward and Elizabeth's son, Prince Edward. George was no better off if his aim was, as had been suggested only a year earlier, to be placed on the throne himself. Furthermore, George was not the only prince of royal blood. Indeed, if the Lancastrian line were to be fully restored and based upon lineage the Dukes of Exeter, Somerset, and Buckingham all held claims that were stronger than his. This meant that George was unlikely to retain high status within the Lancastrian system and there was a risk of being totally isolated or removed.

Arrivall's second point of note here is in relation to the prospect of the Dukes of Clarence and Gloucester having to wage war against one another. There is no talk of duty, loyalty, or kinship here. It is quite simple, blunt, assessment of the scenario:

"...the mortall warre and detestable, lykely to falle betwixt them; and, ovar this, that yt was evident that to what party so evar God woulde graunte the victorye, that, notwithstandynge, the wynner shuld nat be in eny bettar suerty therefore of his owne estate and parson[35]".

There was little to be gained by George, or his brother the Duke of Gloucester, through going to war against each other. At best one would retain their standing, the other would lose everything. And that supposes that both survive any such clash. It is when this is realised by the Duke of Clarence that the Arrivall states George was open to changing sides. Here the *Arrivall* does refer to loyalties, stating that it would be unnatural and against god's laws for the conflict between brothers to continue, and on that basis, there was scope for George to be pacified and agreeable to a return to the fold. The method of obtaining this change of heart is as Commines suggests through covert negotiations. Unlike Commines' recollection, the *Arrivall* states that the driving force for the change was Margaret of York, sister to King Edward and George, Duke of Clarence. Negotiations were facilitated through the Duchess of Exeter, another sibling, and '*by mediacions of certayne priests*[36]'.

The conclusion of these talks was that George would return to the Yorkist fold. An agreement was made whilst Edward was preparing in Holland that upon the landing of Edward's force on the north coast, George would join with them. The *Arrivall* explains that:

"...parfecte accord was appoyntyd, accordyd, concludyd... wherein the sayde Duke of Clalrence full honorably and trwly acquited hym; for, as sune as he was acertaygned of the Kyngs arivall in the north parties, he... drew towards the Kynge, hym to ayde and assyste agaynste all his enemyes...[37]"

When King Edward and his force arrived on the east coast, George did follow through with this agreement and returned to his brother's side. Was this an act of loyalty to his brother? Was he rectifying an unnatural wrong that ought not to have happened in the first place? Or was George simply changing sides on the basis that he stood to gain more in the event of his brother being victorious than he would if his brother failed?

The political situation in England at the time was complex. It is easy to view it as being those in favour of the readeption versus the Yorkists intent on restoring Edward to the throne. Those who were party to the readeption were, however, divided in their own aims and loyalties. There were those like George Duke of Clarence and the Earl of Warwick who had been disgruntled under Edward's Kingship and sought to have better standing under an alternative regime. There was also the Lancastrian elite. The Dukes of Somerset and Exeter, Earls of Pembroke and Richmond were all relatives of Henry VI. The restoration included the return to these branches of the House of Lancaster the titles, lands, and potentially roles that they had held prior to Edward seizing power in 1461. The interests of the former Yorkists and the Lancastrian elite are not mutually compatible. For one set to benefit from the readeption would be at the expense of the other. Lands to be recouped from the followers of Edward IV who were in exile were far from extensive enough to enable a compromise arrangement. And whilst the promise of financial compensation may appear appealing, it was land, retainers, patronage, that the lords craved as this was the basis of their power.

George, Duke of Clarence stood to lose much of the land that he had held under his brother's rule. This perhaps could be accommodated through political offices. But those too were highly prized and with many offices of state already taken, often by supporters of the Duke of Clarence and Earl of Warwick, there was little realistic room for enhancing George's political role. The communication that was opened through his sisters appears to have begun as issues such as patronage, estates, and roles were being put into place by the Council that was ruling with the Earl of Warwick as Lieutenant.

His return to Edward's side is recorded widely. The *Chronicle of London* noting that it was *'contrary to his promyss and othe made vnto the fifrenshe King.[38]'* John Hardyng offers an alternative account. He states that the Earl of Warwick failed to engage Edward's forces, *'for feare that the Duke of Clarence whome he thought bad deceaued hym[39]'*. The *Warkworth Chronicle* notes that the *'Earl of Warwick had a letter from the Duke of Clarence, that he should not fight with him, till he came himself; and all (this) was to the destruction of the Earl of Warwick, as it happened afterward[40]'*. The *Arrivall*, perhaps the best indication as to the way in which King Edward viewed the reunion with his brother, describes the sighting of the Duke of Clarence coming towards the royal party. The King, together with the Duke of Gloucester, Earl Rivers, and Lord Hastings, rode out to greet him:

"And so they met betwixt both hosts, where there was right kind and loving language betwixt them two, with perfect accord knit together for ever hereafter, with as heartily loving cheer and countenance as might be betwixt two brethren of so great nobility and estate[41]".

George's return to the side of his brother saw him participate in the Battles of Barnet and Tewkesbury. In July 1471 he swore allegiance to his new-born nephew, Prince Edward, not only publicly affirming his loyalty but also recognising that the prince was heir to the throne.

The years 1471-75 raised several issues pertaining to George: the lands associated with the now deceased Earl of Warwick, and preparations for War with France. The first of these had a direct bearing on George personally. As he had married Isabel Neville, the way the Earl's estates were dealt with would have had a bearing on the inheritance that may or may not have become his own by right of his wife. Should the inheritance be allowed to stand, it would see the countess retain her own, substantial, lands and a third of the Neville inheritance as dower. The remainder of the Neville lands would pass down the male line, to the son of the Marquess of Montague. George, who had been persuaded to bring his military might to the cause of his brother, would be left with nothing until the death of the countess. If the Earl and his brother were attainted, this would leave the Neville lands to be redistributed. In this scenario, the King could allocate the estates as he saw fit. Legally, this should not include lands inherited by the Countess from her father.

The matter was politically sensitive. More so as the Duke of Gloucester soon made it clear that he intended to marry Anne Neville, Isabel's sister. Any such marriage of Richard Duke of Gloucester to Anne Neville would take time to acquire the required dispensations. The intention to marry gave Richard an interest in the estates though. The King also had to factor in the relative lack of lands held by the Duke of Gloucester and rewards due to him for his youngest brother's loyal service.

The solution was partially enabled by the fact that the countess had entered sanctuary at Beaulieu. In 1472 a settlement was drawn up that acted as though the countess were dead. It split the bulk of the Neville-Beauchamp inheritance between the Dukes of Clarence and Gloucester, before Richard and Anne had married. George's approach to the negotiations was stubborn, protecting his own rights as far as possible, even when that led to dispute with his younger brother. The matter was finally closed in 1474. The Countess of Warwick had left sanctuary which meant that the land settlement needed to be looked at again. The squabbling over rights had taken its toll on the King, who opted to exclude the Duke of Clarence from an Act of Resumption which in effect dispossessed the Duke until a new settlement was agreed. As Michael Hicks noted, George Duke of Clarence was *'faced by a choice of rebellion or submission*[42]*'*.

Whilst the matter of the Neville-Beauchamp inheritance is largely an attempt by the two royal Dukes to maximise the benefit to be gained from landed estates, it does provide some clues as to the motivation that the Duke of Clarence may have had on other matters. George had chosen to fight his corner, disrupting relationships between himself and his two brothers, over status, income, titles, rights. He was single minded in his pursuit of those goals, which is comparable with decisions he made in earlier years regarding his allegiance with the Earl of

Warwick, his attempt to establish a vast household at Tutbury, and his hurt at seeing his Lieutenancy of Ireland being performed by a deputy. The latter of these issues was to recur in late 1473. Ireland, to which the Duke of Clarence had been regranted the Lieutenancy of for a period of twenty years in 1472, required military intervention to restore order. The Duke was once again overlooked. A Chancellor was appointed, and the Duke of Clarence side-lined once again.

1475 was to see the English take up arms and invade France. It was a short campaign with no coming to blows. The French were willing to negotiate, as was King Edward. The Treaty of Picquigny provided pensions for many of the English royal household. The same year had seen the birth of a son to Isabel and George, the couple's third child, the first of whom had died within hours of her birth at sea in 1470. 1476 saw the Clarence household grow once more. A second son was born on 5 October. The couple now had two sons and a daughter. His young family and further disputes with the King over lands and roles saw George increasingly away from court. His life was then turned on its head. Isabel died on 22 December 1476. Then, on 1 January 1477, the couple's son Richard died.

The dual deaths sparked an incredible series of events that, a little over a year later, culminated in the execution of George Duke of Clarence on charges of treason. The events included the death of the Duke of Burgundy, which left his unmarried daughter Mary as heiress. George's arrest, judgement, and execution of Ankarette Twynho, Isabel's midwife. Thomas Burdett, a member of the Duke's household being arrested, tried, and executed on charges of wishing the King dead. A matter further complicated by the Duke of Clarence displaying very public support for Burdett. Along with these events, there were also allegations made against George in relation to his own intentions at this time.

These incidents provided the reasons for the duke being arrested and charged with treason, along with evidence of the motives George had. Elements of this are clearly linked to the issue of betrayal. They also illustrate the duke's state of mind at the time and are useful in terms of understanding his other actions at that time.

The case of Thomas Burdet was significant. Though there is nothing to suggest that George himself was party to the actions of Burdet and his co-accused, it had the potential to embroil the Duke in a scandal. Burdet was charged with treasonable necromancy, and:

"...seeking the death and destruction of the King and Prince... by exciting war and discord between the King and his lieges... [that they did] falsely and treacherously disperse divers seditions and treasonable rhymes and ballads, containing complaints, seditions and treasonable arguments... and rise and make war against the King...[43]*"*

As Burdett was a close associate of the Duke of Clarence there was the potential for George to be linked to the plot. This was serious as the Duke clearly had the opportunity to access the King, had previously plotted to take the throne for himself, and had been party to the readeption of Henry VI. For a member of his household to be facing such charges had implications for the Duke of Clarence. At best it casts serious doubts on his judgement and choice of confidants. At worst, George is implicated in the plot and again the force behind a plot against his brother.

The trial of Thomas Burdett was conducted in the usual manner. There is nothing in the remaining evidence to suggest that the Duke had been implicated or accused, or that the matter had been tried in anything but a fair environment: indeed, one of the three accused was pardoned rather than being sentenced to death. As a senior member of the royal family and magnate, George had a responsibility for the upholding of the justice system. In simple terms, he needed to accept that one of his confidants had been convicted fairly for the most serious of offences. That is not how the Duke of Clarence responded. The day after the execution of Burdett, the Duke of Clarence:

"...came to the council-chamber at Westminster, bringing with him a famous Doctor of the order of Minorities, Master William Goddard by name, in order that he might read the confession and declaration of innocence above-mentioned before the lords in the said council assembled; which he accordingly did.[44]"

This act is hard to comprehend. George, second in line to the throne, holder of offices of state, senior magnate, had walked into the King's council and called into question the justice that had been meted out at its direction. Doing so can only cause disruption and has the potential to incite unrest, one of the very issues Burdett himself had been found guilty of. Had Burdet's plot proven successful the King and Prince of Wales would have been destroyed. That would place the Duke of Clarence on the throne. No matter what the Duke's intentions were when questioning the judgement and sentence, it was only likely to result in only one response. It triggered the arrest of George Duke of Clarence and his imprisonment in the Tower of London. He himself was then charged with treason. The *Croyland Chronicle* notes that King Edward, in George's trial, referenced the act of having questioned the courts findings:

"...the King began, with his own lips, amongst other matters, to i nveigh against the conduct of the before - named Duke, as being derogatory to the laws of the realm, and most dangerous to judges and jurors throughout the Kingdom.[45]*"*

George was not only faced with charges relating to the court case. He was also accused of calling his brother's legitimacy into question. Evidence of Edward's legitimacy being questioned can be traced back to the insurrection of 1469, the rebellion of the Duke of Clarence and Earl of Warwick, and the period of the readeption of Henry VI. The Duke was not alone in being charged with spreading rumours at this time. Bishop Stillington was also arrested, for *'violating his oath of fidelity by some utterance prejudicial to the King[46]'*. The bishop had links to George, and possibly Burdett, through land management and the undertaking of their roles.

What is clear is that at this time in which there were several high-profile cases being brought against people on charges pertaining to sedition. In addition to evidence of arrests and trials, the notion that George was involved in, or at least noted as being the intended beneficiary of such rumours was documented by John Rous, is noted in ballads, features in Edward Hall's chronicles, and popularised by Shakespeare.

The spreading of rumours is typical of the way support for a potential uprising would be encouraged in the 15th century. The Duke of Clarence was known to be interested in pursuing an interest in marriage to his niece, Mary of Burgundy. Upon the Duke's arrest, it emerged that he had held discussions with retainers and members of his household about sending his son, Edward, to Burgundy. These discussions were with John Tapton, Abbot Strensham, and Roger Harewell. All three men who hitherto had been loyal to the Duke. It could be inferred from these conversations that the clandestine nature of the Duke's preparation for sending Edward overseas was a conspiracy.

The lending of support for Thomas Burdett, suggestions of the Duke planning to send his son overseas, and concerns over the motives George may have had for pursuing a marriage to Mary of Burgundy are all serious matters. Inevitably, each is noted in some form in the posthumous attainder of George Duke of Clarence. These are the matters that prompted the arrest, they are simply the combination that pushed George's behaviours beyond a point from which there could be no return.

The mass of accusations levelled at George are all matters of concern because of the events of 1469-71. This is made clear in the text of the attainder document:

"...the said Duke beyng in full purpose to exalte hymself and his Heires to the Regallye and Corone of Englande... uppon oon the falsest and moost unnaturall coloured pretense that man myght imagine, falsely and untruely noysed, published and saide, that the Kyng oure Sovereigne Lorde was a Bastard.[47]*"*

Burdett had conspired to destroy the King and replace him. George defended the guilty party. In doing so, he reminded the King, or council, of his own treasonable acts in 1469 and 1470. Should there be any doubt on that matter, the attainder continues to note that the Duke of Clarence had played a role in the Reedeption parliament, and further, that at that time he had been signatory to a pact by which he stood to inherit the crown in the event of Prince Edward and Anne Neville not producing heirs. The attainder suggests that this was concealed from King Edward IV:

"...which exemplificacion the said Duke hath kepyd with hymself secrete, not doyng the Kyng to have eny knowlegge therof,

therby to have abused the Kynges true Subgetts for the rather execucion of his said false purpose[48]".

The way in which the various elements of the charges levelled at the Duke combine can be seen in the record of his trial.

"He [George Duke of Clarence] planned to send his son and heir abroad to win support, bringing a false child to Warwick castle in his place. He planned to raise war against the King within England and made men promise to be ready at an hour's notice. The Duke has thus shown himself incorrigible and to pardon him would threaten the common weal, which the King is bound to maintain.[49]"

The accuser was the King himself. The documentation pertaining to the trial and attainting of George refers frequently to the expectations of loyalty. Family ties are cited, the King's love for his brother, their natural bonds. As noted previously, the duties and responsibilities of those in elevated positions of state are referenced. The King is bound to maintain the good of the common weal. Dukes such as George are equally bound, it is a matter of duty, and acting in a manner that would undermine the good of the people is a betrayal of the people's trust in their superiors. The Duke, states the Act, was guilty of acting against *'not only by the bond of nature, butt also by the bondes of soo grete benefit'* showing that at the highest level of state the matter of affinity and the two way nature of patronage were held in such regard as to make them matters of guilt or innocence before the highest court in the land.

Rightly or wrongly the King determined that George had betrayed his family, the commons, and loyalty owed to Edward as King, as brother, and through patronage. That it was viewed as betrayal is summed up in the Act of Attainder. George's betrayal was:

"...moch more malicious, more unnaturall and lothely Treason than atte eny tyme hertoforn hath been compassed, purposed and conspired[50]".

Chapter Three. Richard Neville, 16th Earl of Warwick

Richard Neville, 16th Earl of Warwick became known in popular history as 'Warwick the Kingmaker'[1]. He arrayed his forces on behalf of every factional or royal leader between the years of 1452 and his death in the Battle of Barnet in 1471.

Richard was the eldest son of Richard Neville, 5th Earl of Salisbury and Anne Montagu, 5th Countess of Salisbury. His father's title was by right of his wife, who was the heiress to Thomas Montacute 4th Earl of Salisbury. His father in turn was the eldest son of the marriage of Ralph Neville, 1st Earl of Westmoreland and his second wife, Joan Beaufort.

Joan Beaufort was a daughter of John of Gaunt and Katherine Swynford. As a daughter of John of Gaunt, Joan was also half-sister to King Henry IV and subsequently related to Henry V and Henry VI. Ralph's parents were John Neville, 3rd Baron Neville who held Raby Castle and Maud Percy, daughter of Henry Percy, 9th Baron Percy of Topcliffe, 2nd Baron Percy of Alnwick.

A descendant of John of Gaunt, Richard Neville's family had benefitted from enfeoffments during his grandfather's marriage to Joan. These had caused a family feud as the children from this second marriage stood to become far wealthier than those from Ralph's first marriage. The Beaufort descent tied the family to the Lancastrian Kings and the Earls then Dukes of Somerset, to whom they were related. Marriages had also seen potentially powerful bonds formed with their neighbouring major landholding family in the north, the Percy family.

Richard's own marriage, to Anne Beauchamp, resulted in the inheritance of the Earldom of Warwick, its substantial estates, and the legacy of the Beauchamp family. His father's marriage saw the Montacute inheritance pass into the Neville household, again with a powerful legacy to live up to. The aunts and uncles of Richard Neville also consolidated a powerful set of family ties. His aunt Cecily married the Duke of York, Katherine married the Duke of Norfolk, Eleanor married firstly into the Despenser family, and secondly to Henry Percy 2nd Earl of Northumberland and finally Anne married the Duke of Buckingham.

The Earl of Warwick by lineage was very much linked to the Lancastrian regime. Patronage that resulted from being a line of descent from John of Gaunt had seen the family rise. Marriages had built on that. The young Richard Neville was knighted by 1445, possibly at the Coronation of Queen Margaret. In the 1440s he served in campaigns against the Scots and became close to the king. Following, the perhaps unexpected, inheritance of the earldom of Warwick, Richard was appointed as joint Warden of the West March. Patronage and positions were being afforded to Richard by the Lancastrian regime at a relatively early age.

Richard Neville's stock rose with the death first of his brother-in-law, Henry Beauchamp Duke of Warwick in 1446 and then of

Henry's daughter, Anne, who died in childhood in 1449. It resulted in Richard Neville inheriting the earldom of Warwick by right of his wife, Anne Beauchamp. With the title came the inheritance of a large estate. Anne Beauchamp inherited her father's Beauchamp estates, held a share in her mother's Despenser inheritance, and a further joint share in the inheritance of the lordship of Abergavenny.

The inheritance had huge consequences for Richard Neville. He was elevated to the peerage, given a place on Council, and took possession of roles that the Beauchamp family had traditionally held, including the Chamberlainship of the Exchequer. He was also now incredibly wealthy, these lands combining to form one of the largest holdings of any English peer at the time. The inheritance also brought about conflict, as the joint shares in the Despenser and Abergavenny inheritances were disputed.

As England entered the 1450s Richard Neville was consolidating his hold on this inheritance and to a large extent staying out of national politics. When he did, it demonstrated loyalty to the crown. This was most evident in 1452. As the Duke of York marched towards London with a large force, the Earl of Warwick was one of the peers who stood firm in his bond to the crown, attending to the king with retainers and being one of the lords who was in the king's army at the standoff with the Duke of York at Dartford.

The loyalty that the Earl of Warwick had until this point shown to King Henry VI and the council was soon to be challenged. In

1451 the Chamberlain of the Exchequer position was taken from Richard Neville. Then, in June 1453, the Duke of Somerset seized lordships from the Neville inheritance in Wales. It triggered an immediate response, the Earl of Warwick taking armed possession of Cardiff and Cowbridge Castles. His removal from the position of Chamberlain to the Exchequer had been referred to the Exchequer Court. King's Commissioners had been sent to Cardiff and Cowbridge to obtain their surrender, which the Earls men refused. By summer of 1453, the Earl of Warwick was facing challenges to his enormous inheritance. They came largely from Edmund Beaufort, Duke of Somerset. The Duke's wife was an elder half-sister of the Earl of Warwick's wife. Somerset was attempting to change agreements, and common law practices, in relation to the inheritance.

These matters may have been settled through arbitration but for other events. In 1453 King Henry VI suffered his first period of serious illness. This led to a political scenario in which Council had to choose a route forward. For the Earl of Warwick only one option would safeguard his inheritance, a Protectorship by the Duke of York. This tied in with other splits in affinity that were taking place. The 1440s had seen the Neville family itself feud with arguments between the Earls of Salisbury and Westmoreland. Other regional politics had seen the Middleham branch of the Neville family being drawn into disputes. These initially centred around a decade long dispute between the Earl of Northumberland and the Archbishop of York, but in the early

1450s increasingly led to direct disputes between the Neville's and the Percy family.

In retrospect, this may seem to be Richard Neville choosing sides in an almost inevitable civil war. At the time, it was far less clear cut. The Earl of Warwick had enjoyed patronage from all quarters of court as he grew up. He was related to almost all the major players in English politics at this time to some degree. To safeguard his inheritance, it simply made sense for him to join, along with his father, those who supported the Duke of York. Whilst the political arguments over the ruling of the kingdom took centre stage, the Earl of Warwick remained locked in his dispute with the Duke of Somerset. At this point, the Earl of Warwick had the systems of state working against him. The exchequer court had not affirmed his right to a hereditary position. The Council had not admonished the Duke of Somerset with regards his seizing of properties. In simple terms, the Earl was being let down and the responsibilities that Council and the Courts had were not being acted upon.

Matters escalated when the king recovered his senses. The Duke of York's protectorship came to an end in February of 1455. With it came the threat of revenge against the duke and his allies. This was because the duke of Somerset had been placed under arrest by the Duke of York on charges of treason. As an ally of the Duke of York in 1453-54, the Earl of Warwick and his father were faced with a dilemma. They could try to repair their relationship with the Duke of Somerset or remain true to their relatively new bond to the Duke of York.

There was little hope of reconciliation with the Duke of Somerset. The inheritance dispute had been bitter. Neville backing had contributed to Edmund Beaufort's removal from office and imprisonment in the Tower for a year. Furthermore, the Earls father, the Earl of Salisbury, had felt compelled to resign as Chancellor[2] when ordered to release the Duke of Exeter from custody. The political foes of the faction that the Earl of Warwick was now part of were now free, angry, and in the ascendancy at court. It was not surprising then that when Richard 3rd Duke of York chose to stand firm against the *'poor counsel'* that had returned to the forefront of national politics, the Earl of Warwick and his father followed suit.

With the Neville family also embroiled in violent disputes with the Earl of Northumberland and his retainers[3], the stakes were now high. The factions armed themselves. As the king was being escorted to Leicester for a Council meeting by a large armed contingent, they were met at St. Albans by a force including the Earl of Warwick and his retainers, his father, and the Duke of York. The result was the First Battle of St. Albans on 22 May 1455.

"This yere the Lord Egrymond was take by Sir John Nevell, my Lorde of Salysburys sone. And in the same yere (the xxth day of May, beyng Thyrsday was the fyrst batayll at Seint Albonys; and ther was slayne the Duke of Somersett, the Erle of

Northehomberlonde, the Lord Clyfforde, with oþer mo under the kynges baner. And the Duke of Yorke, the Erle oof Warwyke, the Erle of Salysburye wanne the felde, and so came with the kynge to London with mycche ryalte.[4]"

The battle saw the Earl of Warwick lead his men through the alleyways of St. Albans to launch a surprise assault on the royal army. The Duke of Somerset, Earl of Northumberland and Lord Clifford were slain by the Earl of Warwick's men. Prior to this point, the Earl of Warwick had sought to secure his inheritance through courts, by garrisoning castles, by utilising the patronage of the Duke of York. Now, he was responsible for the death of a duke, earl, and a lord. Furthermore, he had taken up arms against a royal army, whilst the king was present.

The act of taking up arms against the king is treason. A betrayal of one's loyalty to the crown, and in the Earl of Warwick's case, kin. It can only be viewed as being anything other than an act of betrayal by the earl and his allies in 1455 if the actions of the Duke of Somerset following his release are seen as being those of the aggressor. However, it was the Yorkists who mobilised their retainers and moved to cut off the royal party. This had prompted the King to summon forces on 18 May 1455. Messages were exchanged between the two parties. The King commanded the Yorkists to disband, they did not and instead issued demands that the Duke of Somerset be handed over as a traitor. The final exchanges saw no change in the stance of either side. Facing one another at St. Albans, it was the Yorkists who began the first battle of the Wars of the Roses. Planned or spur of the moment, the ensuing clash resulted in the Earl of Warwick being the man whose actions would make peace between the two parties hard to maintain in the years that followed.

The aftermath of the First Battle of St. Albans saw a second protectorate established. The Duke of York and his allies were again in the ascendancy. This lasted into 1456, when the King was returned to ruling in his own right by Council. In this time the Earl of Warwick was appointed to the position of Captain of Calais and became a central figure in the running of government. The end of the protectorate soon saw the return of open disputes between the Yorkists and their political foes.

In 1457 the Lord Mayor and Aldermen of London were forced to intervene to prevent a clash between the two affinities:

"This yere as the Duke of Yorke and the Erle of Salysbury lay peaseblye in London, than came to London the Duke of Somersett, and the Erle of Northehomberlond, and the Lord Egrymond, and other lordes of ther affynite, and loged hem from Tempill Bar to Westmester, with myche people all aboute to Seynt Gylis; and they came in that entent for to fight.[5]"

The feuds continued, resulting in a loveday parade and public act of reconciliation being held in March 1458. Despite the public oaths, fines, and bonds under which accompanied the Loveday, clashes continued, both politically and physically. April

1459 saw clashes in London and as lawlessness spread, the Earl of Warwick chose to use his position as Captain of Calais to engage in acts that were viewed as piracy. Recalled from Calais to explain himself, a brawl broke out which the Earl was fortunate to escape from. Retainers of the Duke of Somerset and Earl of Wiltshire had set about the Earl of Warwick's men. Whilst Richard Neville was able to escape in a boat across the Thames, several of his men were killed[6].

The Earl of Warwick returned to Calais following the incident. It was now very clear that the attempts at arbitration between the Earl and the Duke of Somerset, along with others of each affinity, had failed. This resulted in both parties readying themselves for any eventuality. The Queen based herself in Coventry and summoned a Council to attend to her in June. Orders had also been issued for the mustering of forces at Leicester by the 10 May 1459[7]. The Yorkists viewed this as a direct threat and in turn mustered their own forces.

"And þis same yere the kynge and the quene and ther lordes lete make a grete gaderynge in the northe contre, where of was grete noyse. And the Erle of Warwyke came from Caleys thorowe London, and the Erle of Salysbery went from Medlame for to mete withe the Duke of Yorke and Warwyke his sonne with iiij mlmen, and the quene lay by the wey with xiiij ml men to stoppe his wey.[8]"

The Yorkist plan was for the Earl of Salisbury to march his northern force from Middleham to Ludlow, where his force would merge with that of the Duke of York. The Earl of Warwick on his part brought with him a force from Calais. The Queen instructed Lord Audley to intercept the Earl of Salisbury's force, which he did at Blore Heath, Staffordshire on 29 September 1459. Though heavily outnumbered, the Earl of Salisbury's tactics were enough to win the day for his force. It was now clear that both factions were willing to engage in warfare.

From Blore Heath, which had been fought on 23 September 1459, the Yorkist forces met and attempted to make their way to London. A larger royal army forced them to reconsider and, whilst protesting their loyalties to the king, they retreated to Ludlow, where they fortified positions adjacent to Ludford Bridge. On 11 October Henry Stafford, 1st Duke of Buckingham and King Henry VI were seen in the Lancastrian camp in armour. Messages were sent to the Yorkists promising pardons for all who would change sides. The implication was clear, there would be no pardon for those who did not change sides. Overnight Sir Andrew Trollope and 600 men from the Calais Garrison did defect. The risk to the Yorkists was that more men may follow suit, or simply refuse to fight the King. With the odds stacked against them, the three Yorkist lords fled.

The resulting rout at Ludford Bridge was the culmination of the escalation of events that had spiralled out of control in the late 1450s. The killing of the Duke of Somerset at the First Battle of St. Albans had created an animosity between the Queen, the new Duke of Somerset, and their adversary the Earl of Warwick that no amount of appeasement would pacify. The Earl for his part had angered Council through his abuses at sea. 1459 had seen both factions raise armed forces. The Queen had the advantage of being able to use the King's name. The Yorkists did not, and that makes their raising of private armies an act of rebellion.

Of course, it was the case that the Queen had issued her instructions for as many men as possible to muster before the Yorkists opted to do the same. In this sense, mustering a force is not a betrayal as such but was outside of the law. This fact was not lost on the Earl of Warwick. He issued a justification for the actions of the Yorkist Lords. In it, he places the blame for the need to bear arms upon the Court party. His brief explanation stated:

"I. That the Commonweal and good politic laws had been piteously overturned.

II. That the crown property had been outrageously spoiled and robbed.

III. That sufficient was scarcely left for the sustentation of the royal household.

IV. That the merchants and people had, by illegal novelties, suffered great extortions, without payment, from the Ministers of the King's household.

V. That the Government permitted great and abominable murders, robberies, perjuries and extortions; and favoured and cherished instead of punishing them.

VI. That the King from his own blessed conversation, and noble disposition, graciously applied himself to the commonweal; but that certain persons, from their covetousness, and (in order) that they might rule, had hidden all these evils from him[9]*".*

The motivation for opposing the forces raised by the Queen in the King's name is, at least in Warwick's mind or words, the betrayal of the commons of England by corrupt counsellors. This is borne out by other sources. Commines noted in his memoirs that, *"The reason of the Earl of Warwick's espousing the interest of the House of York against King Henry, who was of the Lancastrian family, was upon a difference that happened at court betwixt the Duke of Somerset and the Earl of Warwick.*[10]*"* Furthermore, when the Earl returned to England in 1460, his use of force was seemingly limited to targeting those who were perceived to be at fault. An English Chronicle notes that at Northampton in July 1460, the Earl:

"let cry through the field, that no man should lay hands upon the King nor on the common people, but only on the lords, knights, and squires: then the trumpets blew up, and both hosts encountered and fought together half an hour.[11]*"*

After the Yorkist victory at Northampton there continues to be evidence of the Earl of Warwick portraying himself as being loyal to King Henry VI. Just weeks after the victory, letters were distributed to the shire by the Earls of Warwick, March, and Salisbury. In this example, to the county of Norfolk, the emphasis is clearly on keeping the King's peace:

"RYGHT welbeloved, we grete you wele; and wher, for the tendre love that we have to the concervacion of the Kyngs peas, lawes, and justice in this his realme of Englonde, we have comaunded the Kyngs peeple in his name, be oure letters and diverse writyngs.[12]"

The scenario in 1460 was different to that of 1459. Following the rout at Ludford Bridge, the Yorkist leaders had been attainted by the Coventry 'Parliament of Devils'. The Yorkists now had nothing to lose. For Yorkist leaders, their retainers, and mercantile contacts, the attainders stripped titles, rights, income, political power. Whilst many could contemplate a shift in allegiance, or seek new commercial partnerships, it would take time, be less beneficial, and there was no guarantee of future safety or prosperity. Leaders such as the Earl of Warwick stood to lose everything. So, it was in their interests to force a change. That could be a reversal of attainder, which was possible, but which would take time and was a rather improbable proposition given the enmity between the leaders of the two factions. Coercion was the alternative. Seizing power and ensuring that they, rather than the other party, had control of the king's person, and his government. Ultimately this is regime change without necessarily requiring a usurpation of the throne. To achieve this would take force of arms, moral right, and public support. Without those, any attempt to recover the political higher ground would either fail or be faced with widespread opposition.

The attainders had resulted in an escalation of actions being taken against the Yorkist affinity. The Earl of Warwick had the Captaincy of Calais stripped from him and given to the Duke of Somerset. This resulted in the Duke of Somerset having to attempt to take Calais from the Earl of Warwick by force of arms. Actions went beyond those aimed directly at the Earl and the other lords though. In England, justice was being meted out against men who supported the Yorkists. Nine men were arrested, charged with treason, and hanged, drawn, and quartered for supporting the attainted lords. One of whom was Roger Neville, a lawyer of the Temple who may have been related to the Earl of Warwick:

"and or he went to the see he toke a gentilman of the Temple that was called Nevell, and John Goode felaue, vinter, and oþer viij persones, and bare hem and honde that they were going to Caleys to the Erle of Warwyke with bowestrenges and arowes heded. And here upon thei were dampned of treison, and her hedis sett on London Brige, and ther quarters on the yatis aboute the towne"[13].

It had been clear from the events of 1459 that the government being run in the king's name was intent on the destruction of the Yorkist lords. It was a situation caused by escalation in the tension that had been contributed to by both parties. Whilst King Henry himself was not a target of anger at this moment, the senior magnates were. Survival now meant for the earl of Warwick that he would need to defend himself. This saw pre-emptive moves undertaken by the Calais Fleet, such as the Raid on Sandwich on 15 January 1460, which was followed by the defeat of a Lancastrian assault on Calais in the Battle of Newnham Bridge on 23 April 1460. Is this a betrayal? Clearly in the eyes of the law as it stood at the time, it was an act of rebellion and treasonable. As for betrayal, the Earl of Warwick had himself been wronged by the Duke of Somerset in 1453. This had been escalated by the Earl at St. Albans in 1455. The subsequent political clashes and threats of violence toward Richard Neville were undoubtedly caused by the death of the Duke of Somerset, with the political isolation of the Queen's party in the Duke of York's second protectorate contributing. But the acts of violence in the period 1455-59 were instigated by both factions. This was demonstrated by the ambush at Blore Heath, with a Lancastrian army forcing the Yorkist lords into defensive array at Ludford. And throughout, the Earl of Warwick affirmed his loyalty to the King. Was that genuine, or simple political prudence? That the Earl did not support the immediate succession of Richard Duke of York when he claimed the throne in October of 1460 suggests that he was genuine at this time in his claims.

The events that followed the Battle of Northampton, fought on 10 July 1460, illustrate the notion of the loyal but armed opposition that took place prior to the return from Ireland of the Duke of York. In his memoirs Phillip Commines describes the Earl of Warwick's actions at the time:

"[The Earl of Warwick] took King Henry and brought him directly to London, carrying the naked sword before him, as if he had been his constable; and, upon his arrival at London, he led him straight to the Tower, in which there were four barons of the kingdom of King Henry's party, that were kept prisoners there; to whom King Henry sometime after, and the Earl of Warwick, gave very fair words, and released them out of the Tower, after they had solemnly promised them that their persons should be protected from all manner of danger whatsoever, and in confidence of these fair promises they consented to go out of the Tower[14]"

.

In effect the Earl of Warwick makes use of King Henry's name to obtain submission of Lancastrian nobles. A simple method, but one that at times worked. The Yorkist lords who had fled to Calais following the rout at Ludford Bridge were quite consistent in what they said, and did, prior to the return of the Duke of York. At no point prior to Richard's return was there any reference to the superiority of the York claim to the throne. So much so that Edward, Earl of March, the future Edward IV, put his name to a manifesto issued as the Yorkist invasion of 1460 took place. That manifesto, also signed by the Earl of

Warwick and his father, is quite clear in its view on the position of King Henry VI:

"We therefore, as we suffice, beseche youre sayde good grace, to take, repute, and receyue thervnto oure sayde trouthe and entent, whiche to God ys know, as we shewe it by the seyde tenure of the sayde endenture, and nat apply youre sayde blessednesse ne the grete ryghtewysnesse and equite whereinne God hathe euer endowed youre hyghe nobeley, to thymportune impacience and violence of suche persones as entende of extreme malyce to procede vnder the shadow of youre hyghe myghte and presence to oure destruccione, for suche inordinate couetyse, whereof God ys nat pleased, as they haue to oure landes, offices, and goodes, not lettyng or sparyng therefore to put suche thyngys in alle lamentable and to sorowfulle geopardy, as moot in alle wyse take effect by the mystery of Goddys wille and power, nor nat hauyng regarde to theffusione of Crystyne blood, ne any tendrenesse to the noble blood of thys lond suche as serue to the tuicione and defens therof, ne nat weyng the losse of youre trew liegemenne of youre sayde reame, that God defende whiche knowethe oure entent, and that we haue avoyded therfro, as fer as we may with oure sewertees, nat of any drede that we haue of the sayde persones, but onely of the drede of God and of youre sayde hyghenesse, and nat wylle vse oure sayde defence vnto the tyme that we be provoked of necessyte, whereof we calle heuene and erthe in to wyttenesse and recorde; and therynne beseche God to be oure Juge, and to delyuer vs accordyng to oure sayde entent, and

oure sayde trouthe and dutie to youre seyde hyghenesse, and to the sayde commonewele. Most Crysten Kyng, ryghte hyghe and myghtye Prince, and moste drad souerayne lorde, we beseche oure blessed Lord to preserue youre honoure and estate in ioye and felycite[15]".

The Yorkist lords make it clear that they respect the king. They are his true liegemen. King Henry VI has been betrayed by corrupt nobles who have lost much land, in France, another slur on the Beaufort Dukes of Somerset. For peace and justice to exist in the King's realm the loyal Yorkist lords had been obliged to take up arms in defence of themselves. All they sought was justice, good governance, and the prosperity of King Henry's England. The mantra is almost the same as the Earl of Warwick's justification of the 1459 actions. It would be repeated by him a decade later to justify his and the Duke of Clarence's actions. In 1460, the words were backed with action. King Henry had been taken into the care of the Yorkist lords. They had secured the Tower and taken control of London and Westminster, and with that, parliament. Until the Duke of York landed in north Wales, the actions of the Yorkist party match the words of intent in their declarations.

It is not known is whether the lords who had taken refuge in Calais were aware that the Duke of York would return and state his right to the throne. Known or not, the fact remained that the lords who had sailed from Calais in July 1460 had done so on the basis of being loyal subjects of King Henry VI. Even if there was an agreement in principle that at some stage the king needed to be replaced, it was simply not prudent to support Richard Duke of York in forcing regime change at this time. It had been immediately clear that there was considerable shock at and opposition to Richard's claim, from nobles, clerics, and the commons.

The Earl of Warwick along with other magnates was involved in the compromise of the Act of Accord being agreed. The Duke needed to be persuaded firstly not to proceed with seizing the throne and having himself crowned. Then the arguments for the right to the crown had to be heard and considered[16]. Finally, once the Act of Accord was drawn up and the line of inheritance formally altered from King Henry's seven-year-old son to the Duke of York and his heirs, there was the task of creating a secure Yorkist government.

The Act of Accord was passed and given royal assent by the Yorkist dominated October 1460 parliament[17]. The same parliament confirmed grants to the Earl of Warwick, to be levied from the Duchy of Lancaster, for the purpose of the keeping of the seas. Patronage was also afforded to the Earl, along with other senior Yorkist magnates, to reflect the borrowing and expenses incurred in the upheaval of the previous year. In doing so the rights of Prince Edward had been revoked, viewed by Queen Margaret as a betrayal and slur on her son's hereditary rights.

Richard Neville, 16th Earl of Warwick, was now in receipt of royal patronage as a direct result of his role in enabling the Duke of York's victory of sorts. It was a patronage that would be reinforced in the reign of King Edward IV, seeing large grants bestowed upon the Earl in March 1463[18] along with reversion of rights to estates in the November 1461 Parliament[19] and renewal of all grants under the 1467 Act of Resumption[20].

Patronage was not the only change that resulted from the Act of Accord. Oaths of allegiance and loyalty were also required in a public setting. This saw the Duke of York and his sons the Earls of March and Rutland swear oaths to King Henry: and it is worthy of note that Edward Earl of March had not openly supported his father's claim to the throne in October 1460. The lord's secular and temporal made oaths that recognised King Henry and the right of the House of York to inherit. Loyalties, through oaths made before God, and the people of England, were now owed to the figurehead of both the Houses of Lancaster and York.

The Yorkist lords were under no illusion as to what the response of the Queen and her allies would be to events in Westminster. King Henry may have given royal assent to the Act of Accord and may have been able to present his arguments to the lords, but his argument had not prevailed, and it was the Queen who was the political leader of the Lancastrian faction. This had been recognised by both parties. At Northampton, the King and Queen had parted ways with the King:

'commaundyd hyr that she shulde not com unto hym tylle that [he] sende a specyalle tokyn unto hyr that no man knewe but the kynge and she. For the lordys wolde fayne hadde hyr unto Lundon, for they knewe welle that alle the workyngys that were done growe by hyr, for she was more wyttyer then the kynge, and that apperythe by hys dedys.[21]'

The sequence of events after the Act of Accord was, then, quite expected. The Queen and her affinity agreed to meet in the north and began arming themselves. Richard Duke of York and the Earl of Salisbury marched north to tackle the problem. Perhaps through underestimation of the enemy's strength, through treachery by John Neville, or poor scouting, they were defeated and killed at Wakefield on 30 December 1460. The Earl of Warwick's father had been executed after the battle rather than being ransomed. A relative may have betrayed him. Queen Margaret's force had acted against the legal heir to the throne. Parliament had confirmed changes to the line of inheritance to the throne and confirmed the relative positions of the Duke of York, his sons, and the positions within the government of the Yorkist affinity. Lancastrian's arming themselves was, from a simple legal perspective, treasonable in this instance. Or at least so it could be claimed by the Earl of Warwick for whom the events at Wakefield were perhaps the main turning point in his views on the crown. King Henry had given royal assent to the Act of Accord, but he had little choice in the matter. Did the success of the Duke of York's line of argument over a partisan council of magnates have moral as well as legal credibility?

From the perspective of the Earl of Warwick, the answer to this question, in public at least, was a firm yes. Following the victory of Edward at Mortimer's Cross on 2 February 1461 and the defeat suffered by the Earl of Warwick in the Second Battle of St. Albans on 17 February 1461, the matter of inheritance was broached again by the Earl of Warwick and Edward who was now Duke of York. The situation was such that there was no hope of a peaceful solution. Queen Margaret would not accept the Act of Accord. King Henry, having been left for the Lancastrian army to find in St. Albans, was likely to overturn the legislation. Lords who had seen the Yorkists take up arms in 1459, and plan for it at least a year earlier[22], would not be willing to compromise again. All avenues towards an agreed peace were exhausted. And now both sides had the non-judicial killing of senior nobles to avenge.

When the Earl of Warwick met with Edward, now Duke of York in his father's stead, the matter was discussed, and a solution agreed upon. Edward would be proclaimed king, justified by virtue of King Henry having forfeited his crown by travelling north with the Queen. The solution overlooks the fact that the Earl of Warwick had left King Henry in St. Albans and ignores the fact that the Act of Accord placed no limitations on the movements or behaviour of King Henry. Nonetheless, a justification for seizing the crown was required for public show, and the remaining Yorkist lords knew that they had reached the point of having to eradicate the Lancastrian regime for themselves to survive. The *Brut Chronicle* briefly explains the way in which the decision was justified:

"And when þei wer commyn to London, & had spoken with þe lordes & Astates þat wer ther, þei concluded, for-as-mych as King Henry was gone with þame Northward, þat he had forfeted his Crown), & ought forto be deposed, According to þe Actes made and passed in þe last parlement. And so, by thavice of þe lordes spirituel & temperel þen beyng At London, þerle of Marche, Edward, bi þe grace of God þe oldest son of Richard, Duke of Yorke, As rightful heir & next enheritour to his fadre, þe iiijte day of Marche, þe yere of oure Lorde God M1 cccclix, toke possession of þe Reame of England[23]*"*

The campaign that followed the declaration of Edward as King of England was a success. At Towton, the Lancastrian army was defeated on 29 March 1461. Surviving Lancastrian nobles fled for safety. This resulted in a Lancastrian enclave in the North-East. Utilising castles possessed by the Percy family the Lancastrians put up a staunch defence. Aided by French and Scottish funds, manpower, and munitions, they were able to retain a foothold in England until shortly after the Battle of Hexham, in 1464.

North-Eastern England was the ancestral home of the Neville family. Conflict over dominance in the region between the Neville and Percy families had contributed to factionalism in the 1450's. It was their dispute that had led to Henry VI's vain attempt at arbitration via the Loveday of 1458. With the family having a solid base of support in the region, and designs on expanding their influence, the task of suppressing resistance to the new Yorkist regime in the far north was given to the Earl of Warwick, and his younger brother.

In the period from the Battle of Towton to the mopping up of the final pockets of resistance that remained after the Battle of Hexham, the Earl of Warwick had a range of roles to fulfil. Militarily, he retained oversight of campaigning in the North-East. Calais remained under his captaincy. The position of Great Chamberlain of England was awarded to the Earl. He was also given ambassadorial roles. The Earl's roles included the keeping of the seas, giving him authority over shipping and a mandate to deploy naval resources to protect England's interests. He was commissioned to pursue a truce by sea with France on 28 March 1464, on 5 April of the same year he was appointed to seek a perpetual peace with the Scots, 12 April saw the Earl being appointed to lead negotiations with Burgundy for a truce. May 1464 saw a repeat of attempts at agreeing a truce with the Scots, then in June 1464 as Great Chamberlain, the Earl was appointed to end the war in the North-East by receiving the submission of all rebels, except Ralph Gray and Humphrey Neville, in return for a general pardon[24].

The mid-1460s saw the pursuit of foreign policy objectives. The Earl of Warwick was heavily involved in these diplomatic talks. They included negotiations with the French, Burgundians, and Scots. The aim of the talks was to end disputes with France, end trade wars with Burgundy, and to bring about a truce or perpetual peace with the Scots.

It was a complex mixture of objectives. Burgundy and France had been at war with one another, and France remained in open conflict with Brittany, another traditional ally of England. Should England reach a positive agreement with any party, it may sour the relationship with the others. As it stood, Burgundy was engaging in trading war with England. England having restricted Burgundian foodstuffs entering England in 1463 and the response from Burgundy being to place a trade embargo on English cloth in October 1464. This was damaging to the English woollen trade, and the treasury, and was a consideration for Richard Neville through his role in keeping of the seas. Matters with France had never reached a formal conclusion after English forces had been ousted from Normandy and Gascony. It meant that there was always a possibility of renewed war, with Calais being the likely French target along with the risk of renewed raids along the English Coast: French ships had attacked the south coast in the period following the fall of Normandy, the risk was real.

Negotiations had to take on board these factors, along with the facts that the English still claimed the French crown and had been an ally of the Burgundians until the mid-1430s. There was also a natural leaning towards Burgundy as popular opinion in England remained anti-French, there had been French support for Lancastrian opposition. Rapprochement with France may limit the prospect of further French input into English civil wars, but at what cost? Burgundy also presented a problem in terms of negotiations. Whilst the economic embargoes and tariffs could be traded off until a mutually acceptable agreement was in place, the future of Burgundy itself was not assured. Duke Philip was too ill to treat with envoys himself, his son and heir Charles did so. Furthermore, Burgundy could quite easily become embroiled in another war with France, particularly likely should the Duke pass away.

In 1465 the Earl of Warwick led an embassy onto the continent that included other high-status men such as Lords Hastings and Wenlock. This also enabled the Earl to remain in the limelight and centre of English politics. With Lancastrian resistance in the north-east shattered, managing the complex diplomatic talks was a suitably challenging task for the Earl.

Richard Neville was not the only person looking at the diplomatic scenario. In France, Margaret of Anjou had set up a Lancastrian court in exile. It remained ambitious and had links with the French court. In the French court, the king himself took an interest in affairs in England. The Burgundians on their part stood to benefit from a mutual agreement on trade being found. And the Burgundians now had closer ties to the court in England. Edward IV had married Elizabeth Woodville in May 1464, and once the marriage became public knowledge in September 1464, it formed a bond through marriage between the English and Burgundian courts through the Queen's mother.

The economic need to find agreements on the continent, coupled with a changing role for the Earl in domestic policy, coincided with the period in which the King's marriage seeing an increase in the importance of the Woodville family at court. It was soon to become a mixture of ideals, policies, and egos, which were incompatible. A difference of opinion over foreign policy between the king and a senior noble is far from unusual. In most cases, it would not be an insurmountable problem for either party. From 1465 onwards, it was the issue that provided a spark for discontent.

The French king had noted the changes in the dynamics of the English court as soon as the Lancastrians had been removed from their northern enclave. As the English imposed restrictions on Burgundian imports, King Louis XI sent a member of his household to the English court[25]. The intention was clear, to utilise the dispute between the English and Burgundians for French gain. The method, to win the support of the Earl of Warwick.

Negotiations of treaties, truces, economic arrangements involved embassies travelling, messengers being sent to gain the opinion of the king, or council, and rarely saw a fast resolution to affairs. The foreign policy of England at this time followed that pattern. Negotiations continued for over a year, until in 1467 the Earl of Warwick was once more sent to France as Ambassador. The Earl was welcomed in a manner usually reserved for monarchs. King Louis *'personally greeted Warwick, the Queen was in attendance, lavish banquets and formal boat processions were laid on. Warwick was housed in comfort, next door to Louis*[26]*'*. The talks between the French King and English Earl took place night and day, with no attempts made to hide the fact that the pair were talking at unusual hours. It played on the Earl's preference for an alliance with France.

The Earl of Warwick would have anticipated that his work on agreeing terms with France would come to fruition. The *Milan State Papers*, an archive of newsletters sent by ambassadors and ducal letters, records the progress of talks that the two parties were engaged in. As Early as February 1467 the papers recorded that the French King was incredibly close to Richard Neville, though in this instance it, surprisingly at this moment in time, it suggests the French *'have talked of treating with the Earl of Warwick to restore King Henry in England, and the ambassador of the old queen of England is already here.*[27]*'* By April, the Milanese were aware of the actual contents of Anglo-French discussions. These were far from traitorous on the part of the Earl of Warwick. Instead, the Milanese had learnt that the King and Earl had formulated a plan that would result in:

'perpetual peace between the realms of England and France. King Edward will yield, quit and renounce all rights, actions and claims which belong to him, and which pertain or may pertain upon the kingdom of France[28]*.'*

The agreement that the Earl had reached would have included a diplomatic marriage for Richard Duke of Gloucester and seen the English ally with the French against Burgundy. The result would be a war against Burgundy which, once won, would result in the Low Countries being an Anglo-French conquest. Victory would result in the *'lordship of Holland, Zeeland and Brabant for his brother [Richard Duke of Gloucester] aforesaid.[29]'*

However, as the Earl of Warwick continued formulating these plans with France, an agreement which he no doubt believed was in the best interests of the country, king, economy, and himself, the alternative option of allying with Burgundy was also being explored. This avenue was attractive to the King for a variety of reasons but at total odds with the policy being pursued in France by Richard Neville. In fact, as the Earl of Warwick sailed to France for the negotiations of June 1467, the Burgundians were engaged in talks about a marriage union between the future Duke Charles of Burgundy and King Edward's sister, Margaret of York. Tension with Burgundy had been eased partly because of the link that Queen Elizabeth's mother, Jacquetta of Luxembourg, had to the court of the Dukes of Burgundy.

The Earl would have been aware of the Burgundian talks. A tournament had been arranged which was held at Smithfield on 11/12 June 1467. The centrepiece of the event was the competition between Anthony Woodville, the Queen's brother, and the Bastard of Burgundy. Whilst there was no hiding the visit of the Burgundians, or the fact that they received a very warm welcome, events surrounding the tournament drove a wedge between the Earl and the King. On 8 June, George Neville, brother of the Earl of Warwick, was dismissed from the position of Chancellor of England. Additionally, the tournament followed the announcement in Parliament on 17 May 1468 of the marriage union between Margaret of York and Charles of Burgundy.

Not only had the Earl seen his work at obtaining an agreement with France overturned but he had seen his absence used as a means of quietly dismiss his brother from an office of state. To confound his political loss of face, the Burgundians crossed the Somme invading France whilst he was in talks with King Louis. The Earl returned to England having seen his vision of an Anglo-French alliance shattered. Not only that but the French king upon whose support his own ideas relied on was in a fragile position, having only just overcome a challenge presented by his own brother and now engaged in a fresh war with Burgundy. As if to add insult to injury, messengers captured travelling from Margaret of Anjou to Harlech Castle spoke of the Earl of Warwick scheming[30]. Whilst this may well have been simply messengers relating rumours, it was enough to warrant the Earl having to affirm his loyalty. Whilst there is no firm evidence that the Earl of Warwick was involved in any conspiracy against the king at this stage, it was suggested in the memoirs of Philippe de Commines that the relationship between the pair had broken down prior to the decision by Edward to press ahead with the pro-Burgundy policy. *'By accident the Earl of Warwick had fallen out with his master the year before the Duke of*

Burgundy's expedition against Amiens[31]*'*. This would place the relationship as deteriorating in 1466.

The consequence of the Burgundian marriage and alliance was a change in the relationship between the King and the Earl of Warwick. *Hearne's Fragment*, written in the early 16th century, notes two distinct issues. First, the mindset of the Earl of Warwick, *'his insatiable mind could not be content, and yet before him was there none in England of the half possessions that he had'*. Richard Neville craved power, land, control, and being the central figure. Second, the way in which the Earl acted following his alliance with France being snubbed in favour of the Burgundian marriage and alliance. *"He counselled and enticed the Duke of Clarence, and caused him to wed his eldest daughter, Isabel, without the advice or knowledge of King Edward.*[32]*"*

The marriage of the Duke of Clarence and Isabel Neville took place on 11 July 1469, in Calais. Whilst the Duke, Earl, and others of their party were in Calais for the wedding, a rebellion under 'Robin of Redesdale' broke out in Yorkshire. King Edward was forced to march north to meet the threat. The threat was not only to the King from the north though, safe in the knowledge that Edward IV would be marching north, the Earl of Warwick and Duke of Clarence issued a letter from Calais the day after the Duke's marriage. It bore the hallmarks of the Earl's previous manifestos and proclamations. It stated clearly that the King's cousin and brother had only ever intended things for the good of the crown, commons, and for the ending of any oppression of the poor people of England. And yet they have found themselves in Calais away from their lands and kin. The cause, they note, was:

'the false means and subtle dissimulations of such certain covetous and seditious persons, as such covetous and seditious persons, as have guided... their own singular and insatiable covetousness, and to the magnifying of their friends and adherents, than they had to the Majesty Royal... to the great hurt, impoverishing and the utter destruction of you and the Realm...[33]"

The consequence of the uprisings and proclamation in Calais was that King Edward found himself marching north to face one threat when word of another reached him. At Nottingham, he paused to gather his thoughts, send for aid, and to attempt arbitration. The reinforcements that Edward had called for came in the shape of retinues of the Earls of Devon and Pembroke. The two Earls were tracked by rebel scouts and, whilst arguing amongst themselves, brought to battle by the force of 'Robin of Redesdale'. At Edgcote on 24 July 1469[34] the force loyal to King Edward IV was defeated, and Edward was soon taken into the custody of the Earl of Warwick and Duke of Clarence.

Warwick and Clarence had organised a revolt that resulted in the King being taken into their custody. Men who were retainers of the Earl in the north had been present on the battlefield. Furthermore, the weeks after the battle saw the summary execution of Lord Rivers, the Earl of Pembroke, John Woodville, and others including the Earl of Devon who was captured by a mob in Bridgwater and executed by them on 17 August 1469. As was noted of the Duke of Clarence, this is an act that normally would be treasonable. But the Earl himself had not taken up arms. His manifesto had been clear in its aim of ensuring good governance and had placed a limit on the scope of their intent: the Earl wanted rid of the corrupt counsellors that the king was being ill-advised by. Whilst placing a King under a form of house arrest is highly unusual under any circumstances, Edward was not at any point placed under a strict regime of imprisonment. He was merely moved out of the way to Middleham. The planning of the revolt and subsequent house arrest of the King by the Earl of Warwick and Duke of Clarence is an example of boundaries being pushed as far as possible. It is a betrayal of trust, and a betrayal of their respective roles and duties within the King's council and government.

The Earl and Duke attempted to rule in the King's name. This would fulfil their stated aims of good governance from men who were true liegemen of the king. However, the uprisings that they themselves had provoked were difficult to bring an end to. Additionally, they did not enjoy the support of all the nobility. It was soon clear that they were unable to maintain the façade of ruling in the king's name. When Edward slipped away from his captivity, neither the Duke of Clarence nor Earl of Warwick attempted to stop the king resuming his position in London. The response of rebels and nobles at this time indicates that the Earl of Warwick's plan was far from supported by his peers, or many of the commons who remained in revolt.

The king's response to the events of 1469 was mixed. In public, he demonstrated a policy of rapprochement with his brother and cousin. *'Howbeit that the King our Soveraine Lord graunted unto Georg Due of Clarence, and Richard Erie of Warwyk, his pardon generall of all offences committed and doon ayenst him*[35]*'* . Both were involved in dealing with the uprisings, so remained able to retain armed forces. Neither received admonishment, nor loss of rank or office. Circumstance dictated this policy, and it reflected Edward IV's long-standing approach of appeasing or forgiving magnates who had in some way opposed him[36].

To what extent Edward was doing this because he was compelled to is hard to ascertain. Politically, the King was in a very weak position. Rebellion had taken a hold in several parts of the country. The Duke and Earl had been attempting to tackle these. It was simply prudent to combine forces to bring about a swift resolution to the unrest. Besides, whilst the Duke and Earl had lacked the political clout to rule without the King being present, the King did not have the military resources available to him to challenge his two most powerful subjects. Had he been equipped to do so, the prospect of more fighting after so much disruption would have been frowned upon by many.

Had the Earl of Warwick betrayed the king, or his own responsibilities in orchestrating the revolts? Undoubtedly so with regards the king. There was a risk to the King's person in facing these challenges and no amount of arguing that the actions were for the good governance of the country can detract from the fact that it would be known that Edward himself would lead the response to the Robin of Redesdale revolt. That the Earl of Warwick was not attainted or stripped of roles was not necessarily due to Edward simply accepting the events and moving on. A Parliament would need to be called which could prove to be split. It was also pragmatic for the King to do so; the Earl was simply too powerful and influential to be challenged at that time.

What then was the motivation of the Earl of Warwick in betraying the King at this juncture? Clearly, it was not total regime change. Had that been the case, the King would have as a minimum faced a much more secure imprisonment as had happened to King Henry VI following his capture near Clitheroe in July 1465. The executions carried out during the aftermath of Edgcote make the Earl's motives clear. The people named by the Earl, or rebels, and those executed are a reasonably limited number of nobles. But it is a very specific faction within court. The men who were executed had advocated the Burgundian marriage of Margaret of York and the pro-Burgundian foreign policy of which that was part. All were either members of the Queen's family, or closely aligned to them. Richard Neville had sought an ally in the Duke of Clarence, himself a man who had suffered a rejection by the Burgundians. He had then used this powerful alliance to target those who had challenged his own supremacy within English government. The Earl of Warwick was ensuring that he and his kin retained positions of strength. This is playing off a loyalty to his own family and retainers against his loyalties to the king, crown, and systems of government. It is, however, a major breach of accepted norms and was a betrayal of the king and the responsibilities of a senior earl.

The actions of Edward also need to be considered if assessing a betrayal by the Earl of Warwick. As Earl of March, Edward had been a signatory to manifestos regarding the governance of the realm. He, along with other Yorkist lords, had made their views on favourites, spending, and policies very clear. The statements issued by the Earl of Warwick and Duke of Clarence in 1469 were almost identical to those issued in 1460 by the Earls of March, Salisbury, and Warwick. The justification for Yorkist intervention was little different to the Earl of Warwick's justification for the actions of 1469. Had the king failed in his responsibilities as a monarch? Was it the case that there were favourites? Was the good of the Common Weal being overlooked by a select few advisors? Or was the Earl of Warwick simply acting out of selfishness and greed?

Richard Neville was perceived by the *Croyland Chronicle* as being aggrieved at the King's marriage to Elizabeth Woodville, and the rise of her family[37] and it is also the only contemporary record that suggests that foreign policy was a source of Warwick's disillusionment. *Hearne's Fragment* suggests that the cause of disagreement was the marriage union and Burgundian alliance, which can be inferred as being disgruntlement at the Woodville pre-eminence at court, or at his own policies not being pursued. There are few suggestions within contemporary documents that the marriage of the king to Elizabeth Woodville over the union to Bona of Savoy that had been mooted by the Earl of Warwick. Most references to this possible cause of disenchantment come after the event. *Hearne's Fragment,* Dominic Mancini, John Warkworth, William Worcester, Jean Wavrin and Sir Thomas More all comment after the event and with varying levels of access to people who could reliably inform on the Earl of Warwick's views. In short, we do not know definitively what the true cause of the rift was as it is clouded in political theatre or based on incomplete or one-sided information.

The uprisings of 1469 had seen the County of Lincolnshire experience unrest. In early 1470 rumours began to spread that justice was about to be meted out upon the commons of the county for their part in the rebellions[38]. It resulted in a large force being assembled at the direction of Lord Welles, his son, and Sir Thomas Dymoke. Sir Robert Welles was taken into the King's custody prior to any meeting of armies on the field. His confession states that the guidance to arm themselves and resist was brought to himself by a messenger in the employment of the Duke of Clarence. It then goes on to describe exchanges of messages with the Earl of Warwick. Lord Welles also noted that despite the bidding of the Duke of Clarence and Earl of Warwick, at that time, no commotion or stirring had been undertaken by his kin. *"Also say that ne had beene the said Duc & Erles provoking we at this tyme wold ne durst have maid eny comocon or sturing but upon their comforth we did that we did*[39]*"*. Confessions are hardly the most reliable of sources, so from Welles' word alone it is impossible to discern the extent to which the Earl of Warwick was involved in fuelling discontent in Lincolnshire. Lord Welles and Sir Thomas Dymoke were executed on the field at Empingham on 12 March 1470 when King Edward brought his force forward to face Sir Robert Welles and the rebel army. The battle itself is most referred to as Losecote field[40] due to the rebel force fleeing in the face of the large royal force. The *Chronicle of the Rebellion in Lincolnshire* notes that for those who did stand and fight, *'theire crye was, A Clarence! a Clarence! a Warrewike!*[41]*'*

It was not until the last minute that the King, in public at least, acknowledged the potential complicity of the Earl of Warwick in the Lincolnshire rebellion. Commissions of Array had been issued to the Earl. Messages had been exchanged. Yet there was rumour that the Earl may be intending to participate in the revolt against the king, rather than at his side suppressing it. A letter written by Sir John Paston as the king was making his way north says. *'Item, my Lorde of Warwyk, as it is supposyd, schall goo with the Kynge in to Lyncolne schyre; some men seye that hys goyng shall doo goode, and som seye that it dothe harme.*[42]*'*

It is hard to ascertain whether the Earl of Warwick, or Duke of Clarence, had intended to join with the rebel force at this time. Welles' confession noted the intention of the pair to place the Duke of Clarence on the throne[43], presumably with the Earl of Warwick acting as Lieutenant or similar, as he did in the readeption parliament. Letters found amongst the baggage train at Empingham confirmed that the Duke and Earl were in communication with the rebels. The pairs actions in the aftermath of the royal victory also made their involvement clear: they fled first to the North West where they unsuccessfully attempted to gain the support of the Stanley Family, then made their way south before boarding a ship that, after being turned away at Calais, eventually disembarked in France. *Hearne's Fragment* suggests that the Earl of Warwick had continued to plot against the king. Rather than the Earl, or

Duke of Clarence joining the rebel army, it instead suggests that the plan was to entice the King to:

"a banquet at his [Archbishop of York's] Palace of the Moor besides Langley: whither as the King came, and a little before supper, when they should have washed, John Ratcliff, that after was Lord Fitzwalter, warned the King privily, and bade him beware; for there were ordained privily an 100 men of arms, the which should take him and convey him out of the way[44]".

The rout of the Lincolnshire rebels at Empingham certainly changed the approach of the Earl of Warwick, and the view that the King had of his cousin. *Robert Fabyan's chronicle* summarises the events. He suggests that the Earl and Duke departed for France due to their lack of military might at that time. In France the Earl opened discussions with Louis XI regarding French assistance in an invasion. This in turn included the Earl *'providing for the return into England'* of Queen Margaret, and Prince Edward. Only when, *'the sayd lordes were thus departyd the lande, the kyng comaudyd them to be proclaymed as rebellys & traytours thorugh out his realm[45]'.*

Early 1470 showed that the Earl of Warwick was implicated in further unrest and disruption to the state. It cannot be stated definitively what the intended outcome was. His motive appears once more to have been ensuring his own position at the heart of government. As suggested in *Hearne's Fragment*, the plan may have been to take the king once again into custody and rule in his name. For that to happen successfully would have required a shift in the balance of power. With the

Lincolnshire revolt being foiled, and the Stanley's being unwilling to support the Earl and Duke, there was little hope of this being achievable. Furthermore, the involvement of the Earl of Warwick and Duke of Clarence in the unrest was now known. Whatever the initial intentions of the Earl of Warwick, his options were now limited. Denounced as a traitor by King Edward and seeking refuge in France, the opportunities to remain at the centre of English politics now became reliant upon others.

This period of exile resulted in one of the most extraordinary agreements of convenience that was brokered between any magnates or royals in the history of medieval England. The political scenario in France lent itself to their supporting the Earl of Warwick. Conflict with Burgundy saw the French fleet stretched. The Earl had considerable experience in naval warfare, and despite initially suggesting it was loyal to King Edward, the reality of Calais' loyalty to the Earl of Warwick was soon clear. For Louis XI, financing a fleet and army for the Earl of Warwick's use made good military sense. Louis was also aware of the possibilities to destroy the Anglo-Burgundian alliance. To manage it, he needed regime change in England.

The various parties now in France were an unlikely band of allies. Louis XI was playing host to not only the Earl of Warwick and Duke of Clarence but also to Queen Margaret, Prince Edward, and the Lancastrian court in exile. The Queen and Earl had clashed from the mid-1450s onwards. It was the Earl's men who had captured King Henry on more than one occasion, his leadership that was largely responsible for the Yorkists gaining the political advantage in the South-East in 1460. It was his vast wealth and network that had provided supplies for the campaign of 1461 that saw the Queen and her kin defeated at Towton and put to flight. The last bastions of resistance in England had been wrestled from Lancastrian hands by the Earl of Warwick and his brother. Everything that the Queen had fought for had been denied largely because of the Earl of Warwick. And now, they were both in exile in France.

Whilst the pair clearly had much that would make them very wary of each other, they had several things in common. Both wanted power in England. The Queen wanted the restoration of King Henry and the inheritance of the crown to revert to her son, Prince Edward. The Earl of Warwick had already attempted to enforce his political will on the government of England once, and the recurrence of unrest in areas where he had influence suggest that he had again intended to oust King Edward and ensure that he could rule. Both parties had considerable resources, could draw upon the support of lords, retainers, merchants, and large sections of the commons. However, both parties had discovered that their strength was insufficient to effect lasting change. In short, to succeed, Richard Neville and Queen Margaret would need to work together.

Through suggestions and introductions presented by King Louis XI, the previously bitter rivals were able to come to an agreement that was to the benefit of both the Earl, and the Queen. The Duke of Clarence was also party to the agreement. The Manner and Guiding of the Earl of Warwick at Angers[46], better known as the Angers Agreement, had several key components. It bound the House of Lancaster and Neville families together through a marriage union. Prince Edward and Anne Neville were married as a result. The Earl agreed to invade England, with a Lancastrian force following. King Henry would be returned to the throne. Prince Edward would be his heir, and next in line would be the Duke of Clarence[47]. The Earl of Warwick would hold the position of Lieutenant of England, acting in lieu of King Henry to eradicate the indecisiveness that had plagued earlier periods of Henry's personal rule. As had happened previously, there was a statement from the Earl and Duke outlining the faults of King Edward's reign and justifications for the resumption of Lancastrian rule. In making this agreement with Queen Margaret, the earl of Warwick has abandoned any possibility of a return to the Yorkist fold and is complicit in a further betrayal of his cousin, King Edward IV.

The motivation for the Earl of Warwick remains the desire for status, control, influence, and the safeguarding of his daughter's futures. In this respect, the Earl had remained consistent. His argument that he acted for the good of the common weal also remains consistent, and in many respects his words on issues such as favourites can be backed with examples. On the matter of foreign policy, however, the grievance is one of personal preference more than it being an act of corruption. Richard Neville was remaining true to himself, his immediate family, his retainers, in pursuing policies even via questionable methods that would maintain or improve their lot. Such diligent pursuit of the good fortunes of one's kin and retainers would commonly be regarded as good lordship. Running the risk of incurring the wrath of a king makes it a precarious route, but one that he and other senior magnates had been actively pursuing and seeing others pursue, often with success, for decades.

Where this instance differs from the Earl of Warwick's previous use of military might is in the change of allegiance. Previously, the Earl had in common with other lords, issued manifestos that condemned the actions of corrupt officials and called for true liegemen to be at the heart of government. Those statements actively supported the reigning monarch in words. 1459, 1460, 1469, the manifestos published by Richard Neville had called not for regime change but for better governance. At Angers, that changed.

"The Oath of the Earl of Warwick at Angers sworn to King Henry."

"First, the Earl of Warwick sware upon the verrey (true) Cross in Saint Mary's Church of Angers, that without change he shall always hold the party and quarrel of King Henry, and shall serve him, the Queen and the Prince, as a true and faithful subject oweth to serve his Sovereign Lord[48]*."*

This oath of allegiance was accompanied by a series of propaganda statements issued by the Earl of Warwick and Queen Margaret. These were intended to inform their supporters in England of the pact, to reassure them that the union was a true one, and to foster support for their cause. When the Earl landed in England, the outcome was a swift and relatively peaceful victory. The Earl's supporters were ready.

The King and his supporters seemed to be caught by surprise, resulting in King Edward being forced to flee to Burgundy when the Marquess of Montagu changed his allegiance following the arrival of his brother, the Earl of Warwick. Philippe Commines noted of the ease by which the Earl of Warwick executed his plan:

"Misfortune and danger never go alone: the king's success and his courage were now strangely altered. A fortnight before that man would have been looked upon as mad, who should have told him, "The Earl of Warwick shall drive you out of England, and in eleven days have the supreme power and dominion in his own hands" (for it cost him no more time to bring the whole kingdom to obedience).[49]"

The plan to oust Edward had been well planned. The Yorkist king was warned at the last minute of the duplicity of the Marquess of Montagu and managed to flee, to Burgundy. Commines is perhaps exaggerating the suggestion that the Earl was not viewed as a threat. It was known that he and the Duke of Clarence were in France and that ships were readied. The speed at which he was able to undertake his invasion, the lack of opposition to the Earl, and the ease at which Richard Neville and the Duke of Clarence took control of the South-East and London were achieved quickly. Such a rapid change in fortunes in this region was not unprecedented though, the Earl had achieved similar results in 1460.

There is little doubt about the way in which King Edward viewed the actions of the Earl of Warwick and his brother. The *Arrivall*, compiled with Yorkist approval, opens with a statement about Edward's intentions in 1471. 1471 required King Edward to fight, *'agaynst th'Erle of Warwicke, his traytor and rebell, calling himselfe Lievetenaunte of England, by pretensed auctoritie of the usurpowre Henry, and his complices[50]'*.

However, it is not the case that the Earl was simply dismissed as a traitor and placed in a 'do or die' situation. The matter of responsibilities to the country, lords, clergy, and commons arose. The Earl of Warwick had significant support. It was prudent not to dismiss the rebels and offer them no means of returning to the fold. This level of responsibility meant that on occasion, the show of force could be enough to enact political change: revolt was a means of pressurising the monarchy for which there were several significant precedents[51]. This instance is rather different as the Earl of Warwick had made an oath of allegiance to King Henry, but that was not an unforgivable act so far as King Edward was concerned.

The route to potentially bringing the Earl back into the affinity of King Edward was to come from the Duke of Clarence. As discussed earlier, there is the distinct possibility that the duke had decided to return to the side of his brother prior to Edward landing at Ravenspur in 1471. George's decision and timing shifted the balance of power in 1471, leaving the Earl of Warwick in a scenario where his forces were separated from those of the Lancastrian magnates who had participated in the readeption period at a time before the arrival of Queen Margaret, Prince Edward, and the force that they were bringing to bear from France.

Upon receiving the Duke of Clarence back into the Yorkist fold, the King permitted George to seek:

"a goode accorde betwyxt the Kynge and th'Erle of Warwyke; not only for th'Erle, but also for to reconsyle therby unto the Kyngs good grace many lordes and noble men of his land, of whom many had largly taken parte with th'Erle; and this for the weale of peax and tranquilitie in the land, and in advoydynge of cruell and mortall were, that, of the contrary, was lykly, in shortyme, to enswe; he made, therefore, his mocions, as well to the Kynge as to th'Erle, by messagis sendynge to and fro, bothe for the well above sayde, as to acquite hym trwly and kyndly in the love he bare unto hym.[52]"

Whilst the Earl was within the strongly defended town of Coventry, messages were exchanged with King Edward. They varied in intent. On the one hand the Earl was challenged to fight on an open field, on the other hand, he was offered terms by the King. That Edward offered the Earl terms may seem strange given the events of the previous two years. The King, and Earl, however, had duties that went beyond their own selves. The responsibility of a King, Lieutenant, or senior magnate is to work in the best interests of the people. For that duty to be fulfilled requires of them the ability to compromise for the good of the country. So, despite the Earl having committed acts that Edward would undoubtedly view as treason, it was prudent for the good of the people to attempt to come to an agreement with the Earl. This, according to Arrivall, resulted in Edward offering the Earl a pardon and terms, *"for the wele of peax and tranquilitie of the Realme of England, and for therby to avoyde th'effusyon of Christen bloode.*[53]*"*

The terms that were offered to the Earl by Edward were rejected. The Arrivall addresses possible reasons for the decision to decline the terms and fight on. It suggests that the Earl had either determined that there had been too many offences committed for any pardon to be true. Alternatively, it could have been a matter of honour due to the great number of oaths and promises that he had made to Queen Margaret, the King of France, and at the readeption parliament. Finally, the Arrivall notes that the Earl of Warwick would also have expected to be able to escape to Calais or France, as he had done previously, if required. It cites the example of the Earl of Oxford who had managed to do this in the aftermath of the Battle of Barnet, suggesting that Richard Neville would also have had a plan should he have been able to escape the field of battle[54].

For the Arrivall to suggest that it may have been a matter of honour shows that despite everything, the Yorkist leadership still had some respect for the Earl of Warwick. Richard Neville's decision to spurn the offer of a pardon led to the two sides facing each other in the Battle of Barnet on 14 April 1471. His army included his brother, the Marquess of Montagu, as well as Lancastrian lords including the Duke of Exeter and Earl of

Oxford. It was not an inconsiderable force, but one that through mistakes induced by poor visibility was overcome by their foes. As the army of Warwick retainers and Lancastrian men tried to flee the battlefield, Richard Neville, 16th Earl of Warwick, was found by the Yorkists and killed.

The decision to fight at this time raised some questions in near contemporary accounts. The *memoirs of Phillipe Commines* suggests that there was a fourth possible reason why the Earl chose to fight on. Not a matter of honour, nor a belief that he had angered Edward too much for any pardon to be of questionable value. Instead, Commines states that, *"the fear he had of the Duke of Somerset, whose father and brother he had put to death, and the hatred he bore to Queen Margaret, mother to the Prince of Wales, induced him to fight alone.[55]"*

The Earl of Warwick is known as the Kingmaker due to his changing of allegiance at critical moments in the Wars of the Roses. This can lead to questions being asked about his sense of honour, loyalty, or assertions being made that he had betrayed one, or two, monarchs. In his own words Richard Neville argued consistently for strong and effective government. He stood his ground when parliament's effectiveness seemed to be waning, and monarchs were increasingly influenced by a small group of favoured courtiers. Alongside this argument runs the simple fact that at each of these moments in time, the Earl of Warwick stood to retain or strengthen his own level of power and authority by acting against men he argued were corrupt. Was he always backing the option that gave the country the best form of governance, or the option that provided himself with the greatest amount of power? The former can be justified in many ways, the latter backs claims that the Earl of Warwick betrayed first King Henry VI, then King Edward IV.

Chapter Four. Henry Beaufort, 3rd Duke of Somerset

The House of Beaufort is the family name given to the children of Katherine Swynford during her affair with John of Gaunt. The couple had four children, John, Henry, Thomas, and Joan between the years of 1371 and 1379. After the marriage of John of Gaunt and Katherine Swynford in 1396, the children were legitimised by King Richard II but barred from inheritance to the throne by King Henry IV.

The Beaufort line was therefore very closely aligned with the House of Lancaster. John of Gaunt was also the father of Henry Bolingbroke who became King Henry IV, the first of the Lancastrian kings. The first generation of Beaufort's were half siblings to Bolingbroke, uncles and aunt of King Henry V, and great uncles and aunt to King Henry VI.

Through marriages and appointments, the Beaufort family was able to establish itself as one of England's most important family networks. John Beaufort, 1st Earl of Somerset married Margaret Holland. Margaret was a daughter of Thomas Holland, 2nd Earl of Kent. Thomas was a half-brother to King Richard II. The descendants of John and Margaret include the Dukes of Somerset upon which this chapter concentrates, and Margaret Beaufort, mother of Henry Tudor.

Henry Beaufort entered the church, gaining high rank as Cardinal and acting as Lord Chancellor of England. He was hugely influential in the minority of King Henry VI. Henry Beaufort's loans enabled the continuation of war against France and financed campaigns that his nephew, John 1st Duke of Somerset, commanded.

Thomas Beaufort, married Margaret Neville of Hornby. He held a series of important roles including the position of Lord Chancellor, Lord High Admiral, and Captain of Calais. Thomas and Margaret had one child who predeceased them.

Joan Beaufort married firstly Robert Ferrers, 2nd Baron Ferrers, and secondly Ralph Neville, 1st Earl of Westmoreland. By Ralph Neville, Joan bore five daughters and nine sons. Their daughters married well, including unions to the 2nd Duke of Norfolk, 2nd Earl of Northumberland, 1st Duke of Buckingham, and to the 3rd Duke of York. The couple's sons included Richard Neville, 5th Earl of Salisbury, Robert Neville, Bishop of Salisbury and Durham, William Neville, 1st Earl of Kent, George Neville 1st Baron Latimer, and Edward Neville, 3rd Baron Bergavenny.

Already related closely to the House of Lancaster, their marriages and ecclesiastical appointments soon formed bonds of kinship across the country and with many of the most powerful families in the country. It was a platform that saw the family's position within court rise. John Beaufort was created Earl of Somerset in 1397. He was then appointed to significant roles including that of Warden of the Cinque Ports and Admiral of the Irish and Northern Fleets. He was soon elevated to the rank of Marquess because of the support he gave to Richard II against the Lords Appellant. The seizure of the crown by John's half-brother Henry Bolingbroke could have presented problems for the Marquess of Somerset. The new king had been a Lord Appellant. John's father-in-law was Thomas Holland, 1st Duke of Surrey, who the first Lancastrian king had executed for his role in the epiphany uprising.

John Beaufort faced few sanctions for his role as a counter-appellant, though his elevation to Marquess was rescinded along with other creations from the latter stages of Richard's reign. The Earl of Somerset was one of the key commanders in suppressing the rebellion of Owen Glyndwr and after undertaking several diplomatic missions, he was named as Constable of England in 1404.

John Beaufort had proven his worth and loyalty to his half-brother's regime. Upon his death in 1410 his title passed to his eldest son, Henry Beaufort 2nd Earl of Somerset. Henry was a boy when his father died and the Beaufort lands were managed on his behalf by his mother, Margaret. He took livery of his lands aged 15 and was soon involved in military action in Normandy. Serving under his uncle, Thomas Beaufort, Duke of Exeter, he participated in the Siege of Rouen, in which he was killed on 25 November 1418, aged 16. The Beaufort title was then inherited by his brother John.

Like his elder brother, John Beaufort 3rd Earl of Somerset went to Normandy to participate in the campaigns being fought by his cousin, King Henry V. After participating in the 1419 campaign, he returned and fought at the Battle of Baugé under his stepfather Thomas, Duke of Clarence. The Battle of Baugé was a hugely unexpected reversal for the English. Thomas, Duke of Clarence was killed in the fighting. The young Earl of Somerset was captured and held for ransom. John Beaufort. 3rd Earl of Somerset was to remain in captivity from 1421 until 1438.

The release of John Beaufort, 3rd Earl of Somerset began a series of events that would contribute significantly to the outbreak of the Wars of the Roses. John was soon reassigned to positions in France. He was appointed as captain of numerous fortresses across the north of France. When Richard Beauchamp, 13th Earl of Warwick died, the Earl of Somerset took command of all English forces in France. It was a temporary solution until the Council made a long-term appointment. John's management of England's forces in France was quite successful in this period. Harfleur was retaken, Avranches relieved, Picardy harassed and weakened, and the Duke of Brittany forced to accept terms in the summer of 1440.

Politics at court was soon to begin forcing a divide though. Despite John's successes, the Council chose to appoint Richard, 3rd Duke of York, to the position of Lieutenant-General of France on 2 June 1440. Though the Duke of York was more senior, the reasoning was as much to do with the rift between the Duke of Gloucester, who backed the Duke of York, and Cardinal Beaufort, who had been bankrolling his nephews campaigning.

It left the Beaufort family in England and frustrated by the lack of opportunity in France, whilst the Duke of York was benefitting from work previously undertaken by the Earl of Somerset in France. In this time John married Margaret Beauchamp. The couple had one child, Margaret Beaufort, before events at court and in France took John away from the family home.

1442 presented the Earl with an opportunity. Guyenne was under threat from the French and the Earl was earmarked to lead the expedition for its relief. Though the immediate threat to Guyenne lifted, it was clear to Council that additional forces were needed in France. The Earl once more was to lead the relieving army. The venture raised several questions. First, should the army be dispatched to Guyenne, or Normandy. Second, how would the command of the Earl of Somerset relate to the Duke of York's overall command as Lieutenant in France.

The solution saw the Earl elevated to Duke for parity of rank. It then agreed that the Duke of Somerset would lead a force that would drive south from Normandy, creating a defensive screen and hopefully forcing the French into a pitched battle. The campaign was again financed largely by Cardinal Beaufort, whose financing of military matters in France was a major factor in deciding what policy would be adopted.

Such a campaign affected the Duke of York's ability to undertake his role across all of English held lands in France and denied him reinforcements as they were directed to the Duke of

Somerset's chevauchee. It was a slight on his command that began to drive a wedge between the Duke of York and successive Duke's of Somerset.

The Duke of Somerset's campaign was a failure. Blighted with problems with recruitment and planning, it headed south from Cherbourg and failed in its objective to bring the French to the field of battle. Further to this, the campaign had stopped short of the Loire and instead of pressing into central France or towards Guyenne, it turned to the west and campaigned along the marches of Brittany. Though gains had been made, the venture had been very expensive and had performed a strategic U-turn. When the Duke disbanded his army in January 1444 and returned to England, he found himself barred from attending the royal court. John Beaufort, 1st Duke of Somerset, died shortly afterwards, in May 1444. Though he was known to be unwell there was a suggestion that the Duke had taken his own life.

The death of the Duke whilst in disgrace saw the dukedom extinguished and the original title of Earl passed to his brother, Edmund Beaufort. John's lands were inherited by his infant daughter, Margaret, making her one of the wealthiest wardships of late medieval England.

Edmund Beaufort had grown in importance during his brother's imprisonment in France. He had taken up diplomatic roles and, in 1436, commanded the English defence of Calais. His success in retaining Calais led to him being honoured as a Knight of the

Garter. Other military successes had followed, it was Edmund who had led the campaign in Normandy that recouped lands from the French, including the port of Harfleur. At the time of his brother's death, Edmund had already been created Earl of Dorset, elevated to Marquess, and like many other English nobles, held titles and lands in English controlled parts of France[1].

Edmund Beaufort, like his brother, had benefitted greatly from titles, lands, and patronage from King Henry VI. The same family ties and networks provided for him the political and military opportunities and powers that enabled his Earldom, elevation to Marquess, and the funds with which to engage in operations in France. So highly thought of was the Marquess of Dorset, that he was appointed to the hugely important positions of Lieutenant of France, Guyenne, and Normandy in late 1447. It was followed in March of 1448 by Edmund being created Duke of Somerset.

The positions were among the most important that could be given to an English noble. They enabled the Duke of Somerset to act in the King's name within the occupied areas of France, and in Guyenne and Normandy. Unfortunately for Edmund Beaufort, he was granted the roles at a time when the English grip on these territories was under severe pressure. Under his stewardship Normandy was lost in August 1450. Bordeaux and Guyenne fell the following year, before being briefly recovered by the Earl of Shrewsbury before being lost again in 1453. The loss of France was the result of a wide range of factors, from governance by the King and his Council, through to funding, tactical inadequacies, French ingenuity, the continental alliance systems, and sheer bad luck. In a political setting, there was usually somebody who had to take the blame. This led to conflict between the Duke's of Somerset and York.

The Duke of Somerset's actions in the period leading to the fall of Normandy were called into question. His behaviour and demands with respect to having to cede his lordship of Maine to the French as a result of the terms of the marriage contract drawn up between King Henry and Margaret of Anjou linked him to lords who, by the end of 1450, had been impeached, or murdered. Politically this was a difficult association. However, it was the way Edmund Beaufort defended Normandy that drew the attention of the Duke of York. Despite having large payments for ceding Maine, personal wealth, and funds from Council, he was accused of having done little to improve the defences of the Duchy of Normandy.

The collapse of English defences in Normandy was rapid. The French attacked in July 1449. Rouen was surrendered by the Duke of Somerset himself in October 1449. The following July Caen, and with it the whole of Normandy, was surrendered. The expectation at the time was that defenders of a besieged town would hold out until there was no option but to surrender, on honorable terms. This would require them to endure some degree of discomfort whilst opportunities for relief could be explored, forces gathered, attempts made. Rouen was handed to the French without the opportunity for that to happen. So too was Caen surrendered before a relief force could be sent from England. Defeat without honour was intolerable to many lords. Especially so those who were slighted by it: the Duke of York was nominally the Captain of Rouen; or those who lost estates in Normandy because of the French victories.

Deserved or not, the Duke of Somerset was accused of being responsible for the losses suffered in Normandy in particular. Fabyan recorded that:

"And thus began rumour' & malyce to spryng atwene the lordes of th lande: and specially the duke of Somerset and other of the queues counsayll were hadde in great hateryd for the losynge of Normady, wherof [the] chief cytie Roan was lost or gyuen vp by appoyntement the yere preceding...[2]"

The charge that the Duke of Somerset was responsible for the loss of Normandy was part of a wider complaint about the conduct of Government. 1450 had seen the rebellion led by Jack Cade. That had noted a series of complaints about corruption, poor or wicked counsel, frivolous spending, and unfair taxes. Though the complaints of the commons were raised in revolt, they mirrored many of the concerns of some of the nobility. It led to the Duke of York, frustrated at lack of change and the favouritism within court, arraying his men and marching from his lands in the Welsh Marches, through the south, around London and then towards the capital. It resulted in a show of force by the Duke of York in 1452 that culminated in an armed standoff at Dartford against a force that included the King, Duke of Somerset, and Earls of Salisbury and Warwick amongst others.

When the two sides faced each other at Blackheath in 1452, the complaint made by the Duke of York was once again aimed at the Duke of Somerset. Fabyan's account continues by noting that:

"...his [the Duke of York's] entent & purpose was to remoue from hym a fewe euyll dysposyd persones, by whose meanys the comon people was gretiouslye oppressyd, and the comynaltye greatlye enpouerysshed; of the whiche he namyd for pryncypall the duke of Somerset.[3]"

The dispute between the Duke of Somerset and Duke of York escalated further in 1453. The Duke of Norfolk, aligned to the Duke of York, petitioned for the arrest of Edmund Beaufort. He argued that:

"greete dishonneurs and losses that ben come to thys full noble royaume of England by the fals menes of som persones that have take on theym over grete autoritee in thys royaume shulde be knowen, and that the persones lyvyng that have doon theym shulde be corrected aftyr the merites of her desertes. And to that entent y have denounced and delyverd to you in wrytyng certeyn articles ayenst the Duc of Somerset, whych ys one of theym that ys gylty thereof.[4]"

This renewed attack on the Duke was set against the context of Guyenne having also been lost to France, the King having entered his first period of incapacity, civil unrest between the Neville and Percy families in the north east, and critically with regards the Duke of Somerset, the transferring of affinity to the Yorkist faction of the Earls of Salisbury and Warwick due to inheritance disputes with the Duke of Somerset. The balance of power in court had shifted. The Duke of Somerset could not hide behind support from an incapacitated monarch, instead, he was placed in custody in the Tower of London. He remained there from late 1453 until February 1455[5], shortly after the King's recovery.

The consequence of the King's recovery and the Duke of Somerset's release was an immediate change in the balance of power at court. Once more the Duke of Somerset was in the ascendancy as chief amongst the counsellors to the King and Queen. Having been detained for over a year, the Duke was slighted, and angry. A Great Council was called by the King. It was to be held in Leicester in May 1455.

The tension between the factions headed by Queen Margaret and Duke of Somerset and that led by the Duke of York were heightened. A Great Council in a city loyal to the court party could be taken as a sign that punitive action was about to be taken against the Yorkist lords. Those lords began raising their retainers. In response, the Duke of Somerset and other nobles of that faction raised their retinues. The King was therefore to be accompanied by a large force. It found its way to Leicester blocked by a Yorkist force at St. Albans.

The Yorkists once again made accusations about the Duke of Somerset. Messages were sent that were never passed to the King. Some survive. One letter reminds the King that the Duke of York and his affinity are true and loyal, concerned only for his welfare and that of the commons of England. It asks:

'...sayd Hyghnesse so to take, accept, and repute us [the Yorkists], and not to plese to geve trust or confidence unto the sinistrez, maliciouse, and fraudulent laboures and rapportes of our sayd ennemyes unto our comyng to your sayd moste noble presence[6]*'.*

The Yorkist lords became frustrated with the failings of negotiations. In 1452 the apparent success of Yorkists at forcing change at Blackheath had been almost immediately turned on its head by the Duke of Somerset, resulting in the Duke of York's public humiliation. This wasn't going to happen again, something that perhaps the Duke of Somerset had not contemplated. The result was the First Battle of St. Albans on 22 May 1455. Fought within the streets and squares of the town centre, it was a short but decisive battle. In which the Duke of Somerset, Edmund Beaufort, was killed.

To this stage each of the ennobled Beaufort's had served the Lancastrian kings as commanders. They had enjoyed royal patronage from Henry IV through to Henry VI. The family, as

Earls and Dukes of Somerset, had been central to the courts of the three Lancastrian monarchs. Even when faced with humiliation, in the form of John Beaufort failures and death in questionable circumstances in 1444, the family themselves had remained close to the king and enjoyed ongoing benefits of kinship and patronage. Following the deaths of Henry VI's uncles, John Duke of Bedford and Humphrey Duke of Gloucester, the House of Beaufort had assumed a central role at court, as befitting men who were among the kings closest remaining relatives. Allied closely with Queen Margaret, aiding her dominance at court, and having sided with her when faced with the impeachment then murder of another court loyalist, William de la Pole, Duke of Suffolk, it is perhaps inconceivable to consider that this family could at any point be accused of betrayal. And yet that is a charge that can be levied against Henry Beaufort, 3rd Duke of Somerset.

Henry Beaufort was the eldest son of Edmund Beaufort. He too fought in the First Battle of St. Albans and inherited the Dukedom of Somerset upon his father's death in that clash. The Yorkist affinity were aware of the potential for the young Duke to present them with political or military problems. To counter this, Henry was placed in the care of the Earl of Warwick. The adage of keeping one's friends close but your enemies closer did not prevent conflict for long.

A letter penned by John Gresham to John Paston on 16 October 1456 describes events that took place whilst the magnates of the land were in residence in Coventry for a Great Council. Men of the Duke of Somerset's household caused a *'great affray'* against the watch.

"On Moneday last passed was a gret affray at Coventre bytwene the Duke of Somersets men and the wechemen [watchmen] of the toun, and ij. or iij. men of the toun were kylled there, to gret disturbance of alle the Lords there; for the larom belle was ronge, and the toun arose, and wold have jouperdit to have distressed the Duke of Somerset, &c., ne had the Duke of Buks not have take a direccion therein[7]".

The clashes appear to have been an attempt at asserting some authority over proceedings. It failed and required the intervention of the Duke of Buckingham to prevent the townsfolk targeting the Duke of Somerset. The same source informs us that there was *'opynyon is contrary to the Whenes [Queen's] entent, and many other also, as it is talked'*. The Duke of Somerset, among others, were strengthening their ties to the Queen, factionalism was on the rise again.

The enmity between the Dukes of Somerset and York and their affinities continued throughout 1457. As 1458 began there was a large political divide, further complicated by a threat presented by the French. This threat was significant and impacting on trade.

"John Vyncent of Bentley was at the Priory of Lewes in Sussex this week, and says that sixty sail of Frenchmen were sailing

before the coasts, keeping the sea. The Lord Fauconberg is at Hampton with his navy. Edmund Clere of the King's house has heard from a soldier of Calais that Crowmer and Blakeney is much spoken of among Frenchmen. 'The King's safe conduct is not holden but broken, as it is voiced here, and that will do no good to merchants till it be amended.' Figs and raisins are dear at 18s[8]*".*

That there were 60 French ships at sea was a significant risk. The potential for landing, raiding, and destroying ports or coastal communities was great. In August of 1457 a French flotilla had raided Sandwich, killed the mayor, and burnt much of the town.

With the French at sea, the magnates of England needed to be brought together. Sandwich had been so easily assaulted by the French partly because Council had been distracted by internal divisions. The fleet at Calais had not been paid, an ongoing concern but at this time an issue that was compounded by the Earl of Warwick being Captain of Calais and the ill feeling between the Earl and Duke of Somerset. These matters, and the need to deescalate violence and tension between the factions, led to a series of agreements, bonds, and declarations that culminated in a Loveday Procession that was held at St. Paul's Cathedral.

On 23 March 1458 a series of bonds of recognisance were issued. Issued to the Dukes, Earls, Duchess and Countesses who had suffered or caused losses in the First Battle of St. Albans they saw bonds being required of each individual which would be held on, *'Condition, that [s]he shall abide and obey the king's award touching all controversies, trespasses, debts, debates, actions, offences, condemnations, executions and demands between him and [their opponents][9]'.*

The use of Bonds of recognisance was commonplace as a means of keeping the peace. Rarely, however, had they been issued to so many of the most senior magnates at the same time. These bonds would be lodged with the treasury with as a security for the future good conduct of the individual. Should they break the conditions, the bond would be lost. The amount lodged as a bond was therefore a considerable sum, based upon the wealth of each individual.

Holding the lords to bonds of recognisance was not on its own enough though. There needed to be public awareness of the promises made by these powerful overlords and influential ladies. This was achieved through the Loveday Procession of 25 March 1458.

"Item the xxiiij day of March our lady Eve of Annunciacion the king and quene being at Westminster and divers lordes condescended and agreed and ther made a full unyte and peas betwene the dukes of york and somerset and betwene the Erles Warrewyk Salesbury Northumbrelond and lord Clifford: ^ and the king pardoned all things doon afore aswell at Seint Albons as elles wher and proclamacion made peroi the same day thurgh the citee and therupon on the morn the King and Quene and the

lordes yede a procession at powles (which ^) was a greet gladnes and comfort to the peple[10]".

The Loveday and bonds of recognisances did little to alter the animosity between the Duke of Somerset and his adversaries. 1458 saw the Earl of Warwick set upon. April of 1459 then saw a fatal clash on Fleet Street between men loyal to the two factions[11]. The Queen and her adherents moved Court to Coventry and there was a marked increase in the issuing of the Prince of Wales's livery. A Great Council was called in June that the Yorkists refused to attend. Soon the plans of the Court party were made clear.

As both factions arrayed forces it was clear that the Yorkists would need to converge for them to present a strong enough front. This could be countered by the Court party as they commanded lands through which the Earls of Salisbury and Warwick would need to march if they were to join with the Duke of York.

The Duke of Somerset had a force at his disposal that was arrayed to the north west of Coventry[12]. It was ideally placed to intercept the Earl of Warwick as he marched towards Ludlow. On 21 September 1459, the Earl's force passed the Duke of Somerset's positions unhindered. Two days later Baron Audley ambushed the Earl of Salisbury's army at Blore Heath. The intention to prevent the Yorkists combining their force seems clear. The reasons for the Duke of Somerset having not engaged the Earl of Warwick are unclear.

The Yorkists had managed to unite their forces, the Earl of Salisbury having been victorious at Blore Heath. They were based at Ludlow. The Court Party, with the King present, marched toward the Yorkists. This presented the Duke of York and his affinity with a dilemma. They could not claim to be loyal to the king if they fought against him. Nor could they simply submit as their enemies within the Court party would almost certainly have them arrested on charges of treason. The outcome was the rout at Ludford following the Yorkists lords fleeing in the night.

Following the flight of the Yorkists the Court Party held Parliament in Coventry and attainted the Yorkist leaders. The Duke of Somerset as a leading magnate of the faction was a beneficiary of the reallocation of roles. The Captaincy of Calais was granted to the Duke. He would, however, need to take possession of the port city by force as it remained loyal to the Earl of Warwick.

The appointment as Captain of Calais was one that the Duke attempted to take up almost immediately. Taking Calais would be a hammer blow to Yorkist hopes of a revival and was specifically aimed at the subject of Henry Beaufort's hatred, the Earl of Warwick. The Duke's attempt to take possession was a failure. He,

"with a certeyne nombre of men of armes, hauyng with theym the kynges letters, wente to Caleys to thentent that the seyde duk shulde haue be cap- teyne of Caleys... they of Caleys wolde

haue take hym, and with muche payne he escaped and fled in to the castelle of Guynes...[13]"

Attempting to take the Port of Calais from sea had failed. He now attempted to take it by land. This required reinforcements. This too proved to be a failure. Not only did the Earl of Warwick hear of the plans, but he also managed to sail across the English Channel, attack the fleet in the haven of Sandwich, and capture Earl Rivers, sink several ships, and take possession of others. The Duke of Somerset's siege continued through the winter into spring of 1460.

Two events in April 1460 brought the Duke of Somerset's attempts to seize Calais to an abrupt and embarrassing end. First,

"the duk of Excestre, that was Amyralle, was sent to the see with a grete nauy for to dystresse the seyde erle of Warrewyk and his nauey, and sayled from Sandwyche to Dertemouthe, and there for lack of vetayle and of money hys soudyers were dysparbeled, and wente awey fro hym.[14]"

The Yorkists had managed to gain naval superiority in the Straights of Dover and English Channel. The Duke of Exeter, Admiral of the Fleet, was forced to remove the remaining ships from Sandwich as there was insufficient funds to pay the crews, and the haven was proven to be insecure.

Second, the failure of a frontal assault on Calais on 23 April 1460. Knowing that he had limited resources and time in which he could now take the port, Henry Beaufort opted to attempt to seize the entry to Calais. This attempt at Newnham Bridge was fended off by the garrison and the Duke was forced to withdraw without having had any success against the main fortifications at the Port of Calais.

There were major political consequences of the failure to oust the Yorkists from Calais. The Earl of Warwick was able to sail to Ireland to meet with the Duke of York. Lancastrian shipping and forces were attacked on more than one occasion. Yorkist support in the south-east was made aware of plans. And in June 1460, the Yorkists were able to sail from Calais to Sandwich, take the town, and march on London. The Court Party found its dominance shattered, and following the Battle of Northampton on 10 July 1460, it was they who found parliament being used against them. As the Yorkists pulled off this extraordinary turn around in their fortunes, the Duke of Somerset had been based in the castle at Guines in the Pale of Calais, unable to intervene.

For the Duke of Somerset, the series of events led to him leaving Guines for the safety of France. Henry Beaufort was therefore in France as the Yorkists consolidated their hold on power. So too was he overseas as Richard 3rd Duke of York returned, claiming the throne for himself. The outcome, the Act of Accord of 25 October 1460, was a compromise that suited nobody in the short term. Least of all those like Henry Beaufort whose rank, income, and roles were all due to his families ongoing patronage from the House of Lancaster.

The Duke of Somerset, and others in the affinity of Queen Margaret and Prince Edward, now faced a dilemma. If the Act of Accord were to remain, the bond to the Queen would weaken over time, then, with the accession of a Yorkist, be either broken or potentially worthless. Magnates such as the Duke of Somerset who had been proactive in seeking the attainting of the Yorkists would almost certainly lose their status, and possibly life, if the Act of Accord was to take effect. The system of patronage had benefitted the Beaufort family greatly. They had risen to the highest echelons of Government and Church. Patronage from each of the Lancastrian kings had bound them firmly to family now effectively headed by Queen Margaret on behalf of King Henry VI and Prince Edward. Bound by patronage, forced by circumstance, the Duke of Somerset and others of the Queen's affinity chose to combat the Act of Accord through force of arms.

The consequences of the Yorkist revival were clear to the Duke of Somerset and others in the Queen's affinity. A letter dated 12 October 1460 from Christopher Hansson to John Paston notes that:

"As for tythyngs here, the Kyng is way at Eltham and at Grenewych to hunt and to sport hym there, bydyng the Parlement, and the Quene and the Prynce byth in Walys alway. And is with hir the Duc of Excestre and other, with a fewe mayne, as men seythe here.

"...the Duc of Somerset he is in Depe [Dieppe]; withe hym Maister John Ormound, Wyttyngham, Andrew Trollyp, and other dyvers of the garyson of Gyanys, under the Kyng of Fraunce safcondyte, and they seythe here, he porpose hym to go to Walys to the Quene. And the Erle of Wyltschyre is stylle in pece at Otryght at the Frerys [Friars], whiche is seyntwary[15]".

In the same way that the Yorkists had chosen to avoid Great Council and Parliamentary sessions, so too had the Court party chosen to do so in October of 1460. As the Yorkists had done, the leaders had separated, in the case of the Duke of Somerset to Dieppe, others to Wales, and the Earl of Wiltshire into Sanctuary.

Bales chronicle notes of the actions that nobles including the Dukes of Somerset and Exeter who, *"wer sett of affnite and purposed as was reported and seid to have doon greet myschief and hurtes as they afore had used undre counciles and colour of supporting the kings right which proved evermore contrary as shewed be their werke[16]"*. The bond of affinity to the faction led by the Queen had, therefore, held firm after the Act of Accord was passed. Despite the Act being a compromise in Council and, it being granted royal assent by King Henry VI, the faction continued to be 'supporting the kings right' and that of what they perceived to be the true heir to the throne, Prince Edward. In simple terms, those in the affinity of the Queen and Prince Edward continued to support the prince and remained true to each other as a faction.

The Duke of Somerset now took charge of the forces arrayed against the Yorkists. At Wakefield on 30 December 1460, he commanded a Lancastrian army that defeated the Duke of York's force. The Duke of York was killed in the battle. His son, the Earl of Rutland, was killed in the immediate aftermath of the battle. The Earl of Salisbury was taken prisoner, then beheaded at Pontefract Castle. The Duke of Somerset had avenged the death of his own father five years earlier, proven his loyalty to the Queen and Prince Edward, and dealt the Yorkists a blow from which the Lancastrians must have believed their foes would not recover from.

This was the beginning of a series of battles that would determine the kingship of England for the next decade. Following the victory at Wakefield the Duke of Somerset went to York. From here the Lancastrian army, with Queen Margaret now present, marched south. The objective was to take London, recover King Henry VI from the Yorkists, and deal with the Earl of Warwick and other Yorkists in a decisive manner. The advance saw the Duke of Somerset command at the Second Battle of St. Albans. Here, on 17 February 1461, the prize of King Henry was won, as the Yorkists left the king behind as they fled from the field, having been outwitted in battle.

Victory at St. Albans was not decisive. The Earl of Warwick had retreated to London, and the Duke of York's heir, Edward, had defeated a Lancastrian force at Mortimer's Cross. There was now a large Lancastrian army, with the Dukes of Somerset and

Exeter as the battlefield commanders, approaching London. The Yorkists had the remnants of the Earl of Warwick's force, and that of Edward Earl of March. London was the prize for both. With the Yorkists inside London, the City of London refused Queen Margaret's army entry into to the city. In the meantime, the Yorkists declared Edward King of England, effective from 4 March 1461.

England now had King Henry VI, an anointed king who was with lords loyal to him and to Prince Edward's birthright. It also had King Edward IV. Edward's claim was based on the principle that in joining the Queen and Prince Edward on the field of battle at St. Albans, King Henry VI had broken the Act of Accord. According to the Yorkist argument when his kingship was ratified, this was justification for immediately enacting the inheritance of the throne as the Act had stated it would upon the death of King Henry VI[17]. It was in essence a political power play by the Yorkists to gain additional support through an argument of legitimacy.

The matter of kingship aside, the Act of Accord had been ignored by a series of nobles, including the Duke of Somerset. The Act had been passed by Parliament and was English law. The lords in the affinity of the Queen were loyal to the crown but not to the partisan parliamentary and state processes that had enacted the change in succession. In this scenario each noble was at odds with the norms of loyalties. The nature of what was now a civil war made it impossible for those in the

Court party to retain bonds to both Lancastrian kingship and the Parliamentary process. To work with one would mean exclusion from the other, as had been the case for the Yorkists in exile.

When the Lancastrians found themselves denied access to the City of London they chose to retire to the north, returning to York. The City of York, despite the dukedom in its name, was largely surrounded by estates of nobles who were adherents of Queen Margaret. The Yorkists, when they chose to march north to face the Lancastrians, would be faced with fierce resistance at the crossing points of the River Aire, need to pass through lands that were loyal to the Queen, pass close to Castles that were held by men of the Queen's affinity. And would be doing so after provisions had been acquired by the retreating army of the Lancastrians. Furthermore, there was hope that agreements could be made with the Scots, should the talks of Christmas 1460 be progressed. Strategically there was much logic in the decision to head north, a choice that must have been at least in part been influenced by senior commanders such as Henry Beaufort.

That there would be a major clash between the two sides was inevitable. Both factions stood to lose everything if they did not resolve matters in a decisive manner. Neither side would be willing to trust the other and the chivalric expectation of a noble being taken prisoner and held securely until a ransom was paid had been put to one side at Wakefield, so mercy could not be expected by either side. It had become a 'do or die' situation for the leading magnates.

The expectation of crushing the Yorkists in battle must have been high. Superior in numbers and on a field of their own choosing, the Duke of Somerset and other Lancastrian commanders would have been confident that their army would prevail. It was not to be, after a bloody battle to take control of Ferrybridge the Yorkists had advanced north of the Aire. The Battle of Towton that followed on Palm Sunday 1461 was said to be long and bloody. Eventually the Yorkist force, bolstered by the arrival of fresh soldiers under the command of the Duke of Norfolk, seized the initiative. *Hearne's Fragment* summarises the events succinctly:

"This field was sore fought. For there were slain on both parts 33,000[18] *men, and all the season it snowed. There were slain the Earls of Northumberland and Westmorland with others and Sir Andrew Troloppe; and taken the Earls of Devonshire and Wiltshire and beheaded there; The Earls of and the deposed King Harry, his Queen, with Henry, Duke of Somerset, and others, in great haste fled into Scotland*[19]*".*

As it became clear that the day was lost, the Duke escaped the field of battle and made his way to York. From here he, in the company of King Henry VI, Queen Margaret, and a number from the royal household, made their way to the safety of Scotland. This was simply the best option for the senior members of the Lancastrian leadership. Those who could, escaped to fight another day. In Scotland they were assured of a reasonably warm and secure welcome.

Exile in Scotland also provided an opportunity for the Queen to communicate with her French relatives. Now was an opportunity for the Lancastrians in exile to make use of the Auld Alliance as best they could. The *Paston Letters* includes correspondence from Lord Hungerford and Robert Whittingham[20] to Queen Margaret that notes the Duke of Somerset had travelled to Dieppe by August 1461, whilst the Royal family remained in Scotland with a small but notable group of their supporters. Henry Beaufort was still in France in October, being noted in correspondence[21] as being near Calais whilst other leading Lancastrians were engaged in actions in Wales and Scotland. The Duke of Somerset was clearly a leading figure in the coordination of the attempts to regain the initiative against the Yorkists.

This period illustrates the various ways in which the matters of loyalty, responsibility, rights, and honour were viewed by the leaders of both the Lancastrian and Yorkist factions. Both sides had summarily executed captured nobles in 1460/61. There had been defections either in the face of battle, or during the fighting itself. Acts of Parliament and attainders had been ignored or overturned. Yet there was still some semblance of honorable behaviour. Whilst Henry Beaufort was working with Queen Margaret and others such as the Duke of Exeter and Jasper Tudor to keep the Lancastrian cause alive, Edward IV issued an, *"Order to pay to Margaret Duchess of Somerset 166l. 13s. 4d. a year for life; as the king has learned how that she holds that yearly sum for life by endowment of John Duke of Somerset her husband and assignment of the late king as dower of an annuity of 500l. of the said custom[22]"*. A grant that was respectful of the awards of King Henry VI's reign and that was reiterated in further orders whilst her son was still preparing to wage war against Edward IV[23].

By March of 1462 the Duke of Somerset had returned to Scotland[24]. The period was one of frenetic diplomacy by both sides. The Lancastrians following up the Duke's talks in France with a visit by Margaret of Anjou herself, which resulted in French money and aid being promised. At the same time the Yorkist regime was busy making secret pacts with John of Islay, Earl of Ross, Lord of the Isles which was designed to undermine King James III. The fluidity of the situation meant that coordinated assaults against the Yorkist regime were hard to achieve. In autumn of 1462 though there was a breakthrough of sorts for the Lancastrians.

Queen Margaret had obtained the use of forty two ships under the command of Pierre de Brézé. This fleet put to sea with a thousand French soldiers and made for North East England. The Duke of Somerset also set sail, from Scotland, and landed at Bamburgh with a force of exiles and Scots. With the area having been part of the Earl of Northumberland's lands, it was hoped that the locals would rise against the Yorkists in support of the invading force. That wasn't to be, but the garrisons at several of the North Eastern sea facing castles did declare their loyalty to King Henry VI whilst others soon fell to the Lancastrian force.

The result was a fortified enclave in the North East that ensured that King Henry ruled over at least a portion of his domain. To survive, these castles needed supplies and more men from Scotland. Queen Margaret heading north to arrange this, the Duke of Somerset remained to take charge of Bamburgh Castle.

The response of the Yorkists to the return of Lancastrian forces in the North East was swift. We learn from a letter from John Paston Junior to his father that by 1 November 1462, *"my Lord of Warwyk yed forward in to Scotland as on saturday last past with xx.ml. [20,000] men; and Syr Wylliam Tunstale is tak with the garyson of Bamborowth, and is lyke to be hedyd, and by the menys of Sir Rychard Tunstale is owne brodyr[25]"*.

Militarily the defenders of Bamburgh could realistically only hold out if they were supplied and reinforced by sea. The Earl of Warwick had a large army and had large calibre cannon available. The duty of the Duke of Somerset was to hold the castle for as long as was possible, to wait and hope for reinforcement, or for a discreet opportunity for escape being provided by his Scottish and French allies. Attitudes of the day looked unfavourably on men who surrendered. Henry Beaufort only needed to look at the way in which his own predecessors had been viewed when surrendering or failing to follow orders properly. The latter had seen the dukedom degraded to an earldom; the former had seen widespread derision. As a simple matter of honour, as a chivalric norm, as a military approach, the only acceptable course of action was for the Duke of Somerset and his men to hold Bamburgh Castle for as long as possible. Furthermore, was the personal aspect. The Duke of Somerset had actively attempted to oust the Earl of Warwick from his position at Calais, had contributed to the increased animosity between the two factions, had been in overall command when the Earl of Salisbury and Earl of Rutland were executed, or butchered. Anything other than fighting to the bitter end would be unacceptable and humiliating. Yet the Duke of Somerset chose to take the Earl of Warwick at his word on a promise of pardon in return for his surrender.

Hearne's Fragment paints a slightly different picture. In this account the taking of Bamburgh was accidental, as the ship was forced ashore there by inclement weather. Nonetheless, the Duke and Sir Ralph Percy made little attempt at escaping, going as far as suggesting that the men had sought no remedy to escape. In burning their own ships, the Lancastrian lords were eliminating the possibility of a tactical withdrawal and placing themselves at the mercy of the Earl of Warwick[26].

What we have then is a surrender on terms. The questions surrounding accepting these terms are whether the terms were accepted after sufficient attempts to withhold assault, whether the Queen and Lancastrian affinity stood to gain from prolonged resistance, and whether or not there was ever any intention on the part of the Duke of Somerset to adhere to the terms of the pardon.

What is clear is that despite the adoption of a no mercy policy in the immediate aftermath of the Battle of Towton, both King Edward IV and the Earl of Warwick were now willing to countenance the granting of a pardon to the man who had commanded the Lancastrian army in the field and been central to the Court parties ongoing feuds with the Yorkists. It is an extraordinary turn around by both sides. The Yorkist change of heart is explained by the news that a relief force was heading to the North East from Scotland, that there was unrest and the last vestiges of resistance in Wales, and that King Edward was unwell with measles. In short, they wanted a fast resolution so that other matters could be addressed. The acceptance of the terms by the Duke of Somerset was after six weeks of defence. Enough time to dismiss charges of having simply given up. It was also in the face of a more concerted siege effort by the Yorkists who had moved ordnance into position. Not knowing that a relief force was en route, the fate of the castle may have seemed to be inevitable. In which case, the Duke's acceptance of a pardon may be viewed as being somewhat more honourable.

The Duke of Somerset attended court following his submission to the Earl of Warwick and receipt of his pardon from the King. Naturally, his presence was a moot point amongst the Yorkist affinity, many of whom did not trust him and had suffered losses because of his actions as a member of the Queen's affinity. This put a strain on the king's policy of rapprochement. Whilst it is a responsibility of those in power to wield it for the greater good, it ought perhaps not be extended to forgiveness of all sins and favour being granted to those who had seemingly done nought to deserve it.

After some time, it became clear that the presence of the Duke at court was likely to provoke incidents rather than lead to wounds being healed. Consequently, the Duke of Somerset was moved, with his pardon wholly intact, into a safer location in Wales. Here, some aspects of the terms of the surrender and pardon became unstuck. The Duke had been *'in to King Edwardes grace, by whiche graunted to hym a [thousand] marke by yere, whereof he was not payde.' The Duke 'therefore departed oute of England after halfe yere into Scotlonde.*[27]*'*

Whilst the *Warkworth Chronicle* suggests that it was the non-payment of the thousand marks per year annuity that led to the Duke of Somerset absconding and making his way north, the reality is that he had been plotting with his Lancastrian kin. An uprising in the Newcastle area began, and failed, as the Duke made his escape[28]. That the Duke had been conspiring is supported by a reference in a letter from John Paston the Youngest to John Paston Senior, that noted that, *"my Lord hathe gret labore and cost here in Walys for to take dyvers gentyllmen here whyche wer consentyng and helpyng on to the Duke of Somersettys goyng; and they were apelyd of othyr se[r]teyn poyntys of treson, and thys mater" and that, "The Comenys in Lancasher and Chescher wer up to the nombyr of a x. ml. [10,000] or more[29]".* The suggestion is that people were being arrested for having aided the Duke of Somerset in his treasonable return to the Lancastrian fold, and that some ten thousand men had risen in Lancashire and Cheshire in 1463.

The Duke of Somerset made his way to Scotland and then into North Eastern England. In his absence the Scots had invaded in support of the Lancastrians. This force had been pushed back over the border but there remained a loyal band of Lancastrians who were willing to fight under the Duke of Somerset's command. In April 1464 the Lancastrians attempted to ambush John Neville, Lord Montagu as he marched north to escort a Scottish delegation from the border to York. The attempt failed on Hedgely Moor, where on 25 April 1464 the two sides clashed. The Lancastrian force quickly faltered, with many fleeing the battlefield when the extent of Lord Montagu's force was realised. Henry Beaufort was among those who escaped, with a rear-guard of Sir Ralph Percy and his retainers being cut down by the Yorkist force.

The Yorkist force was now intent of tracking down the Lancastrians and putting an end to the persistent threat that they posed in the region. On the night of 12/13 May 1464 Montagu's army crossed the Tyne. On the 14 May he marched towards Hexham where the Lancastrian force was encamped. The following day saw a rapid Yorkist advance on the Duke of

Somerset's encampment. The speed of the assault took the defenders by surprise leading to the encounter being a chaotic rout. During the clash the Duke of Somerset and other leading Lancastrians were captured by Montagu's men. They were taken into Hexham and that same evening the Duke of Somerset was beheaded. Further executions followed, leaving the Lancastrians leaderless in the region.

Henry Beaufort had been executed for having reneged on the terms of his surrender and for resuming resistance to Yorkist rule. The Yorkists were unwilling to allow the Duke another chance. His demise then was for the Lancastrian cause for which he had been a leading protagonist since his father's death. It was not a glorious end but one at the hand of an axeman. In his time as Duke, Henry had shown a steadfast resolve, at times, to seek retribution for his personal loss. Yet had then set aside honour and surrendered to the very man whom he held most responsible for the crimes against his family. If it was a calculated gamble to enable him to fight another day, it was of limited success. Instead, his presence in the North East resulted in a bolstering of Yorkist resolve to destroy Lancastrian resistance, in which he himself was captured and executed. The days that followed his defeat at Hexham saw all remaining castles that were in Lancastrian hands submit to Yorkist nobles.

Henry Beaufort was then posthumously attainted with his estates becoming crown property and the dukedom of Somerset in abeyance. The title was claimed, in exile, by Henry's brother, Edmund. Edmund was in exile in France where he remained until the readeption. Following Edward IV's flight to Flanders in 1470 Edmund Beaufort, being acknowledged by the restored Lancastrian regime as the 4th Duke of Somerset, returned to London. He was not enthusiastic about the decision to work with the Earl of Warwick and as the Earl and Edward IV both headed towards London, he marched to the South West to be at Queen Margaret's side when she and Prince Edward landed. Edmund's decision to leave London was a contributory factor in London being willing and able to permit Edward IV entry into the city which in turn led to the Yorkists ability to engage and defeat the Earl of Warwick at Barnet.

Edmund Beaufort, like his elder brother, took command of the army assembled by Queen Margaret and Prince Edward. He had input into decision making about the routes to be marched, the length of stays at each encamping location, and the determination to try to cross the River Severn to merge forces with the more experienced warrior, Jasper Tudor. Those decisions resulted in Edward IV being able to engage the Lancastrian army at Tewkesbury before it had been able to cross the River Severn to safety and a position of significant advantage. Like his elder brother, mistakes were made in underestimating the speed, guile, and ruthless nature of Edward IV on campaign. This carried onto the battlefield, where Edmund Beaufort broke from a carefully prepared defensive position and left his force vulnerable to assault by battles commanded by King Edward IV and that of Richard Duke of

Gloucester. Edmund, realising that the battle was lost, sought refuge in Tewkesbury Abbey. He and other nobles may have hoped for traditional rights of Sanctuary within the Abbey church. They were to be disappointed, after two days they were forced out of the Abbey church and the last of the male Beaufort line was briefly tried, then executed, by the town cross in the centre of Tewkesbury.

The Beaufort family were the kin of the Lancastrian regime. This had resulted in patronage and positions of state being bestowed upon members of the family. For Henry Beaufort, 2nd Duke of Somerset to temporarily accept Yorkist rule therefore raises questions about his loyalty and honour. Was he acting in the best interests of the Lancastrian cause? Or was he simply acting in the interests of self-preservation?

Chapter Five. Henry Percy, 4th Earl of Northumberland

The Percy family were one of the dominant forces in northern politics throughout the fourteenth and fifteenth centuries. The family's estates were vast, with manors held throughout Northumbria and Yorkshire along with some lands in the south. Through merit, marriage, military success, and appointment, the Percy family was hugely influential, and bound by blood, patronage, and roles to a complex web of noble associates.

During the Wars of the Roses the 2nd and 3rd Percy Earls of Northumberland were killed in battle whilst fighting for the Lancastrians. The 4th Earl of Northumberland was held as a prisoner by the Yorkists following his father's death. He was then released with a pardon after pledging allegiance to King Edward IV, which he honoured by *'uttarly takynge parte with the Kynge[1]'*. This was followed some 14 years later, on the field of battle at Bosworth, with the 4th Earl taking the field at Richard III's side, but of his men's attempts to engage Henry Tudor, it has been said that *'there was no opposition made[2]'*.

The story of the Percy family is inextricably linked with the story of rebellion and civil wars in England and Wales from the deposition of King Richard II in 1399 to the murder of the 4th Earl of Northumberland in 1489. There were extended periods of steadfast loyalty to the crown with the family holding a series of significant positions of state, ecclesiastical positions, and military commands in Calais, and as Wardens of the Western and Eastern Marches along the Anglo-Scottish Borders.

Each of the first four Percy Earls died a violent death, as did Henry 'Hotspur' Percy who predeceased his father, the 1st Earl, when killed fighting against King Henry IV in the battle of Shrewsbury in 1403. This was a family who backed their thoughts and feelings with action. Yet in the space of 85 years the family changed its allegiance on numerous occasions. To whom, then, did Henry Percy, 4th Earl of Northumberland owe allegiance? And to what extent did he, or his father and grandfather, betray those people during the Wars of the Roses?

The Earldom of Northumberland was created in 1377 and awarded to Henry Percy, who was promoted from the baronial ranks. Percy had fought in France aged 18, become Warden of the Eastern March aged 20, and been appointed Marshall in 1376. As such, he was an important figure in the final years of Edward III's reign, which led to his elevation to the rank of Earl at the coronation of King Richard II. Henry Percy was a son of the 3rd Baron Percy and Margaret of Lancaster. He was descended from King Henry III and grew up in and around the Royal Household and that of his uncle, Henry of Grosmont 1st Duke of Lancaster.

Henry Percy was soon granted the position of captain of Calais, a role reserved for trusted and competent men. However, a variety of issues led to the 1st Earl of Northumberland leaving these posts and returning to Northumberland, where cross border raids by the Scots had become increasingly significant. It led to a dispute between Henry Percy, 1st Earl of Northumberland and John of Gaunt, whom the King had appointed as Lieutenant of the Marches, above the Wardens. It saw the Earl refuse John of Gaunt entry to Alnwick Castle, followed by an incident at the Royal Council in November 1481 that resulted in Henry Percy being arrested for having offended the King. The matter was not forgotten, resulting in spats between the Royal Prince and Earl that lasted until John of Gaunt left England to pursue his goal of becoming King of Castile.

The 1st Earl of Northumberland continued to keep a watchful eye on the Scottish border throughout the political problems that Richard II faced in the 1380s and 1390s. His son, known as 'Hotspur', was appointed as Warden of the Eastern March in 1388 for a period of three years, meaning that the Percy family had effective control of the defence of the border. A source of discontent arose in 1391 when the Eastern March was then awarded to a courtier who held no northern lands and had no direct experience of defending the borders. Changes to the wardenship would continue to be a problem that would arise as they were influential roles that were financially lucrative at times. That financial incentive depended, however, on ongoing clashes across the border. In the 1390s King Richard II sought to make diplomatic arrangements with his neighbours to the North and across the English Channel. The result of which was that the

1st Earl of Northumberland and his son, Henry 'Hotspur' Percy, were disgruntled.

After serving Richard II as soldiers, administrators, and diplomats, throughout his reign, the Percy family saw an opportunity to improve their lot through aiding Henry Bolingbroke in his seizing of the crown in 1399. Despite Henry Bolingbroke being the eldest son of John of Gaunt, the earlier arguments were put aside. The Earl of Northumberland was once again appointed as Warden of the Western March, under the seal of the Duchy of Lancaster rather than the Great Seal[3]. When Richard II was ousted, Henry Percy 1st Earl of Northumberland was one of the two magnates to receive the king's abdication. He then played a senior role in the coronation of Henry IV and was shortly afterwards appointed Constable of England for life. The support shown by the Percy family resulted in additional grants of lands and appointments to roles for Henry 'Hotspur' and for the Earl's brother, Thomas Percy, Earl of Worcester. These awards created a Percy powerbase in Cheshire and North Wales, giving them extensive control over the Marches of Wales as well as their historical role on the Scottish border.

The early history of the Percy Earldom of Northumberland then is one of conflict with the crown when there was interference in what they perceived to be their rightful role in the north. This had extended as far as being complicit in the removal of King Richard II. The Earl held significant roles at various points in the reigns of Richard II and Henry IV yet appears to have valued the Wardenships of the Northern marches, and the Percy Hegemony in the north east, above all else. That the Percy family valued their northern roles is hardly surprising, it was a lucrative role, enabled military might, and was a position of influence over the affairs of the north and in relation to Anglo-Scottish relations.

The Percy rise was extraordinary in the first years of the reign of Henry IV. Estates and roles were expanded quite significantly. It was a situation that did not last. In quick succession there were disputes or disgruntlement over payment for defending the marches, the granting of the captaincy of Roxburgh to the Earl of Westmorland, the King refusing the Percy's permission to pay for the ransom of their brother-in-law, Sir Edmund Mortimer, and a ban on releasing prisoners taken at the battle of Homildon Hill for ransom. This was, however, countered with further land grants by King Henry IV in 1402.

The Percy dominance of the north was being challenged, their role in Cheshire and Northern Wales was being undermined. The result was a Percy family rebellion against King Henry IV that culminated in the Battle of Shrewsbury in 1403. The chronicler Hardyng was a member of the Percy household and was present at the battle, he summarised the cause and the outcome: *'Howe for therle of Marche his right, sir Henry Percy and sir Thomas Percy his vncle, erle of Worcester, faught with the kyng, and were slain at the battaill of Shrewesbury*[4]*'.*

'Hotspur' died in the battle. His uncle Thomas, Earl of Worcester, was captured and executed. The Earl of Northumberland, however, was still in the north when the battle was fought. Prevented from marching south by the presence of a force of the Earl of Westmorland's his complicity is easy to assume. He was not, though, charged with treason. The Earl lost his position as Constable of England, the Wardenship of the Western March, fines were levied, his strongholds ordered to submit to the control of the crown, and the Earl held in custody until February 1404.

The 1st Earl of Northumberland was then involved in the Tripartite Indenture alongside Owain GlynDŵr and Sir Edmund Mortimer. If the plan was for a three pronged assault on the crown, it failed very early. Henry Percy marched on the Earl of Westmorland in May 1405. His foe was forewarned and escaped, leading to Henry Percy to take flight to Scotland. After travelling from Scotland to Wales, and then France, Percy returned to Scotland in 1407. He launched an invasion in early 1408 in which he was killed at Bramham Moor.

The result of the 1403, 1405 and 1408 campaigns against King Henry IV was the posthumous attainder of the Earl. His grandson and heir, Henry, son of 'Hotspur', was detained in Scotland for some ten years following his grandfather's flight into Scotland in 1405. He returned to England and was restored as 2nd Earl of Northumberland early in the reign of King Henry V. Perhaps to ease tensions in the north, Henry 2nd Earl of

Northumberland was married to Eleanor Neville, a widowed daughter of Ralph Neville 1st Earl of Westmorland and Joan Beaufort.

Gradually the Earl was returned to positions associated with the Percy family, being commissioned to treat with the Scots and having a role in the defence of the border. He was not, though, returned to the position of Warden of either March until 1421. The Earl also inherited estates that were depleted. In the period of his absence, many parcels of the Percy lands had been granted to other nobles. These included men as notable as the Duke of Bedford, making it a drawn out and at times contentious process for the Earl to recover lands.

The 1420s and 30s saw those lands being recovered and the north was managed without major disagreement between the noble families of the region. Percy-Neville links were strengthened through a marriage of the Earl's sister to Ralph Neville, 2nd Earl of Westmorland. Relationships at court were also amicable, for example Cardinal Beaufort joined Henry Percy on an embassy, then later paid a pension to the 2nd Earl. The major gripe of the Percy household was one the family had in common with the Neville family: the Council's failure to ensure payment for service as Wardens of the Marches.

By the end of the 1430s the 2nd Earl of Northumberland had recouped many parts of the Percy estates. This had been done without there being any significant dispute. Patronage came from the courts of both Henry V and Henry VI via allocation of annuities, appointment to positions, and seniority within Council. He enjoyed ties of kinship with his Neville neighbours in the north, with the Beaufort's, Mortimer family, and to the Duke of York.

When peace in the north was broken in the 1440s, it was not through conflict with the Neville family as some may presume but through a dispute with the Archbishop of York. Archbishop Kemp set about making a series of claims on lands he argued were held by the church. This included manors that were held by the Earldom of Northumberland. It was a contest that went beyond litigation, with violent clashes between men loyal to the archbishop and those of the Earl at Thornton Bridge in 1441 and again at Stamford Bridge in 1447[5].

Friction with the church, though violent on occasion, was not continuous, nor was it a matter of serious concern for the Great Council after the Earl was castigated for his men's actions in 1443. The Earl remained active at Council, and though his roles changed, he was largely busying himself with the defence of the border as the 1450s began. It soon changed, because of the actions of his second eldest son, Thomas Percy Lord Egremont, and those of the Earl of Salisbury's second eldest son, John Neville [later Lord Montagu].

Land was once more a bone of contention and it saw a violent feud begin. Lord Egremont began raiding Neville manors, destroying property, and damaging produce. It was met with retaliatory action. With the two families holding lands across the whole of the north, the feud impacted on many retainers, seeing tensions rise, and the number of men willing to take up arms increase.

The Neville-Percy feud came to a head in a skirmish in 1453. Lands in Lincolnshire and Yorkshire that had once been held by the Percy family had been granted to Lord Cromwell. Lord Cromwell had two daughters as his heirs. An agreement was made for one of these daughters to marry Thomas Neville, one of the Earl of Salisbury's sons. The union made it likely that the manors of Wressle in Yorkshire and Burwell in Lincolnshire would be inherited by Thomas Neville by right of his wife. Having spent some 35 years slowly recovering lands that had been lost because of the 1st Earl's attainder, this was something that incensed Lord Egremont. His response was violent. The Neville family had travelled to Lincolnshire for the wedding ceremony. As they made their way north, Lord Egremont ambushed them at Heworth Moor.

It was clear that violence between the families was now out of hand. So much so that the Earls of Northumberland and Salisbury were both summoned to attend Council to answer for their son's behaviour. Neither attended and instead there was further confrontation. A consequence of the disputes over land was that both Earls began looking for support. Henry Percy (2nd Earl) found support in the form of the Duke of Exeter, who also had an interest in estates held by Lord Cromwell. Thus from 1453 onwards, the Percy family were being drawn into an alliance based on their land interests. Similarly, the Neville family looked for support in their own land disputes. As they had separate disputes with the Duke of Somerset they drifted into an alliance with the Duke of York.

The Duke of York's appointment as Protector and Earl of Salisbury as Chancellor during the illness of King Henry VI did little to deescalate the situation in the north. As soon as news of the Protectorship reached the north there were plans put into place to oppose it. Lord Egremont and the Duke of Exeter based themselves in Spofforth in Yorkshire and raised their retainers. From this base they launched an uprising. The Duke of Exeter was taken into the Duke of York's custody on 23 July. Lord Egremont was intercepted by John Neville near Stamford Bridge in late October 1454 and after a skirmish, taken into custody. There had been six months of on-off violence and destruction directed at Neville property. Lord Egremont was placed in Newgate gaol with orders that he stay there until an extraordinarily large fine of £11,000 was paid.

Family rights and justice with regards land grants were the primary factors in determining the way in which allegiances in this period were formed, or broken, by the Percy family. Much of the dispute was perhaps thrust upon the 2nd Earl by the actions of some of his sons. It saw the Earl of Northumberland draw closer to those in the affinity of Queen Margaret and King Henry VI. Men like the Duke of Exeter, and by association, the Duke of Somerset. Henry Percy was related to many within this affinity, and he had gained patronage from the Beaufort family. He was though now on a course that set his family against that into which his wife had been born, though the families previous experiences of combatting the crown may also have influenced this change in affinity.

From 1402 to 1408 the Percy family had been allied with the Mortimer family amongst others. They had argued via a manifesto that the Earl of March was rightful king of England. This had resulted in the death in the battle of Shrewsbury in 1403 of the 2nd Earl of Northumberland's father, and soon afterwards the execution of his uncle, the Earl of Worcester. Similarly, the 1st Earl had died in battle against a Lancastrian king at Bramham Moor in 1408. The bond of kinship to these powerful families remained strong, the 2nd Earl's mother was a Mortimer. The Earl's own marriage saw further links to the Mortimer line, as well as the more striking link to the Neville family. Kinship to the Neville family and the Duke of York were strong, yet the Percy family found itself having changed its allegiances to join the affinity of men with whom they would have been opposed to, despite also having family links to, just two generations earlier.

This shows that the belief in the rights of a noble family can result in a shift in affinity. Though the early stages of the disputes were perhaps beyond the control of either the Earl of Northumberland or Salisbury, both stood firm and looked at immediate and historic family interests first and foremost as matters escalated.

Feuding over lands in the north and the subsequent unrest directed at the national governance by the Duke of York, Earl of Salisbury, and Earl of Warwick during the first Protectorate resulted in the Percy family being closely aligned with the court party of nobles in the affinity of Queen Margaret. The range of feuds between members of these rival factions created a scenario in which localised problems became intertwined with national politics. As such, Henry Percy's options when the King resumed personal rule were constrained by these allegiances. It meant that the rivalry between the Duke of Somerset and Duke of York would impact on the politics of the north. In turn the Beaufort-Neville dispute also influenced the politics of the north, despite the origins of that dispute being lands held largely in Wales. Both factions had seen loose ties become tightly knit bonds where a threat to one member of the faction was a threat to all. And so, when the Duke of Somerset was released from the custody that the Duke of York, as Protector, had placed him in, the 2nd Earl of Northumberland was duty bound to support the Queen and Duke of Somerset in righting the wrongs that had been done to them on a national level.

This meant that the Earl of Northumberland was one of the court party nobles who travelled with their retinues from London for a Great Council meeting in Leicester in May 1455. At St. Albans on 22 May 1455, the court party were challenged by the Duke of York and his adherents. Parley was attempted and failed as the demands were simply not passed to the king for his consideration. Instead of a tense standoff such as the 1452 encounter at Dartford, this occasion turned violent. The barricades put up by the court party initially held firm against Yorkist attack. Then, the Earl of Warwick led a group of his men through alleyways, emerging in a square full of unprepared Lancastrians. Surprised and unable to organise any defence, the court party were quickly defeated. The animosity between the rival factions was made clear in this encounter. The 2nd Earl of Northumberland was killed in the battle, paying with his life for having allied with the court party and for his part in allowing the escalation of the Percy-Neville feud.

Henry Percy, Lord Poynings, inherited his father's title and earldom as 3rd Earl of Northumberland. He was faced with a politically awkward scenario. His father had just been killed in battle. This was largely due to the family feud with the Nevilles having escalated. The Neville family and Duke of York now held the ascendancy in government. Several of his father's political allies had also been slain at St. Albans. The new generation of nobles had to weigh up their response to the events. And this was complicated by other factors. The 3rd Earl of Northumberland had inherited his father's title and lands, and his responsibilities. Henry had little time to adjust to his elevation. In July 1455 King James II of Scotland attacked Berwick. This required his immediate attention, and following his successful defence of Berwick, he was confirmed as Warden of the Eastern March.

The threat from Scotland had a consequence of removing the Earl from court politics for several years. It was not until 1458 that the 3rd Earl of Northumberland attended court. He travelled with his brother, Lord Egremont, who had escaped gaol in 1456, along with a large following of his retainers and their retinues. By 1458 the ascendancy of the Yorkists was largely over. The Queen and her affinity had resumed control of many aspects of government, but there remained a great deal of tension. The purpose of the visit, backed with force, was two-fold. First, to ensure that the settlements that were to accompany the Loveday parade were debated and agreed without the Yorkists having scope to resort to superior force. Second, a French fleet was harassing the south coast, so there was a military reason other than factional feuds for the magnates having arrayed their retainers and retinues.

March 1458 saw the settlements concluded between the feuding parties in the north. Henry Percy (3rd Earl) then focussed on dealing with the continued threat to the border from Scotland. His brother, Lord Egremont, was less compliant with agreements. As the feud between the two factions at court once again deteriorated[6], Henry Percy made it clear that he would continue to support the Lancastrian regime. In the period following the Loveday it is well documented that the Earl of Salisbury began putting into motion the preparations for war.

A.J. Pollard notes that there were meetings of Salisbury's retainers almost as soon as news of the settlements reached the north[7]. There were also attempts made to attract new retainers. That the 3rd Earl of Northumberland ensured that he was ready to challenge the Nevilles if needed is clear. The Earl of Salisbury marched south and fought a battle at Blore Heath on 23 September 1459. His force was at Ludlow prior to the rout on 12 October. The royal army that challenged the Yorkists at Ludlow that day contained Henry Percy at the head of a large contingent of retainers and men.

That Henry Percy would choose to raise an army and follow the Earl of Salisbury south was not a given. As Earl of Northumberland and Warden of the Eastern March his responsibilities required him to ensure the safety of the border. From his father's death until the Loveday he had focussed on this. Bonds of recognisance had been put in place regarding any actions taken against him, or by him, with regards the Nevilles. Percy's power was based on his ability to secure the Scottish border, and he stood to lose lots if he were to take a sizeable number of his retainers away from the marches. His lands and those of his retainers would be placed at risk from the Scots. For four years he had not responded through use of force to the death of his father. Was there any compulsion to do so at this moment in time? An argument can be made that he had to remain loyal to the crown, even that he had to avenge his father's death. However, that would ignore the fact that for the first half of the 15th century the Percy family had a positive relationship with the Neville family, and that his grandfather and great grandfather, along with a great uncle, had all died in rebellion against the Lancastrian kings. A matter further complicated by the fact that in terms of kin, Henry Percy was more closely related to the Earls of Salisbury and Warwick, and Duke and Duchess of York, than he was to his more distant Beaufort relations. In 1459 Henry Percy had to determine what his primary loyalties and duties were. He chose to be active in the ensuing conflict, in the faction that his father had aligned to.

Historic allegiances and kinship through immediate and extended family are important considerations for magnates when deciding what the best course of action is. In 1459 the bonds of allegiance forged in the previous 9 years far outweighed those of earlier generations. And whilst it may have been prudent to continue the policy of attending largely to the defence of the border, as had been the focus from 1455-58, there was logic to the Earl's decision to take up arms. Not only was it a prudent defensive measure within his own estates, but it was also a sound political move.

For years the Percy family had sought to recover estates lost when the 1st Earl was attainted. Being on the winning side in a clash against the Earl of Salisbury could result in many of those estates being available for the king to redistribute. There was also scope to extend beyond that through additional grants. This could place the Percy family in a position of undisputed dominance in the north. Knowing that the intention was to attain the Yorkists, it made sense to participate in the campaign. The benefit of ousting the Yorkist faction would not only be land grants and a potential reduction in friction, but as is shown by Parliamentary Rolls, the likely payment of owed monies. Wardens of the Marches regularly paid for the costs of defending the border themselves and were reimbursed by the treasury. This was often a slow, sometimes failing, system. The seizure of Yorkist goods though enabled the 3rd Earl of Northumberland to successfully petition the Coventry parliament of November 1459 for the sum of £16,985 5s 7d[8] for the maintenance of Berwick and accrued costs. In the weeks following this payment there was a series of appointments and land grants made in Henry Percy's (3rrd Earl) favour. His loyalty to the Lancastrian cause was being rewarded with patronage.

The benefits of the land grants and appointments were not to be enjoyed by the 3rd Earl. The Yorkist lords had fled the country as a consequence of the rout at Ludford. Events soon ensured that the Earl of Northumberland was occupied with defending the Lancastrian regime. The Yorkists soon regained the military and political initiative. Having fended off attempts to oust them from Calais, the earls of March, Salisbury, and Warwick had landed a force at Sandwich. From here they went to London where the City granted them favour and only a small garrison in the Tower of London held out for the Lancastrian cause. Unperturbed by the resistance of that garrison, the bulk of the Yorkist force headed north and on 10 July 1460 overcame a Lancastrian army at Northampton. Several nobles of the

Queen's affinity fell in battle, including Northumberland's younger brother Thomas Lord Egremont, and King Henry VI was taken into custody of the Yorkists. Queen Margaret and the remnant of the force were forced to retreat north.

The strategic retreat of the Queen into the north increased the importance of Henry Percy (3rd Earl). The arraying of a force to combat this Yorkist threat was to take place in and around York, which in general terms was an area under the control of the Earl of Northumberland. As political events in London unfolded, the authority of the Queen, rights of the Prince of Wales, and the political future of any lord who had been a loyal servant of the Queen and her cause were all under threat. The Act of Accord would transform the balance of power across large parts of England and Wales. It pushed men like the Earl of Northumberland into a position where they had nothing to lose by fighting.

When Richard 3rd Duke of York heard of opposition to the Act of Accord in the north, he raised a force and, with his son the Earl of Rutland, and Earl of Salisbury, marched towards Sandal Castle, near Wakefield, from where he could direct operations against any rebels. It provided an opportunity for those loyal to Queen Margaret to take firm action against several of the leading Yorkists. Historians disagree as to why the duke chose to leave the safety of his castle at Sandal but on 30 December 1460 that is precisely what happened. Together with his retinue he entered Wakefield Green. Sources do not provide a wholly coherent account of the battle, but all are clear that the Duke of York had led his men into a fight that they simply could not win. The Earl of Northumberland and his close allies took to the field of battle along with those of southern lords such as the Duke of Somerset. The Duke of York was slain, his son was killed in the rout, and the earl of Salisbury captured. The prisoner was taken to Pontefract Castle where he was beheaded.

Following the Lancastrian success at Wakefield the Queen's army marched south, intent on taking London, recovering the King, and destroying the Yorkists. The Earl of Northumberland and men were part of this army. At St. Albans the Lancastrian force gained a victory over the Earl of Warwick, and rescued Henry VI from Yorkist control, though the battle was indecisive and the Earl of Warwick evaded capture. At London, the Lancastrian force found the gates barred to them, and the city sympathetic to the Yorkists. Rather than risk the wrath of the citizens of London through attempting a lengthy siege, the Lancastrian army turned north once again.

The Lancastrian army made its way back to York. It left defended positions at the crossing of the River Aire at Ferrybridge, and its commanders chose a position near the villages of Towton and Saxton where they could form up and meet the advance of the Yorkist army that was to follow them north. The City of York was several miles behind this position, providing somewhere for the royal party and a guard to stay in safety.

Despite the faults of Henry VI's kingship, he and his Queen had retained the support of most nobles. Many of these now rallied to the cause. The Lancastrians had a large army, a battlefield of choice, defendable river crossings to guard, and the means to deny the enemy provisions through most of the lands it had to march through. As such, the Lancastrian command had good reason to be confident that they would win what promised to be a winner takes all clash for the crown.

As a senior magnate in the Lancastrian army, The Percy's stood to gain lots through victory. In a winner takes all scenario, in an area that you are the most powerful magnate, the benefits of being on the right side promise to be enormous. The Earl of Salisbury was already dead. For the Yorkists there was little option but for them to go on the offensive. Consequently, there was a good chance that the Earl of Warwick would soon be eliminated. Henry Percy and retainers stood to gain total control of the north in that event.

Loyalty comes with the promise of a prize, but the price of loyalty in war can be high. Henry Percy, 3rd Earl of Northumberland, was to discover that the latter was true. A letter from Thomas Playters to Master John Paston notes not only the death of Henry Percy in the Battle of Towton, but also the lengths to which a magnate's bond of loyalty would go to.

"Item, sir, I herd of Sir John Borceter and Christofer Hanson, that Herry the sext is in a place in York schire is calle Coroumbr; suche a name it hath, or muche lyke. And there is sege leyde

abowte, and dyvers squyers of the Erle of Northumbrelands, and gadered them to geder, a v. or vj.ml. [five or six thousand] men, to byger [bicker] with the sege, that in the mene while Herry the sexte myght have ben stole a way at a lytyll posterne on the bak syde; at whiche byker ben slayn iij.ml. [3000] men of the North. Sir Robert of Ocle and Conyrs leyth the sege on our syde, and thei it is that have do this acte. Sum say the Qwen, Somerset and the Prince schuld be there. Item, it is talked now for trouthe, the Erle of Northumberland is ded[9]".

Henry Percy, if this letter is accurate, had arrayed five or six thousand men. Of these three thousand had been slain. Despite this, and the death of the Earl himself, the remaining men *'have [to] do this act'* of readying for a siege. The decision to take up arms was one with huge rewards, or dire consequences.

Born in 1449, the eldest son of the 4th Earl of Northumberland was a minor at the time of his father's death. He took no personal part in the politics or fighting in the north east between 1461 and 1464. When the last of the Percy Castles surrendered to the Yorkists shortly after the Battle of Hexham the young heir of the 3rd Earl was taken into custody and moved to London. An attainder was passed that forfeited the lands of the 3rd Earl, which saw the Earldom granted to John Neville, previously known as Lord Montagu.

The young Henry Percy remained a comfortable prisoner[10] until 1469. Uprisings in the north, some of which called for the reinstating of the Percy Earldom, and the rift between the King and the Earl of Warwick contributed to this decision. Henry Percy was released on 27 October 1469 subject to a bond until March of 1470 and him paying homage to the king[11]. In March 1470 Henry Percy was then restored as 4th Earl of Northumberland. The arrangements and context are briefly summarised in the Paston Letters:

"And whan the King harde they wer departed and gon, he went to York, and came theder the Thoresday next aftr, and ther camme in to hym all the gentilmen of the shire; and uppon our Lady Day (2nd February - Candlemas) [he] made Percy Erle of Northumberland, and he that was Erle affore Markeys Muntakew [Montagu]. And [so] the King is purposed to come southwarde, God send hym god spede.[12]"

Edward IV had restored Henry Percy to his inheritance as 4th Earl at a time of unrest. As noted in the Paston Letter, the King dispensed with the formalities of restoring Henry Percy to the Earldom and then needed to travel southwards for urgent matters. The urgency was because of the Lincolnshire Uprising and its aftermath. Henry Percy's position was difficult. He had full rights to his earldom now but was faced with revolt before he had the chance to establish bonds with the lords and gentry of the region. Whilst there was loyalty to the Percy family, the structure for the 4th Earl's management of a large region had been managed by John Neville for 6 years.

A dilemma faced the newly restored Earl as to where his loyalties lay. His father had died fighting against Edward IV at

Towton. His family had lost lands to the Beaufort line of the Neville family. There had been calls for Percy reinstatement as a prime mover in the north. An uprising against the king against whom his father had fought and died was underway, should his loyalty be to those in revolt[13]? Or should they be to the king who had just reinstated him? The Neville issue was complicated by the fact that the Earl of Warwick was not only a neighbour in the north but also behind the uprisings. His lands were likely to be seized by the crown. How should he respond to this? John Neville, Marquess of Montagu, had been Earl of Northumberland for a period of five years whilst Lord Percy was imprisoned. He had instigated much of the Percy-Neville feud but had managed the Earldom well. Was he a friend, or a foe? There were lesser barons, members of the gentry, and the commons who wanted a return of Percy lordship and stability. Equally, there were several significant nobles who had been forced to submit to the king just a fortnight before the Earl's restoration. Henry, 4th Earl of Northumberland, had to consider all these questions whilst also stamping his own authority and style to the workings of the vast estates he had inherited.

Clearly the 4th Earl of Northumberland needed some time to impose his style on the structures of estate management and border defences. Time, however, was not something that the Earl was given. At the same time as Henry Percy was learning the craft of being a northern Earl, the Earl of Warwick was plotting further unrest. Richard Neville and the Duke of Clarence had taken flight and eventually found themselves in France. The consequence of the Angers Agreement for the new Earl of Northumberland was that just three months after being restored to the title, he was surrounded by rebellious Neville retainers.

In late July and early August uprisings began in Cumberland and Richmondshire. These were areas with close ties to the Earl of Warwick, and his brother-in-law, Lord Fitzhugh, was implicated, as were his retainers around Middleham. That the Earl of Warwick and Duke of Clarence would invade was a certainty, where was an unknown. The uprisings in the north could be a diversion, or preparation for a landing on the east coast. News of these uprisings had reached London by 5 August, Sir John Paston writing that:

"Ther be many ffolkes uppe in the northe, soo that Percy is not able to recyst them; and soo the Kynge hathe sente ffor hys ffeeodmen to koom to hym, for he woll goo to putt them downe. And soom seye that the Kynge sholde come ageyn to London, and that in haste, and as it is sayde Cortenayes be londyd in Devenschyr, and ther rewle.

Item, that the Lordes Clarance and Warwyk woll assaye to londe in Inglonde evyrye daye, as ffolkes ffeer.[14]".

The uprising was significant enough for King Edward IV to march north in person. He had reached Ripon by 14 August 1470 and with assistance from the 4th Earl of Northumberland, suppressed the uprisings to the extent that 200 pardons were issued as early as 10 September. Analysis of the pardons illustrates that those behind the unrest were closely associated to the Earl of Warwick[15]. The situation changed quite quickly after the suppression of this revolt. Just three days later, the Earl of Warwick landed in the south west. The king was stranded in the north and needed to address the threat quickly. Edward IV, though, was outmanoeuvred and in October 1470 he and a small band of his closest kin and household had to flee to Flanders.

For the 4th Earl of Northumberland, the period of the readeption was one in which his position was potentially complex. He had just aided King Edward IV in suppressing the rebellions planned by the Earl of Warwick. This and the family history of feuding posed a risk of renewed unrest in the north. On the other hand, the Lancastrian nobility who returned to England following the return to the throne of Henry VI were conscious of the sacrifices that the Percy family had made for the Lancastrian cause from 1455 to 1464. This led to a perhaps uneasy standoff in the north, with Percy able to continue developing his relationship with his retainers and learning the craft of regional governance.

The matter of loyalty and responsibilities was one thrust upon the Earl from the off. He had pledged allegiance to Edward IV, the Yorkist king against whom his father had fought and died. Then he had faced a scenario in the north where rebellions saw him pitted against the retainers of one Neville, the Earl of Warwick, whilst having to work with another, the Marquess of

Montagu, the man whose actions years earlier had done so much to fuel the Percy-Neville feud. He had then seen both Nevilles unite and participate in the governance of the land in the name of King Henry VI, the same king that his father and grandfather had been in the affinity of, in opposition to both Nevilles. It perhaps left the Earl with the option of doing what he felt was best for his own, and his retainers', positions. Loyalty based on sound regional governance that could adapt to national politics as required.

That good governance included keeping his political options open. In February 1471 Edward IV dispatched a messenger, Nicholas Leventhorpe, from Flanders to visit the Earl of Northumberland[16]. Whilst it is not known what the precise details of the message from King to Earl were, it seems that Edward and the Earl were able to come to an agreement through Leventhorpe. *Warkworth's Chronicle* tells us that when Edward and his party landed at Ravenspur he was challenged by a *'Sere Jhon Westerdale' who asked what Edward's purpose was. Edward 'answeryde that he came thedere by the Erle of Northumberlondes avyse [advice], and schewede the Erles letter y-send to hym, & undre his seal.*[17]*'*

The insinuation here is that the Earl had advised Edward to land on the Yorkshire coastline. This does not marry up well with Edward's ships having first attempted to land on the East Anglian coast. However, it does fit with the reception that the Yorkist group received whilst in Percy lands. *The Arrivall*, the story of Edward IV's restoration as commissioned by the king, notes of the Yorkists' passage through Yorkshire that:

"it may be reasonably judged that this was a notable good service, and politiquely done, by th'Erle. For his sittynge still caused the citie of Yorke to do as they did, and no werse, and every man in all thos northe partes to sit still also, and suffre the Kynge to passe as he dyd nat with standyne many were right evill disposed to them selfe agaynes the Kynge, and, in expeciall, in his quarrel[18]".

Whilst it looks as though the Earl of Northumberland had decided to remain loyal to the oath of allegiance that he had sworn to King Edward IV a year earlier, the suggestion that Percy could control the East Riding of Yorkshire has been challenged. Instead of the Earl of Northumberland, it has been posited that the decision was made by the Marquess of Montagu[19]. The logic for this claim being that Henry Percy did not raise any retainers from the East Riding in support of Edward, so cannot have had control of the area. Nor indeed did Montagu, who fought against Edward a little over a month later.

The Earl of Northumberland's control over the region may not have been as strong as it had been under earlier Percy Earls. He simply had not had the time to impose his will and patronage on the region. As noted in *Arrivall*, it was politically prudent of the Earl of Northumberland to play little role in events surrounding Edward's landing at Ravenspur. Edward's return, if successful, would remove the Nevilles from the north, increasing his status.

If Edward were to fail, the Earl had to have deniability. The added complication was that a significant number of men who were retainers of the Earl of Northumberland had lost family members in the Battle of Towton. Whilst these men may not like the Neville family having any influence over them through their roles in the readeption, they were equally unwilling to fight for Edward. Whilst they may wish to see the end of the Marquess of Montagu and Earl of Warwick, they retained sympathies for the Lancastrian regime. The lands through which Edward passed after his visit to York are all rich in examples of Lancastrian loyalists. These men had no desire to aid the Marquess of Montagu or the Earl of Warwick.

No matter what the reason for not challenging Edward in the East and West Ridings was, after a year as Earl, Henry Percy could have gathered a force of substance. There were systems in place for the defence of the northern borders which could simply be turned, as they had been in 1460, towards the more southerly parts of the Earl's domain. Even if one accepts that this southern region may have been somewhat undecided in where its loyalties lay, the same is not true of the North Riding. Much is made of the Marquess of Montagu not engaging the Yorkist force as it passed Pontefract. It may have been influenced by the inaction of Henry Percy, or by the lack of support Montagu had in the area. What is often overlooked is the fact that the retainers of the Earl of Warwick in the north riding of Yorkshire and Northumberland were unable to mount an opposition to Edward when he was at his most vulnerable.

The only plausible reasons for this are the terms of their pardons, poor communications, or the regional influence of the Earl of Northumberland. Edward's need to regroup following his fleet being forced to land at different points on the Yorkshire coast provided the time for news to spread and a response to be prepared. The terms of the pardon were hardly likely to be a serious consideration. These men could array forces quickly, they did it quite legitimately to combat the Scots and had done it quickly in the revolts of the previous two years. Raise a force, challenge Edward, and victory is almost certain. At worst, they could merge with the Marquess of Montagu or march south and participate in the Battle of Barnet. None of those things happened, strongly suggesting that the lack of involvement of the Neville's northern retainers was due to the inaction, or threat posed, by the Earl of Northumberland.

The influence of Henry Percy in this matter is recorded in the *Arrivall*:

"the cheftaynes of them that were maliciowsly dysposed, and, for evell entent, as above, have com- moned and begone to assemble the people, anon, upon thies knowledge and considerations, they withdrew them from any ferthar preceding to theyr said rebellyon, as folks not lykly to maintayne theire fals qwarell and partye. They lefte theyr bands, and compaignes, and dyvars of them made menes to th'Erle of Northumbarland, besechinge hym to be good meane to the Kynge for his grace and pardone[20]".

Whether through loyalty to Edward, betrayal of the Lancastrians, dislike of the Neville brothers, ambivalence, or a policy of simply remaining neutral, Henry Percy was viewed as being an important factor in the success of the Yorkists' return to England in 1471.

Victory in 1471 for the Yorkists meant that the key players in the campaigns would expect to be rewarded. The estates of the Earl of Warwick in the north were prime real estate that could be used for this purpose. Henry Percy no doubt hoped to gain from preventing Edward being attacked. However, the king had a range of other things to consider. The Duke of Clarence had a claim to the Neville inheritance through marriage, and his return to the Yorkist fold with his large retinue had been hugely significance at Barnet and Tewkesbury. The Duke of Gloucester had been active in the King's court since 1469, gone into exile with him, and commanded at Barnet and Tewkesbury. He had not yet been granted estates to match his rank though. Added to this was the complexity of duties and roles in the north. The border needed to be defended, and men who had been significant in the household of the Earl of Warwick, such as Sir John Conyers and Sir James Strangeways, needed to be integrated into the remodelling of the north's lines of patronage.

Henry Percy was still a relative unknown. His family history would cast some doubts on his loyalties, and his ability to work effectively with those who had been so closely aligned to the

Neville family during the feuds of the 1450s. Another complication was that the attainder of the 3rd Earl of Northumberland had yet to be overturned, limiting the legal rights of the 4th Earl.

King Edward's solution was to place a lot of faith in his youngest brother, the Duke of Gloucester. After much wrangling, Richard was granted much of the Neville lands and was given administrative oversight of the north. This gave him effective control of the region through the Council of the North and placed him above the Earl of Northumberland in terms of authority, decision making, and through lines of patronage. It was a period in which disputes over rights and responsibilities were quite frequent. Whilst Henry Percy had been appointed as a Warden of the March as early as June 1471 and seen his father's attainder overturned by the parliament of that year, he also lost his position as justice of the Forests to the north of the Trent. Overlordship of several estates were disputed, resulting in the Duke of Gloucester and Earl of Northumberland being summoned to attend the king at York in 1473 to settle matters through mediation.

The Earl's status remained high though. In 1474 he was appointed Constable of Newcastle and Sherriff of Northumberland and installed as a Knight of the Garter. All are signs of favour in court. The following year the Earl participated in the campaign into France, taking a force of 50 esquires and 350 archers[21]. It was followed in 1482 by his involvement at the head of some 6000 of his men in the Invasion of Scotland, after which he was awarded the command of Berwick.

Henry Percy's role in the reign of Richard III continued as being a major force in the north. However, the politics of the north changed in an unprecedented manner. As King, Richard chose to rule the north through a council. This allowed him to make the most of his own estates in the region to exert his personal and regal rights and control. In this respect, Richard was breaking new ground. It is quite likely that the Earl of Northumberland, and to a lesser extent the Earl of Westmorland, would have expected Richard's elevation to result in their own promotions in the north. It didn't happen. This is not to say Percy was not rewarded. He was appointed Great Chamberlain, and Richard saw to it that the Earl was restored to his rightful inheritance of the de Brian estates. These, however, were all roles and estates away from the north, where the Percy family had the basis of their authority.

The relationship between Richard and Henry was strong enough for the pair to work together though. As political events unravelled in the wake of the death of King Edward IV, it was to Henry Percy whom Richard turned to ensure that the north was secured. It is telling that the high value prisoner Anthony Woodville, Earl Rivers, and his aides were sent to the Royal Castle of Pontefract which was in an area that Percy had control over at this time. When Richard became king, Percy was recognised in the king's coronation, at which the Earl had a ceremonial role[22].

When the king faced rebellion, the Earl of Northumberland remained loyal. He was subsequently granted the lordship of Holderness following the execution of the Duke of Buckingham[23]. The evidence suggests that the Earl of Northumberland had, throughout the reign of Edward IV and into that of Richard III, remained a loyal servant of the crown. He had been recognised for his role in Edward IV's restoration, fought against the Scots, campaigned in France, and held multiple administrative and defensive roles, and his lordship over his estates in the north had been consistent with the wishes of the crown.

It is therefore perhaps strange that the Earl of Northumberland is charged with having been disloyal to Richard III when it mattered the most, on the battlefield. An opinion that gained popularity in the late 19th and early 20th century was that *'the Earl of Northumberland, who led one wing of Richard's host, drew aside and would not fight...[24]'*. There is contemporary evidence that hints at this having been the case, the *Croyland Chronicle* noting that, 'in the part where the earl of Northumberland was posted, with a large and well provided body of troops, there was no opposition made, as not a blow was given or received during the battle[25]'. This interpretation goes on to use the murder of the Earl of Northumberland in 1489 as evidence of him having betrayed King Richard III, the logic being that his murder was a belated response to the act by his followers.

Neither the reasons for failing to engage in battle, or the motive for his murder, are proven though. The battlefield deployment at Bosworth is the potential reason for the earl not engaging. Richard III had deployed with his vanguard under the Duke of Norfolk at the front, forming a wide front designed to enable the outflanking of any alternative method deployed by Henry Tudor, and to maximise the advantage of Richard having the larger army. Behind this vanguard was Richard III's own battle, consisting of his household knights and experienced and trusted soldiers. The Earl of Northumberland was deployed behind these in the rear, with a force that had varied levels of military experience. To the left of the Earl of Northumberland's battle was the royal artillery. For the Earl of Northumberland to have fought would have meant that either the Tudor force had broken through the vanguard and Richard's elite force, or for the engagement to be enabled or forced through a wide outflanking manoeuvre by either a part of the Tudor army, or by the Earl's force. There is insufficient evidence to state that either happened. Nor would the Earl make such a move as he had to be wary of the 'third army' of the Stanleys and be ready to engage in support of the King's own battle should it require reinforcement. The Tudor army did make an outflanking attack. Led by the Earl of Oxford, this hit the vanguard of King Richard's army. Whether or not there was opportunity for the Earl of Northumberland to advance on this force is difficult to establish. It would have required the battle commanded by the king himself to have moved from its starting position, otherwise there would have been no space through which the reserve could advance. If that had happened, the battle was in its final phase as Richard's force advanced in the fatal charge that was attempted on Henry Tudor's position.

Clearly it is possible that the Earl may have wished to remain as neutral as practical in the summer of 1485. However, he had attended to Richard III and taken the field of battle. Furthermore, the *Croyland Chronicle* tells us that in the aftermath of the Battle of Bosworth, *'While these events were taking place, many nobles and others were taken prisoners; and in especial, Henry, Earl of Northumberland*[26]*'.*

Whether or not the Earl had deliberately failed to engage in battle, it was a view that at least some people appear to have had at the time. Though imprisonment by Henry VII suggests that there was no complicity with the invader prior to Bosworth, that imprisonment was short. Henry Tudor had practical reasons to restore the Earl at an early stage. The border, and the north, needed to be secure. For that to happen needed an element of continuity and led to the restoration of Henry Percy at an early stage.

The Earl did not enjoy the same degree of autonomy as he had held prior to Bosworth. His positions were subject to renewal on an annual basis, for example. It is perhaps the way Henry Percy acted in the years 1486-89 that reinforces the belief that he betrayed Richard III. There was insurrection in the north in 1486. In 1487 the army of Lambert Simnel, the Earl of Lincoln, and Viscount Lovell, landed in the North, marching from Piel Island to York and onwards to the south. In 1488 problems arose relating to taxation, which rumbled on into 1489.

Each of these led to the repression of men who had been loyal to Richard III, had sympathies with the Yorkist cause, or who had showed any form of ambivalence toward the fledgling Tudor regime. And Henry Percy had played an active role in suppression of this opposition. For the Earl, it meant that for him to remain loyal to the new regime would place him in some degree of conflict with those who had previously been within his, or Richard III's, affinity.

In 1486, for example, the Earl had crushed rebellion swiftly and decisively. The *Croyland Chronicle* recorded that, *'The Earl of Northumberland, however, prudently quelled this insurrection at its first beginning, and caused certain of those who had prompted the movement to be hanged on the gallows.*[27]*'* Such swift action would endear the Earl to the new King but perhaps undermined the loyalty that the people of the north had to the Earl.

The following year, Henry Percy took control of the defence of York as the invading army approached. The events surrounding this invasion illustrate quite clearly how the Earl of Northumberland, City of York, other local magnates, and the crown, worked together to coordinate a defence of the region.

Here we see that not only did the Earl play a leading role in the defence of the City of York, but also that to a large extent, he had no choice as correspondence within the region is strongly suggestive of the area being supportive of the Tudor regime over those of the claims of Lambert Simnel and the nobles in his invading army.

The City of York learnt of the treason of the Earl of Lincoln on 31 March 1487. The City wrote the same day to the Earl of Northumberland. Henry Percy's response was prompt, responding positively to the requests of the City and reminding them of their duty to ensure *'the good rule and peaux of that citie*[28]*'*. There followed further correspondence on 13 April, then a formal request to the King for assistance in repairing the defences and arming of the castle on 23 April. There is then a flurry of correspondence between the City, Earl, King, and the Castle at Scarborough relating to the way in which York would be defended against the Earl of Lincoln and the invading army.

Henry Percy was an integral part of the arrangements that were made. His men played a large part in the defence. It was his networks that ensured that the region was kept as peaceful as possible: though there were murders of note at this time, the north was not entirely peaceful, and not entirely supportive[29]. It was to the Earl that the City of York turned on 8 June 1487 when the rebels wrote to the City of York. In all his actions in the summer of 1487, Henry Percy was unflinchingly loyal to the Tudor regime.

Ongoing involvement in ensuring that the policies of the Tudor regime were implemented did influence the way in which the Earl was viewed by his retainers and people in the region. This came to a head during the tax related uprising of 1489. The Earl of Northumberland issued orders to his retainers to attend to him at Thirsk. This is recorded in a letter sent to Sir Robert Plompton:

"...charg you, and on my desire pray you, that ye with such a company, and as many as ye may bring with your ease, such as ye trust, having bowes and arrowes, and pryvy harnest, com with my nepvew, Sir William Gascougne, so that ye be with me upon munday next comeing at nyght, in the towne of Thirske...[30]*"*

The Earl's retainers did attend to him. However, when faced with a riotous crowd, they did not come to the aid of their master, instead, standing aside as he was murdered. That the retainers allowed Henry Percy to be attacked and killed is recorded in the near contemporary poetry of John Skelton[31].

Chapter Six. Richard Woodville, 1st Earl Rivers

Richard Woodville, 1st Earl Rivers, is best known for being the father of Elizabeth Woodville, the wife of King Edward IV. He is also remembered for his own marriage, to Jacquetta of Luxembourg, dowager Duchess of Bedford. He himself held offices of state, was a close confidant of King Edward IV, and met his end through summary execution during the revolts instigated by the Duke of Clarence and Earl of Warwick in 1469.

This is suggestive of Richard being born into a noble family, having affinity based on family kinship and bloodlines. This, however, is far from the case. Richard Woodville's parents were Richard Woodville (senior) and Joan Bedlisgate. Richard snr was a professional soldier. He was clearly valued by the Lancastrian kings, and it is suggested he may have been raised alongside the future King Henry V[1] but he was born into a family of the gentry rather than nobility. The Earl of Warwick noted this when berating the younger Richard Woodville, in 1460, when, according to the Paston Letters, *'my Lord of Warrewykre hetyd [berated] hym, and seyd that his fader was but a squyer, and broute up with Kyng Herry the V[2]'*.

The lifestyle that the younger Richard was born into was then one of a child in a military family who had connections to senior nobles. These links may have come from Richard's uncle, Thomas, or his great-grandfather, who both had dealings with branches of the House of Lancaster[3].Consequently, his parents received *'of the king when prince dated at Hereford, 27 June, 9 Henry IV, granting to them for life 40l yearly from the issue of the manor and lordship of Kirketon in Lyndesey, co. Lincoln; so that they cannot be retained with anyone else*[4]*'*.

Richard snr and Joan had accommodation in Calais, some land in Kent and later some in Northamptonshire. It provided an environment in which the younger Richard would quickly learn the workings of the English garrison systems, be familiar with many tasks undertaken by soldiers, and be raised alongside other boys for whom expectations would have been similar. It meant that as his father's career progressed, the young Richard was ideally placed to enter service of the crown.

His father served in Normandy and Picardy during the English conquest and occupation of the Lancastrian phase of the Hundred Years War[5]. Having been part of Thomas, Duke of Clarence's garrison at Guines in 1411 the shift towards conquest in the north of France saw Richard snr being raised to the position of captain for the campaigns of 1415 and 1417. He was then a bailiff before progressing to more senior administrative roles. Richard snr was appointed seneschal of Normandy in 1420 and became the Duke of Bedford's chamberlain and treasurer in 1423. His organisational skills, loyalty and all-round ability were clearly noted. It was Richard Woodville snr who was appointed as Lieutenant of Calais in 1435[6] as the Burgundian threat increased. This was a position he had also held in 1427. Richard Woodville snr also gained positions of note in England, becoming MP for Kent in 1433 and sheriff of Northamptonshire in 1437. He was also appointed as constable of Rochester Castle which is a key location in the south east of England[7].

Richard Snr's value to the Lancastrian regime was illustrated clearly in a dispute in 1425. London was tense as Humphrey, Duke of Gloucester and Archbishop Beaufort clashed. Foreigners had been leaving London as the implications of Duke Humphrey's military failure on the continent were becoming apparent. For a time, the capital was seen as being at risk. And so, the King's Council decided that the Tower of London and its treasures needed to be secured. To do this, they turned to Richard Woodville esquire. The matter is covered in the *Appendix to the 1426 Parliament*:

"For the surer keeping of the Tower, Richard Woodville esquire who had been much trusted by the late king, as is well known, who also was chamberlain and councillor of my lord of Bedford, was deputed into the assent of the King's council then in London to garrison the Tower with a certain number of troops, for its safekeeping, and he was strictly charged by the said council that during the time of his charge he should suffer no man to be allowed into the Tower who was stronger than himself, unless he had the special charge or command of the king and by the advice of the council[8]".

This was no straightforward task. It involved a great deal of political acumen and diplomacy as Duke Humphrey, one of the infant king's uncles, was the man trying to enter the Tower of London. Richard Woodville snr had enough respect from the Duke, the remainder of the King's Council, and the garrison, to be able to manage the situation without it escalating. All indicative of him having a very good working relationship with the men at the heart of the court in the early years of King Henry VI's reign.

Whilst Richard Woodville snr was never knighted, his son was at an early age. The younger Richard Woodville was knighted as part of the series of knighthoods bestowed in 1426 alongside the dubbing of King Henry VI himself[9]. That he was chosen illustrates the esteem in which the Woodville family were held at the time, placing him alongside boys of noble birth at a ceremony that held much value to the Lancastrian regime. As these decisions were taken as the issues at the Tower of London took place, the political acumen and loyalty to the crown of Richard Woodville snr were clearly being noted as worthy of family advancement.

The Woodville family spent the rest of the 1420s and into the 1430s largely working for the crown in English possessions in France. Richard jnr gained experience, rising in rank and influence: a captain in 1429, retained by the crown in 1433, and appointed to the household of the Regent of France, John, Duke of Bedford, in 1435. These are positions of note, reflecting his father's rise, his own ability, and perhaps being disproportionately generous to a man of the young knight's rank, or kinship ties.

They were to provide Sir Richard Woodville with an opportunity for advancement that would rarely be possible, or taken, by men of his station. When the Duke of Bedford died in 1435, Sir Richard was a part of his household; he was acquainted, therefore, with Jacquetta of Luxembourg, the Duchess. A romance that is ill documented soon flourished between the Dowager Duchess and the young knight. They married secretly, without the required consent of the King, no later than 1437.

Jacquetta had, until her late husband's death, stood to become Queen Consort of England should the young King Henry VI succumb to any illness in childhood. And whilst based in Paris serving as King Henry's representatives, she was the consort to the Regent. Therefore, her rank until the Duke of Bedford's passing, had been that of the most powerful woman within the Lancastrian hierarchy.

The wide gap in rank between Richard Woodville and Jacquetta posed problems. It was frowned upon by nobles in England, and by Jacquetta's family in the House of Burgundy. Instead of her hand being used for a diplomatic marriage, she was now tied to, *'Richard Wideville, knight bachelor in the regentes court*[10]*'*. This frustrated the King's Council, resulting in a fine of £1000 being imposed on Richard[11].

Notwithstanding the large fine that was imposed on Sir Richard, the union with Jacquetta of Luxembourg, Duchess of Bedford, transformed his fortunes. From a knight with a retinue of 20 men and 60 archers in 1434[12], he was now a member of the royal family through marriage. This was a position that was fortified when King Henry VI married Margaret of Anjou, as Jacquetta's sister was married to the Queen's uncle, Charles duc d' Anjou.

Marriage into the royal family itself did not result in instant reward, patronage, or elevation to the peerage for Sir Richard. In 1437 he was appointed as chief rider of the forest of Salcey, Northampton[13] but his creation as Baron Rivers was not until 1448, he was elected as a Knight of the Garter in 1450, and the further promotion to Earl did not take place until the Wars of the Roses had seen the Lancastrian regime replaced by that of King Edward IV.

As a baron, Richard Woodville began to be appointed to senior military roles. In October 1450 he was appointed as Seneschal of Gascony amid fears of a French invasion[14]. It was an important role, effectively managing the administration of military matters in the duchy. However, news of the actual French invasion arrived in London just weeks later[15]. Preparations were made for Lord Rivers to travel to Gascony but by February 1451 parliament was authorising steps to be taken to repay the loans that it had taken out to finance his expedition, Gascony having, for the time being, been lost[16].

Plans to send Lord Rivers and an expeditionary force to Gascony were finally ended in August of 1451. This was because of the need for the funds, and men, to be diverted toward the defence of Calais. The threat of the French attacking Calais was perceived to be high. So high that King Henry VI himself proposed to lead a campaign in its defence[17]. Though this anticipated assault never materialised, it resulted in Calais' defence being prioritised and with that came Lord Rivers' next military appointment, as Lieutenant of Calais, in 1454.

Richard, Lord Rivers, had then come from a background that was firmly tied to the Lancastrian regime. His family had built relationships with court, taken up military commands, become part of the establishment through administrative roles and as Members of Parliament. He himself had continued that rise through his being knighted alongside the King, his own captaincy in the king's service, and promotion into positions within the Regents household in English controlled France in 1435. His marriage owed itself to those connections and despite the match being viewed by some as being very unequal, it tied the Woodville's very firmly to the crown. Now, Richard Woodville had not only benefitted from appointments based on loyal service of his father and himself but was bound to the Royal House of Lancaster through marriage. His promotions following his marriage to the Duchess of Bedford were gradual and he was a man who clearly possessed the skill set to undertake them.

Events of 1455 saw the Yorkist affinity assume the ascendancy in court. One aspect of that change was the appointment of the Earl of Warwick as Captain of Calais. When this happened, Lord Rivers left his position as Lieutenant of Calais. Returning to England, Lord Rivers assisted in diplomatic affairs, and as the Queen's affinity regained the initiative following the king's resumption of personal rule, he began to be appointed to roles in the South East. These included being appointed as Constable of Rochester Castle in 1457 and as a commissioner in Kent, along with more traditional Woodville commissions in Northamptonshire.

One of the commissions that Lord Rivers received was a delicate matter. On 31 July 1457 he, along with others, was appointed to investigate, *'a conflict on the sea between Richard, earl of Warwick and his retinue and certain of Lubye [Lubeck] under the king's friendship, and to certify the king and council of their examination before 13 August next'*[18].This saw Lord Rivers involved in addressing the actions of the Earl of Warwick in the English Channel which had implications for foreign relations.

Whilst that commission was underway, not being completed until the summer of 1458, the French raided Sandwich, and the government's attempts to address the security of the seas failed. A consequence was the Earl of Warwick being appointed as Keeper of the Seas for three years, but with Lord Rivers one of the men who would be entrusted with aspects of the defence of the south eastern coast.

Therefore, as national political matters spiralled out of control in 1458 and 1459, Lord Rivers was in a position of trust in the South East. Directly opposite Calais, and the potential threat of a fleet under the Earl of Warwick. As the Wars of the Roses sparked into life at Blore Heath, then Ludford, Lord Rivers seems to have been in Kent. There is no record of his attendance at the Coventry parliament of 1459 which attainted the Yorkist Lords. Soon, though, he was involved in implementing the outcome of those attainders.

14 October 1459 saw him commissioned to participate in the seizure of the Duke of York's lands in Lincolnshire. On 30 October 1459, in his capacity as Sherriff of Kent, he was commissioned to, *'resist Richard, Duke of York, Edward, Earl of March, and Richard, Earl of Warwick, and Richard, Earl of Salisbury, and all their accomplices... [and to] arrest all ships and other vessels late of the said earl of Warwick[19]'*. By 10 December the commission was extended to Lord Rivers being ordered to *'take near Sandwich the muster of the man at arms and archers ordered to go on the safeguarding of the sea[20]'*.

Following the rout at Ludford the Yorkist lords had fled. The Earls of March, Salisbury, and Warwick, making their way to Calais, where they retained the confidence of the bulk of the garrison and had taken possession of the town. Meanwhile the Duke of Somerset had been appointed as the Earl of Warwick's replacement as Captain of Calais. To take up his position, he would need to oust the Earl of Warwick. It was in support of these attempts that Lord Rivers was gathering a force in Sandwich. It led to him being in command of a small fleet that was readying itself to depart from the haven at Sandwich to cross the Channel.

Aware of this, the Earl of Warwick had Sir John Dynham launch a daring raid on the Lancastrian fleet. A contemporary letter written by William Botoner notes the assault:

"As for tydyngs here, I sende som of hend wreten to you and othyrs how the Lord Ryvers, Sir Antonye, hys son, and othyrs hafe wonne Calixbe a feble assault made at Sandwich by Denham, Squyer, with the nombre of viijc. men, on Twyesday between iiij. and v. at cloksyn the mornyng. But my Lady Duchesseys stille ayen receved Kent[21]".

The raids consequence was one of humiliation for Lord Rivers. Caught unawares by the attack, the Yorkists, *'took the sayde lorde Ryuers and Antony his sone, in theyre beddes, and lad theym oner to Caleys, and took with theym alle the grete shyppes, saue on called "Grace Dieu' the whyche myghtenat be had awey because she was broke in the botome[22]'.*

Once in Calais, Lord Rivers and his son were possibly berated by the Yorkist lords.

"my Lord Ryvers was brougth to Caleys, and by for the Lords with viijxx. [eight score] torches, and there my Lord of Salesbury reheted [rated] hym, calling hym knaves son, that he schuld be so rude to calle hym and these other Lords traytors, for they

schall be found the Kyngs treue liege men, whan he schuld be found a traytour, &c. And my Lord of Warrewykre hetyd [berated] hym, and seyd that his fader was but a squyer, and broute up with Kyng Herry the VIe, and sethen hymself made by maryage, and also made Lord, and that it was not his parte to have swychelangage of Lords, beyng of the Kyngs blood. And my Lord of Marche reheted hym in lykewyse. And Sir Antony was reheted for his langage of all iij. Lords in lykewyse[23]".

The exchange, if accurate, is illustrative of the attitude that on occasion the senior and established nobility had towards anybody who had risen above their birthright. Here, Lord Rivers is castigated as being a mere knave who made himself through marriage. It notes that his father was a squire, essentially a nobody so far as the three Earl's were concerned. This shows that as late as January 1460, the Yorkist earls in Calais were viewing Lord Rivers as a man beneath them and as someone who had no established lines of kinship to the established noble families. He was of a background where he ought simply to do his captain's bidding, loyalty through obedience. It must be noted though that none of the chronicle accounts of Lord Rivers being taken include an exchange of this nature, they note only the capture of himself and his son, Anthony, with one chronicle suggesting that the Duchess of Bedford was also taken to Calais[24].

Lord Rivers though was worthy of being castigated. He clearly held enough of the Earl's respect to be deemed important enough to put in his place. Perhaps due to the Duchess of Bedford's rank and the noble's respect for her, Lord Rivers and his son were released, perhaps as part of the agreements that brought an end to the failed attempts of the Duke of Somerset to enter Calais.

The possible berating of Lord Rivers used terminology that is quite targeted. Whether the public speech happened or not, the letter itself is contemporary so those assertions were at least being thought about by reasonably well-informed men with ties to Calais. The earl of Warwick notes that he and the other Yorkist lords are, *'Lords, beyng of the Kyngs blood'*. Those blood ties are through the descent from Edward III that each of those men could claim. They are royal themselves and therefore acting loyally as 'true' kinsmen. It matters because many of the complaints that had arisen throughout the 1450s was fuelled by suggestions that there was corruption and self-aggrandizement at the heart of the court.

Nothing is entirely clear about the nature of exchanges between the various nobles in Calais. Jean Wavrin however suggests that there was an exchange of words, but that it was instigated by Lord Rivers and aimed at the Earl of March[25]. There is also the fact that Lord Rivers had very close ties to the Calais Garrison and for the Earl of Warwick to denigrate him in public would potentially incite unrest whilst Calais was being attacked. Would the Earl of Warwick really test the garrison's loyalty to him over that to a former Lieutenant whilst under attack from a duke who had been appointed as the new Captain by the king?

Following the Yorkists gaining the upper hand in Calais they returned to England. It seems probable that as the Yorkist force landed at Sandwich and made its way to London, then Northampton, that prisoners such as Lord Rivers would have returned as honourable captives at this time. Sources do not provide clear evidence as to how Lord Rivers and his son, Anthony, were released, but this had certainly taken place prior to the Battles of Ferrybridge and Towton in 1461 as both Lord Rivers and his son are noted as being with King Henry VI at several moments in the campaigning.

Lord Rivers' loyalty to King Henry VI appears to be absolute at that time. The *Milanese State Papers* noted that, *'King Henry, the queen and the prince are said to have fled to Newcastle, sixty miles from York, accompanied by the Dukes of Exeter and Somerset, and by Lords de Ros and de Rivers*[26]*.'* The same collection of state papers also, incorrectly, notes the death of Anthony Woodville during the Battle of Towton, and the capture of Lord Rivers.

These records from April 1461 show that Lord Rivers and Anthony, his son, had both returned to the side of the king and under the command of the Duke of Somerset once they had obtained their freedom from the Earl of Warwick. Both had been either in the battle, or with the King in York, when the two sides clashed at Towton. Their loyalty to the Lancastrian cause also seems assured as they are noted as being part of the party that accompanied the King and Queen to Newcastle. Everything points to a stoic and loyal service to the King whom he is related to through marriage, and from whom he had received rank and positions of note.

The last of those entries was dated 18 April 1461. Lord Rivers was with the royal party at Newcastle as the Lancastrian defence of the north east was about to begin. A little over four months later, on 30 August 1461. The Milanese reported something quite different:

"The lords adherent to King Henry are all quitting him, and come to tender obedience to this king, and at this present one of the chief of them has come, by name Lord de Rivers, with one of his sons, men of very great valour. I held several conversations with this Lord de Rivers about King Henry's cause, and what he thought of it, and he answered me that the cause was lost irretrievably[27]".

By the time Lord Rivers came to this conclusion, the Yorkists had already moved to strip him of his lands and wealth. At Lincoln on 14 May 1461, he along with several other nobles and knights were subject to a commission to the escheator of the counties of Northampton and Rutland that ordered his possessions to be seized[28]. It made Lord Rivers a marked man. He had already been a prisoner of the Earl of Warwick, had possibly been released on a bond to not fight against the Earl: which may have been broken at Towton, and was bound through his wife to the

Lancastrian regime. His loyalties had been firmly with King Henry VI, Queen Margaret, and the Duke of Somerset to this point. An experienced administrator and military official he had the capacity to inflict damage on the Yorkists in much the same way that Andrew Trollope had done should the chance arise.

In mid-April 1461, Lord Rivers had been attending to King Henry in Newcastle. A month later, the Yorkists named him as one of the men whose possessions had to be stripped. On 12 July he was pardoned by King Edward IV, with Anthony Woodville, Lord Scales, also being pardoned and the rights and dower of the Duchess of Bedford being reconfirmed on 10 December 1461[29].

Soon Lord Rivers was being appointed to Commissions and being accepted into the Yorkist regime. This, just a year after he had been captured by the Earl of Warwick and held at Calais. Possibly subjected to derision if the Paston Letters are accurate. He had possibly spoken against the then Earl of March if the account of Jean Wavrin is to be believed. Lord Rivers was a part of the extended royal family that King Henry VI had set out to construct in the late 1440s. And now, after the execution of many other lords at or shortly after the Battle of Towton, Lord Rivers was accepted and integrated into the new regime quickly and quietly.

How and why would a lord with such ties to the Lancastrian regime change heart so quickly? Why would the Yorkists trust Lord Rivers after the actions of Andrew Trollope in 1459? Was it possible for a change of this nature to be made without any loyalties being betrayed?

Men who had served in the Calais garrison may have felt obliged to serve the crown. Richard Woodville, as a knight, then lord, had done this loyally. He had defended the rights of the men under his control and acted as ordered by his superiors. This may have brought him into conflict with the Yorkists, but as military men themselves, they would appreciate that he was quite simply doing his duty to King Henry VI. This may go some way towards explaining why Lord Rivers was pardoned.

How though, could he justifiably abandon King Henry VI just months after leaving York with him for Newcastle? The logical answer is that Lord Rivers, like the other nobles noted in the Milanese papers, has simply decided that the cause is lost. To justify it, however, is another matter. Was Richard Woodville bound to serve the crown, or a bearer of the crown? If it is the former, his duty could be seen as to the incumbent and following the Battle of Towton, it became quite apparent that this man was Edward IV, not King Henry VI. If the duty is to one king, and to any patronage received through commissions, land grants, or otherwise, then surely Lord Rivers was bound to support the Lancastrian cause. Afterall, at this point there remained an enclave in the north east, was a promise of support from the Scots and French, and resistance to Edward IV's rule was present in several regions.

The question of whether it was a betrayal of any kind assumes that Lord Rivers and his family were tied exclusively to the House of Lancaster. On the face of it, that was the case. The Duchess of Bedford was a clear tie, the roles within the regency household in France and service to the King in the 1450s are another. It must be remembered that much of Richard Woodville's time serving in Calais came under the Lieutenancy of France held by Richard, Duke of York. He worked diplomatically and within the justice system. Those tasks required him to work fairly, for both sides of the factional divide of the 1450s. Had he not done so, the Yorkist lords would not have entertained Lord Rivers, likewise he would not have entertained working with them. But he already had, through governance of areas in which his father then himself had held positions of note. Even matters as potentially damaging to his relationship with senior Yorkists as the commission to investigate the Earl of Warwick's activities in the English Channel would be seen as fulfilment of a role, rather than a personal affront.

Evidence of this bi-partisan approach of the Woodville's in the 1450s and into the early stages of the Yorkist era is not hard to find. Despite holding positions within the justice system in Kent, Lord Rivers was not named by the rebels of 1450 as being a corrupt man who needed to be removed from the king's presence. Commissions in Northamptonshire, as well as Kent, throughout the decade resulted in no lasting grievances, in a period when disputes were becoming increasingly bitter and extra-judicial in their nature. As domestic politics had descended into chaos, Lord Rivers had been assigned tasks dealing with foreign affairs. Put simply, he was somebody who could be trusted to get a job done by not only the crown in its Lancastrian form, but also by the Yorkist party.

Further evidence of this is shown soon after Lord Rivers and his son were pardoned. In 1462, Anthony Woodville married Elizabeth, Baroness Scales. Though Elizabeth herself was from a Lancastrian family, she was related through marriage to the Bourchier family. The Bourchiers' had seen one family member die fighting as part of the Duke of York's force at the Battle of Wakefield and others were prominent members of Edward IV's council. It is illustrative of the fact that in general, families were not entirely partisan and most had good working relationships with nobles, knights, the gentry, or merchants of both factions.

The nature and scale of Lord Rivers assimilation into the Yorkist structure of government shows that he continued to benefit from his marriage to Jacquetta. September 1462 saw further reversions of the Duchesses rights[30] and again in January 1463 there were reversions for the lifetime of the Duchess of lands held in Barton upon Humber and Stewton, Lincolnshire[31]. Lord Rivers' experience as an administrator was also utilised. In June 1463 Lord Rivers was noted as being one of the *'king's kinsmen'* who was appointed to a commission of oyer and terminer to investigate crimes within the City of London. This was no minor undertaking, others issued with that commission included the earl of Warwick, Viscount Bourchier, Lord Hastings and John Tiptoft, earl of Worcester and the incumbent Constable of England[32]. He was then similarly appointed to a commission, with a similarly high standing of others called, for Northamptonshire in January of 1464.

It is perhaps then that Lord Rivers' loyalty was to service of the state, rather than of either faction over the other. True, his marriage tied him in ways to the House of Lancaster, but the Yorkists had never taken issue with the Duchess of Bedford's rank or position within society, and she had remained in London, and was used as an envoy by the City, when Queen Margaret's forces approached in 1461. However, he had been raised to serve as a soldier and administrator, and that is precisely what he continued to do. Is it then a betrayal of loyalty to anybody if he realises that government is now in the hands of the Yorkists, and simply opts to continue fulfilling these roles under a different regime?

Richard, Lord Rivers, was clearly considered competent and trustworthy by King Edward and the upper echelons of the Yorkist government. Though he received no high value patronages from the King in this period, he was brought onto the Royal Council in 1463[33]. He was then as well positioned, and similarly ranked, under Edward IV in early 1464 as he had been under Henry VI in the late 1450s.

This rather functional assimilation into the system of government eschewed by Edward IV meant that Lord Rivers was a likely candidate for more senior positions. He was experienced and capable enough, and as a Royal Council member of a political rank suitable for leading or greeting embassies, organising military campaigns, or should a vacancy arise, assuming one of the key positions of state.

May 1464 enhanced the likelihood of those things happening. If the marital union of Richard Woodville and the Duchess of Bedford had been unexpected and of equal rank, that of Lord Rivers' widowed daughter was to exceed it in terms of inequal status and impact. *Hearne's Fragment* summarised what took place in spring of 1464:

"King Edward... with a little company came unto the Manor of Grafton, beside Stony Stratford, whereat Sir Richard Woodville, Earl of Rivers, and Dame Jacqueline, Duchess-dowager of Bedford, were then dwelling; and after resorting at divers [several] times, seeing the constant and stable mind of the said Dame Elizabeth, early in a morning the said King Edward wedded the foresaid Dame Elizabeth there...[34]*"*

The marriage of his daughter to King Edward IV did not result in instant promotion. Patent Rolls record very standard inclusion in enfeoffments in Northamptonshire in 1465[35] but it was not until the following year that Lord Rivers saw personal patronage or promotion being bestowed. Those positions recognised his ability, and his position as father of the Queen Consort. In March 1466 Lord Rivers became treasurer of England. He was elevated to the rank of Earl in May of the same year, and in

August 1467 he became Constable of England. The promotions provided him with an income in excess of £1500 a year, in addition to the monies derived from Jacquetta's dower lands.

Earl Rivers' promotions were carefully planned though. Positions were already held, and in the case of the Constableship of England, was sold by its incumbent, John Tiptoft, Earl of Worcester, to enable it to be granted to Richard Woodville. His position as father of the queen was being rewarded, which alongside political differences with established Earls, was to have a major consequence for the Woodville family.

Alongside Richard's own advancement came a series of marriages for his kin. These were advanced not only by Earl Rivers and his daughter, now Queen Elizabeth, but also by King Edward who sought to strengthen the affinity around him through carefully arranged unions. Anne Woodville was married to William, Viscount Bourchier in 1467, 19 year old Richard Woodville was married to the 65 year old dowager Duchess of Norfolk in 1465; Margaret Woodville married Thomas, Earl of Arundel; and Catherine Woodville was married in childhood to Henry Stafford, Duke of Buckingham. Additionally, members of the extended Woodville family benefitted from elevated marriages. As a family, they had in just a few years married into many of the most senior and established noble families in England.

The rapid advancement of the Woodville family caused resentment among some of the established baronial families. They challenged a long established tradition of precedence and were a threat to the political power of some senior nobles, including the Duke of Clarence, and Earl of Warwick. That political aspect was almost immediately one that presented problems. Whilst Earl Rivers had been utilised on diplomatic duties for many years, the rise to the upper table of himself and his kin presented an opportunity to influence policy, rather than be simply be guided by it as a more junior member of the Royal Council.

The combination of the clandestine marriage of Elizabeth Grey (Woodville) to the King and the rapid rise of Lord Rivers and his family caused political tensions from the off. The King's marriage prevented a diplomatic match being found, a matter that could have possible consequences. This was at a time shortly after a truce had been arranged with France, with follow up embassies cancelled later in 1464, after the news of the King's marriage became public but whilst other matters also influenced diplomacy.

With a French truce in place and several prominent advocates of a pro-French policy on the continent, the scene was set for a clash of wills. Earl Rivers had connections with Burgundy through his wife. The Earl of Warwick on the other hand had led the negotiations for a truce, remained an advocate of a bond with France, and had political, military, and economic interests in pursuing a French pact over one with Burgundy. It set the two Earl's against one another politically.

Woodville backed proposals in 1468 included one, which was taken up, of Margaret of York wedding the then heir to the Duchy of Burgundy, Charles. A suggestion that was not taken forward was for the Duke of Clarence to also marry into the House of Burgundy. Whilst the Woodville family courted the Burgundians in the presence of King Edward, the Earl of Warwick was in France on a fully sanctioned diplomatic embassy. By the time Richard Neville returned to England, having reached agreements in principle with the King of France, the decision as to whether it would be France or Burgundy to whom Yorkist England would ally itself had already been taken. The Woodville instigated promotion of Burgundian interests had won the day without the Earl of Warwick's negotiations in France being given due consideration.

The relationship between Earl Rivers and his son-in-law was therefore now one of influence. Policy in Europe shifted towards Burgundy, the court of which the Dowager Duchess of Bedford was related to. Politically and economically, there were strong arguments to be had for the match, as indeed there were for the Earl of Warwick's preference of a French alliance. Richard, Earl Rivers, and his kin had acted possibly in the best interests of the country, possibly in the best interests of their family network. Either way, it strengthened their position within court and as diplomats. At the expense of the Earl of Warwick and with a consequence of the Duke of Clarence being passed over as a marriage prospect by the Burgundians.

Whilst Earl Rivers and his kin may have been acting in good faith, the result was the widening of a rift between the crown and the Earl of Warwick, who along with the Duke of Clarence, had reason to feel aggrieved. The way the king had gone about negotiations, and the fait accompli presented to the Earl of Warwick upon his return from talks in France, were not issues of disloyalty by Earl Rivers. They were though matters in which the decisions could be viewed as being disrespectful to the immense role that Richard Neville, 16th Earl of Warwick, had played in placing Edward IV on the throne; his work in ensuring that the Yorkist throne was secured following 1461; and left the Duke of Clarence isolated and in need of alternative methods of funding the household that he was building at Tutbury.

Edward's apparent shift in loyalty to the family of his wife over that of his own brother and cousin led to the resumption of conflict. Rebellion was planned at the behest of the Earl of Warwick. Uprisings in the north leading to the defeat of an army loyal to King Edward at Edgcote in July 1469. Few of the major protagonists in national politics were present on the field of battle. Most were soon involved in the aftermath. The victory was perhaps more stunning off the field of battle than it was on it. The forces in support of the Earl of Warwick and Duke of Clarence soon had King Edward in their care. Further to the King's captivity, Warwick's supporters, *'imprisoned his master*

Kings father (the Lord Rivers) and two of his sons to death, and the third was in great danger (though all of them were great favourites of the king.) He also caused several knights to be put to death[36]*'.*

Earl Rivers and his sons had been sought out and those who were captured, were summarily executed. Richard Woodville paid the price of being the leading adherent of a policy that angered the Earl of Warwick.

Were the actions of Richard Woodville a betrayal at any point in his working life? He had been brought up in a military household, benefitting from patronage earned by his father whilst a boy with his knighting. He held commands in France under the Lancastrian kingship of Henry VI, whilst also taking up administration positions in England. His marriage was advantageous and added a bond of kinship to King Henry VI via the status of Jacquetta, Duchess of Bedford. In 1460 and 1461 he served alongside the Duke of Somerset, was captured, and held prisoner by the Yorkists, yet released when other men with ties to the Calais garrison were put to death. He attended to the Lancastrian royals in York in March 1461 and accompanied the king and queen into the north following defeat at the Battle of Towton.

His service to this point was entirely loyal to the Lancastrian cause. And then he transferred his allegiance. He was noted by the Milanese ambassador as saying that the Lancastrian cause was lost. Was his primary duty to serve the crown in terms of the man wielding the most power, at that time Edward, or the king whose reign he had benefitted from to this point, Henry? If his primary loyalty is to his family, does he look at kinship networks which have ties to the Lancastrians, or to preservation of the family's status as far is possible through accepting defeat once it is obvious? These are intriguing questions for a man of Richard Woodville's rank. Like Andrew Trollope, he had an instilled sense of military duty. Unlike Trollope, he survived the battle of Towton and was in place to see whether the remnants of the Lancastrian nobility had the resources to resist for long. Baron Rivers was not alone in submitting to the Yorkists in the months after the Battle of Towton, and he, like others was accepted into the new regime's structures relatively quickly and smoothly. He, like other professional soldiers, knew that honour determined that you needed to withstand a siege, as the Lancastrians were in the north-east, until it was clear that relief was not coming. To surrender after putting up a fight, as they had at Towton, and after sufficient time had been given for assistance to be found, was not disloyal, nor dishonourable. This had been well established in the Hundred Years War, when his military training would have made the rights and wrongs of any surrender well known to all in command positions.

What is not known of the decision that Baron Rivers made to change sides, is what the views of King Henry VI and Queen Margaret were. Negotiations with France and Scotland were ongoing. There was supply of the castles along the Northumbrian coast. They and those who remained defiant may well have disagreed that the honorable time to surrender had arrived.

Following his abandonment of the Lancastrian cause Earl Rivers' position was bolstered by the marriage of his daughter, Elizabeth, to the king. It strengthened his family's position through the marriages that it brought and increased his level of influence within court. Whilst his contemporaries may have frowned at the way in which the Woodville family grew in stature, it is hardly a lack of loyalty to anybody for him to have played a part in their advancement.

His end was the result of perceptions of betrayal to some degree. A betrayal of the natural order through his over elevated status. An argument of corruption perpetrated by himself and his family. But at the same time, these suggestions need to be weighed against the Earl of Warwick's own ambitions for himself and his daughters and the way King Edward IV appointed men to positions and rewarded his magnates. Additionally, the role of Council and attitudes of all senior advisors to the king, and the king himself, to open discussion and debate of policy options needs consideration. Were views considered? Was one argument heard whilst the other paid lip service to? Was there manipulation of events to undermine other senior nobles?

Chapter Seven. Thomas Stanley, 1st Earl of Derby

Thomas, second Lord Stanley, succeeded his father to the barony In February 1459. For the remainder of the Wars of the Roses he played a prominent, and controversial, role in regional and national politics. As the wars progressed and political fortunes of more senior nobles changed, Lord Stanley adapted, changed sides, and played a role that can be seen as self-serving, treacherous, or true to the loyalties that his family owed through long term patronage. As such, he is a figure who divides opinion. The actions of Lord Stanley and his brother, Sir William Stanley, in 1485 are among the most controversial of the late medieval age in England. The degree to which these acts were a betrayal is easily affected by a modern readers affinity to either side in the conflict of 1485. In the context of the day and the history of patronage, promotion, and politics on a regional level, the issue of betrayal is complex, and his methods and reasoning are not unique, simply being better known than many other nobles.

The political position, titles, responsibilities, and patronage that Thomas 2nd Lord Stanley inherited upon his father's death were the result of a rapid rise in the family's fortunes in the preceding six decades. As the Lancastrian regime came to power in 1399 the Stanley family were of gentry class. By the time of Thomas inheriting, they had been ennobled, were one of the largest landowning families in the north-west of England and had one of the largest retinues in the country.

This rise was the result of Thomas' grandfather, Sir John Stanley, and his father, Thomas, 1st Lord Stanley, receiving patronage, benefitting from well-chosen marriages, and through good lordship and administration in the lands that they held.

The family acquired the kingship of the Isle of Man from King Henry IV which was granted in perpetuity in 1406. They held lands in Liverpool, including a Tower from which they 'ruled' their island kingdom. Sir John Stanley was appointed to administrative roles in Ireland. The family had established links with court, Sir John's grandfather having held positions in the courts of Richard II and Henry IV. The family participated in the French campaigns of Henry V and retained good relations with the crown throughout the reigns of Henry IV and Henry V.

These links enabled Thomas Stanley, the future first Lord Stanley, to be awarded administrative roles at a relatively early age. In January 1431 Thomas Stanley was appointed Lieutenant of Ireland, a role he was to hold for six years. Before the end of his tenure in Ireland Thomas had been knighted, was part of the king's household from 1436, and in 1439 became controller of the king's household. As Thomas Stanley inherited his father's titles in 1437, he was well placed to improve the standing of the family within the north-west and on a national stage. Politically this came from a series of appointments. 1437 saw Thomas appointed as Constable of Chester Castle; 1439 he became

Chamberlain of North Wales; 1441 saw a grant of a £40 annuity from Haworden and Moldsdale; 1443 saw his appointment as Justiciar of Chester and North Wales, grants of the castle and lordship of Mold and Moldsdale in Clwyd; 1445 saw the lease of Le Kyngs Pole on the River Dee; his ties at court enabled the trading of manors to acquire Bosley from the Duke of Buckingham; and, in 1447 Sir Thomas Stanley was appointed as Chief Steward of the southern parts of the Duchy of Lancaster, which included large parts of north Wales.

Though still not ennobled, Sir Thomas Stanley had, by 1447, become a major player in regional politics in the north west, northern Wales, the Welsh Marches, and in Ireland. He was close to the King and the Duke of Suffolk. That he was considered a man loyal to King Henry VI, and the political leadership of the Duke of Suffolk, is shown by his appointment as custodian of the disgraced former Duchess of Gloucester, Eleanor Cobham, from her conviction in 1442 until her death. Sir Thomas was also one of those responsible, in 1447, for the arrest on charges of treason of Humphrey, Duke of Gloucester. In brief, he was at the heart of the Lancastrian government.

Sir Thomas's rise was not simply through being capable. He benefitted from ties to major noble families through marriage. His wife, Joan, was a half-sister to the Duke of Norfolk and her family pedigree included distant royal heritage and ties to several contemporary Earldoms.

This association with and loyalty to the crown associated Sir Thomas with the *'wicked counsellors'* whom the rebels led by Jack Cade wished to remove. It also placed him politically in opposition to the Duke of York.

The revolts of 1450 placed Sir Thomas Stanley in a precarious position. Closely aligned to the Duke of Suffolk, he was politically vulnerable as his senior ally was impeached, exiled, then murdered. Furthermore, the Stanley's attempted to prevent Richard 3rd Duke of York from returning to England from Ireland in 1450. Alongside this, Sir Thomas had angered several members of parliament when he led his retinue from the north-west to Kent to ensure that the rebellion led by Jack Cade was quashed, with his methods being seen as excessive.

Whilst enthusiastically suppressing opposition may be viewed as an example of total loyalty to the crown, it was to have political consequences. The Duke of York's affinity rose in influence in the aftermath of the revolt led by Jack Cade. It allowed the members of parliament who were aggrieved by Stanley's actions to force him, and others, from court. He also resigned his position as Justiciar and Chamberlain of North Wales and saw some of the royal grants that he had received as patronage removed in the Act of Resumption of 1451.

The political clash with the Yorkists was potentially damaging. The Duke of York wrote to King Henry VI that:

"Please it your Excellency to know that as well before my departing out of this your realm for to go into your land of Ireland in your full noble service, as since, certain persons have lain in wait for to hearken upon me, as Sir John Talbot, knight, at the castle of Holt, Sir Thomas Stanley, knight, in Cheshire, Pulford at Chester, Elton at Worcester, Brooke at Gloucester, and Richard, groom of your chamber, at Beaumaris; which had in charge, as I am informed, to take me, and put me into your castle of Conway.[1]"

The division between the two factions was therefore quite wide, and for men such as Sir Thomas to navigate the periods in which the Duke of York and his associates were in the ascendency illustrates a degree of political acumen. One way in which the Stanley family improved their lot with the Yorkists was through marriage, with Sir Thomas' son, the future 2nd Lord Stanley, marrying Eleanor Neville, daughter of the Earl of Salisbury and sister to the Earl of Warwick. This meant that the Stanley family now had incredibly strong ties with both factions as the country headed towards open conflict.

Sir Thomas, though, had by this time become a significant part of the regional administration of the north west and northern Wales, so whilst he was temporarily isolated from court, he remained an important figure. By 1454 he had gained enough trust from the Duke of York to become a member of the council in place during the first of the duke's periods as protector and retained his position on council following the resumption of personal rule by Henry VI. In this period Sir Thomas' men prevented an attempted revolt by the Duke of Exeter, and he marched to St. Alban's, arriving after the battle had been won by the Yorkists[2].

It was in this period that he returned to favour at court. In 1454 his son, Thomas, was a squire to King Henry VI. In 1456 Sir Thomas was elevated to the peerage as the 1st Lord Stanley and appointed as the King's Chamberlain. Whilst he had clearly made his peace with the Yorkist affinity during the two protectorates, it was the House of Lancaster to which he continued to owe loyalty through patronage. 1457-8 saw Lord Stanley attending the royal council, and as a sign of his closeness to the regime he was one of the nobles chosen to form the council of the young Prince of Wales in 1457.

The decision of the Duke of York to call Thomas Stanley to parliament in 1455 may seem strange given the history between the men and Sir Thomas' raising of his retinue. The decision shows that patronage works in several ways. The Duke, as Protector, recognised the need for good administration, for justice to be dispensed efficiently and fairly, and that for the good of the state that he was governing on the King's behalf.

This is illustrated through two sources. The first is an entry in the parliamentary roll of the July 1455 Parliament. The importance of Sir Thomas Stanley in achieving this cannot be understated, his influence and retainers were needed to fulfil this task:

"15. Item, to ordain and provide for peaceful and sober rule in Wales, and to prevent such riots and disobedience as have arisen there in the past.[3]"

The second reason is exemplified in the commentary contained in the *Chronicles of the White Rose of York*. For effective management of the country and to increase the chances of ongoing peace, whilst enhancing his own position, the Duke of York needed to appease men who were powerful and most likely to be amenable to his governance. Sir Thomas is a stand out contender for this, dominant in a region in which there was potential for unrest and related through the marriage of his son to the Neville Earls.

"The Duke of York, to render his high station the more secure, had inserted a clause in the patent, by which it was enacted that he should only be removed by the voice of parliament. He now took steps to retain a majority in that Assembly. He called Sir Thomas Stanley and Sir Richard Welles to the house of Peers, the one as Lord Stanley of Latham, and the other as Lord Willoughby.[4]"

Thus, the Stanley family are elevated to the peerage by the protectorate led by the Duke of York. It recognises the worth of men, attempts to bring them closer into one affinity over the other, and in the case of Thomas Stanley, rewards him for having been an effective administrator and landholder.

This was a period of great instability though. And as Thomas, 1st Lord Stanley, passed away in February 1459, the country was once again on the verge of armed conflict. Very soon his son. Thomas, 2nd Lord Stanley, would need to make decisions about how to navigate the outbreak of war.

The outbreak of war was in September of 1459. The Yorkist lords had travelled to their lands to raise armies with a view to uniting at Ludlow. The Lancastrians were alert to this and themselves raised forces. For the regime led by Queen Margaret, the method of raising forces was through royal summons. Letters requiring lords to raise their retinues to defend the crown against rebels were issued. Thomas 2nd Lord Stanley was a recipient of one of these summonses and as a man capable of raising a large retinue was expected to play a key role in preventing the three main Yorkist forces from merging into one large army.

This placed Lord Stanley in a politically uncomfortable position. He had strong ties to the crown but was related to the Earls of Salisbury and Warwick, leading Yorkists, through marriage. Joining either side could damage his relationship with the other, and if he chose the losing side, his life, lands, titles, or roles were all potentially at risk.

The retinue requested by Queen Margaret was raised. Some 2000 men formed this retinue, a considerable number that could have a major impact on a battlefield. When the Earl of Salisbury led his force into lands close to the Stanley retinue the opportunity was there to defend the crown as requested. The Stanley force was close to Queen Margaret and the army that had gathered around her. When the Queen dispatched Lords Audley and Dudley to intercept the Earl of Salisbury's force the expectation was the Lord Stanley would join them. In the event, when the Battle of Blore Heath took place on 23 September 1459, Lord Stanley chose to keep his retinue uncommitted, later being accused in Parliament of:

"But the said Lord Stanley was within six miles of the said heath at the same time, accompanied by 2,000 men, and stayed with the same company for the next three days at Newcastle [under Lyme], just six miles outside Eccleshall where the queen and the prince then were; and the said Lord Stanley, on the morning after the defeat at Blore Heath, sent a letter by way of excuse to our sovereign lady the queen and the said noble prince; which was the letter your said highness had sent to him, commanding him by the same to come to your said highness with his company in all haste. But he came neither to your highness, to the queen, nor to the said prince, but thus departed for home again[5]."

Lord Stanley had chosen to not take sides in the conflict. In the aftermath of the battle, he wrote to the Earl of Salisbury offering his congratulations at his victory, and to the Queen offering his reasons for having not been at the Battle. It is an episode that illustrates how difficult it was for many lords with ties to both political factions to make decisions that would bind them to one side or the other. It essentially allows Lord Stanley to retain a position of neutral whilst observing events. As a strategy it was one that bore risks.

The response of the crown and parliament to Thomas Stanley's nonattendance was mixed. At the November 1459 'Parliament of Devils' Lord Stanley was present to take the Oath of Allegiance to the king. So, he was welcome enough at the seat of government. Conversely, the same Parliament sought to impeach Lord Stanley. Citing examples of his servants and brother having fought alongside the Earl of Salisbury; of having falsely excused himself; of ignoring requests to attend the field of Battle and take command of the vanguard against the Earl of Salisbury; and of preventing supporters of the crown having passage to the Lancastrian army.

The list of accusations made by the Commons is long, and damning. It ends with a simple request to the King:

"Of all of which matters done and committed by the said Lord Stanley, we your said commons accuse and impeach him; and pray your most high regality that the same lord be committed to prison, to remain there after the form of the law[6]"

Despite the commons having delivered eight detailed accusations against Lord Stanley in their request for his impeachment and imprisonment, the Queen opted to pardon him and overlook the case against him[7]. Does this mean that the Queen and senior Lancastrian nobles did not view his actions as an act of Betrayal? Or is the decision to pardon the Lord one based on the need to minimise the risk of another powerful magnate joining the Yorkist cause? Impeaching or attainting Lord Stanley would have implications in a region that was very close to the base of power of the Duke of York. There is also the link that Lord Stanley had to the court to consider. Was his previous good service to the crown a major factor? Whatever the definitive reason for the pardon, in the context of the day opting not to fight was not something that would result in the Queen and senior nobles opting to take the most serious of actions against a lord, that was reserved for those who bore arms against the crown. Thomas Stanley had opted for a route that minimised the risks to himself. It was a course of action that was not risk free. He could have been attainted. He could have been forced into battle. That neither happened is illustrative of how complex the situation was in autumn of 1459. Loyalties of the nobles were being tested, and the patronage and marriage links that Lord Stanley had with both factions were strong. His actions in terms of communicating with both sides before and after the Battle of Blore Heath demonstrate that he was politically savvy. That he then avoided impeachment further illustrates that, he had become respected enough for his possible slight on the Queen to be pardoned.

The months following the Parliament of Devils saw the Yorkist lords in exile plotting their next move. The crown lay siege to Calais and had retinues at the ready to face any Yorkist invasion. And when that invasion came, Thomas 2nd Lord Stanley was at the king's side at Northampton, though whilst he was present no sources mention him as having fought. His apparent loyalty to the crown was evident in the fact that one of his sons, Thomas, was knighted by King Henry VI immediately prior to the battle commencing[8].

What is particularly interesting is the way in which Lord Stanley's retainers acted after the battle. As the Lancastrians fled the field:

"Upon this Queen Margaret with the Prince fled The Queen from Eccleshall towards Chester, and was nearly taken the Prince to prisoner by John Cleyer, a retainer of Lord Stanley[9]"

Whether or not Lord Stanley himself played a role in attempting to capture the Queen is unclear but that his retainers were willing to do so shows that men of rank would seek to gain advantage of a situation, even when the magnate who retained them had attended the battle on the side of the Lancastrians.

Lord Stanley himself soon cooperated with the now dominant Yorkists. When the Duke of York returned from Ireland there was no repeat of the earlier Stanley attempts to thwart his passage. Instead, Lord Stanley participated in the Yorkist parliament and was involved in creating the settlement known as the Act of Accord on 25 October 1460 that changed the inheritance of the throne from Henry VI's heirs to Richard 3rd Duke of York and his heirs. A little over three months after standing alongside King Henry VI at Northampton watching his own son being knighted by the Lancastrian king, Lord Stanley was participating in the very act that would remove the rights of Prince Edward, around whose court Queen Margaret had orchestrated much of the Lancastrian response to the Yorkist threat. Further, he sat on the Yorkist Council alongside members of the Neville family. Lord Stanley was proving very adept at retaining political influence, even when he had been alongside the king on the losing side at Northampton.

Lord Stanley now was faced with another dilemma. He was ensuring that he retained political power by working with the Yorkist government but had not made any firm commitment to their cause. The Act of Accord still recognised Henry VI as king and in many ways was an act of appeasement. Nobles involved in the negotiations that led to the Act of Accord had been shocked by the Duke of York's claiming of the throne. Negotiating a settlement would pacify the Duke in the short term but the Queen and her closest allies were not going to accept it and that there would be further bloodshed was almost certain. For lords like Thomas Stanley the time had come to make decisions as to which side they were going to take as the Queen began to raise a force at York.

For Lord Stanley the considerations were patronage, retention of roles and rights, family ties, and the maintenance of lands under his control. He had received patronage from the Lancastrians, the expansion of Stanley lands had been via grants given by King Henry. Yet it had been Richard 3rd Duke of York who had elevated Thomas Stanley's father to the peerage whilst he was Protector. Family ties were strong with the Yorkist lords, his wife being a Neville, but this familial link is balanced by the prominence that Lord Stanley's father had within the household of King Henry VI and the roles that Thomas himself had been given. In short, Lord Stanley owed some allegiance to both factions.

That Lord Stanley had strong ties to both parties may explain his reluctance to declare openly for either party. So too may he have simply opted to remain neutral as far as was practical on the simple basis of self-preservation. Not declaring, however, was not the norm in the period from the Act of Accord to the Yorkist victory at Towton. Most members of the nobility participated in some way for one side or the other. Lord Stanley on the other hand is not recorded as having fought at St. Albans, Ferrybridge, or at Towton. It is noted by some leading historians that Lord Stanley most probably returned to his lands in the north west and remained there through the winter of 1460-61[10]. That Thomas, 2nd Lord Stanley remained in his lands during the period in which feuds turned to open warfare does not in itself mean that Lord Stanley was not involved in the conflict. His lands were strategically significant. Forces from south Wales travelling north to join the Queen would need to travel through or close to Stanley lands. Areas to the north of his control were Lancastrian, as were ones to the east and south east. By remaining in his territories with his large retinue, Lord Stanley may well have simply been fulfilling a role of limiting the ability of Lancastrians to wage war. The importance of maintaining control over large parts of the north west is not to be underestimated. It was significant enough for Lord Stanley's role in maintaining the peace in the region to be rewarded in the Act of Resumption passed in the first of Edward IV's parliaments[11].

The situation in 1461 presented Lord Stanley with choices. With lands adjacent to pockets of Lancastrian resistance in north Wales and in the north west of England he was in a position of some strength. He could work with the new Yorkist regime and assist in putting down the Lancastrian resistance, or he could side with the rebels which had the potential to pose the Yorkists a major problem in securing the region. Thomas, Lord Stanley chose to work with the Yorkists. This is reflected in not only his rights being confirmed in the Act of Resumption but also through confirmation of his roles in the north west and in Wales. Though he was not a close confidant of the new Yorkist king, he was clearly seen as a man of great importance. And throughout most of the 1460s he remained loyal to Edward IV. He participated in sieges in the north east and joined his brother-in-law the Earl of Warwick in facing the invasion from Scotland in 1464[12]. His men also suppressed a pro-Lancastrian uprising in Lancashire in 1464 and in 1465 King Henry VI's capture at Clitheroe was by men who were partially under the administrative control of the Stanley brothers[13].

Lord Stanley continued to maintain good administrative control over a large area that had the potential present problems throughout the 1460s and was held in high enough regard to participate in royal tournaments, being champion in one held in 1465[14]. His loyalty to the crown or kin was then put to the test in 1469 when the Duke of Clarence and Earl of Warwick rebelled against King Edward IV. Lord Stanley faced another dilemma as this took place. Was he to remain loyal to the crown, or was a bond of kinship to the Earl of Warwick a more important tie? On a practical level, Lord Stanley would assess the likelihood of the rebels succeeding. This judgement would be important in terms of ensuring that he was in a position of strength in the aftermath of any prolonged unrest or open warfare.

The matter was brought to Lord Stanley's doorstep following the Battle of Losecoat Field which took place on 12 March 1470. Seeking the support of Lord Stanley, the Duke of Clarence and Earl of Warwick made their way to plead with him for military assistance. Hardyng's chronicle summarises the exchange:

"then despayryng and geuyng themselfe to flight, beganne to make a newe hoste, and with many faire promyses did wowe his brother in lawe Thomas Stanley to take his parte. But when said Thomas would by no meanes fight or rebel Agaynste kyng Edward[15]"

This is further confirmed in the *Paston Letters*, which noted:

'And then (when) the Duke of Clarence and the Earl of Warwick heard that the king was coming to themward, incontinent (immediately) they departed, and went to Manchester in Lancashire, hoping to have had help and succour from the Lord Stanley; but in conclusion there they had little favour, as it was informed the king; and so men say they went westward...[16]*'*

Faced with a request from his brother-in-law for military assistance, Lord Stanley opted to decline. Is this a show of loyalty to the crown? Possibly, but it is equally as likely that Lord Stanley discussed options with the Duke of Clarence and Earl of Warwick. At that moment in time the forces of the Duke and Earl were in disarray and even with the Stanley retinue would perhaps struggle to create a large enough coherent force to face a royal army. That is pure speculation but events that followed suggest that there may be some truth in the suggestion. The Duke and Earl made their way to France, regrouped, and launched an invasion. When they did, Lord Stanley met them at Bristol with his retinue, to help in securing the readeption of King Henry VI[17].

Grafton's Chronicle records Thomas, 2nd Lord Stanley's involvement in the release of King Henry VI to secure his readeption:

"On the 25th of October, the Duke of Clarence accompanied by the Earls of Warwick, Shrewsbury, and the Lord Stanley, and other Lords and Gentlemen, some for fear, and some for love, and some only to gaze at the wavering world, resorted with

great company to the Tower of London, and tiience with great pomp brought King Henry VI. apparelled in a long gown of blue velvet, through the lUgh streets of London, to the Cathedral Church of St. Paul, the people on the right hand, and on the left hand, rejoicing and crying: "God save the King l[18]"

After a decade in which he had largely been a loyal servant of the Yorkist regime and a pivotal part of Edward IV's control of the north west, Lord Stanley had opted to join with the forces of the Duke of Clarence and Earl of Warwick to support the restoration of Henry VI at the expense of Edward IV. Whilst there were clear links between Lord Stanley and the Earl of Warwick, supporting the readeption at this time was also opportunistic. The restoration of Henry VI enabled Lord Stanley to force his own governance over Hornby Castle. This was a rift arising from counter claims to the Castle by Lord Stanley another notable family of the region, the Harrington's. The turmoil of 1469-71 allowed the issue to be forced in his favour. *Rymer's Feodora* tells us that on 5 March 1471:

"Thomas Maynwaryng, and four others, are ordered to convey the cannon called Mile Ende from Bristol to Sir Thomas Stanley, who is besieging Horneby Castle.[19]"

This was conducted against a loyal supporter of the House of York at the same time as Edward IV was preparing for his invasion of England. That landing, at Ravenspur on 14 March 1471 saw Sir William Stanley ride to the side of Edward, meeting him at Nottingham, whilst Lord Stanley's forces continued to besiege the Yorkist castle at Hornby.

The siege led to conflict with senior Yorkists following Edward's restoration. Richard Duke of Gloucester intervened on behalf of the Harrington family. It was an issue that ultimately required King Edward IV's intervention, and which had Richard's time as king been more peaceful, may well have led to the case being reopened.

The intervention of the future King Richard III in the dispute, and its wider implications for the Duke and Lords relative strengths within the north, is an interesting sub plot to their relationship. It may have contributed to the mutual suspicion between the two in Richard's reign. It did not, however, prevent Lord Stanley from receiving patronage and roles from King Edward IV. Thomas, Lord Stanley held roles in the administration of the Duchy of Lancaster, providing him with a great degree of autonomy in Duchy lands in the North West. In 1474 the Ducal Council ordered Lord Stanley, in his role as receiver, to seize manors and in the same year he was entrusted with overseeing the repair of the castle at Liverpool.[20]

The following year Lord Stanley was one of the nobles who joined Edward in the Invasion of France. On this expedition Thomas played an important role. The *chronicle of Edward Hall* notes that when French Heralds arrived to treat with the English:

"...the sayd Herauld should first report to the lord Stanley, or to the lord Howard, for the conducting of him to the kinges presence...[21]"

Lord Stanley was then once again at the heart of government and trusted by King Edward IV. His role in the Duchy of Lancaster further illustrates his uses to the crown, which were also beneficial for himself. In 1476 Thomas oversaw a Ducal Council tour of the Duchies estates. This was designed to check that affairs were being properly managed and to ensure that revenue was as it should be. The figures illustrate just how effectively this task was undertaken by Lord Stanley. Revenue from Michelmas 1476 to 1477 amounted to £347 3s 1.5d. Following the progress this role in the following accountancy year to £800 18s 8.5d with further rises in the following two years[22]. Clearly, Thomas Lord Stanley was highly valuable to the Yorkist regime, and this was evidenced by confirmation of his rights within the Duchy in 1476 in a letter that noted that:

"Upon the kings highnesse, and in his absence upon the Lord Stanley, steward there, obeying him in all thinges that he shall' commaunde[23]"

The loyal service in the second of Edward IV's reigns went on to include a further military expedition. When Richard Duke of Gloucester was placed in charge of the 1482 Invasion of Scotland, it was to Lord Stanley that he turned for assistance in raising a sufficiently large army. With the Duke of Gloucester in overall command and the large Stanley retinue commanded by

Thomas, it saw the Lancastrian and Cheshire forces of Lord Stanley recapture the town of Berwick whilst the duke advanced on Edinburgh. Clearly at this point, the Duke of Gloucester and Lord Stanley were able to work together and coordinated an invasion that, though limited in its scope due to changes in Scottish politics, recovered Berwick which had been in Scottish hands since the early 1460s.

From Edward IV's restoration in 1471 until the King's death in 1483, Thomas 2nd Lord Stanley had been an effective administrator, soldier, respected politically, and had received patronage from the crown. His rights and roles had been confirmed, and despite previous disagreements with the Duke of Gloucester, both men were able to work together on campaigning. The same period had also seen Lord Stanley's influence grow beyond the traditional Stanley lands. His marriage to Lady Margaret Beaufort had brought together two large estates, with Margaret's including many in the south of England. It had led to negotiations for the safe return of Margaret's son, Henry Tudor, Earl of Richmond, from exile.

The death of Edward IV transformed English politics. The mistrust amongst senior nobles, the Queen's family, and members of King Edward's household led to political unrest, arrest of Earl Rivers, and the taking up of sanctuary by the Dowager Queen. The series of events surrounding the decision to declare Edward IV's children as illegitimate are for discussion elsewhere. However, of relevance is the fact that Thomas, Lord

Stanley, was one of the men arrested on Richard's orders at a Council meeting held in London on 13 June 1483[24].

Whilst Lord Hastings was executed almost immediately, Lord Stanley was imprisoned in the Tower of London. The implication of being arrested at the same time as Lord Hastings, and others, is that Thomas Stanley must have been suspected of partaking in plots against the then Lord Protector, the Duke of Gloucester. Stanley, unlike Lord Hastings, did not suffer any great consequences. Polydor Virgil explains the reasons for this as follows:

"But the duke after this, being satisfyed with the death leased William lord Hastinges, delyveryd Thomas lord Stanley safe and sownd, fearing, perchance, least yf he showld have doone him any wrong George lord Strange his soon showld have stirred upp the people to armes soomwher agaynst him[25]".

Lord Stanley was released for fear of revolt by his son, Lord Strange, if Virgil's account is accurate. Therefore, it can be surmised that Richard, who was to become king just two weeks after having Lord Stanley arrested, did not trust him. As such you would imagine that Lord Stanley would be a prime candidate to join the rebellion of autumn 1483. Yet quite the opposite was true. Lord Stanley was one of the nobles who accompanied the king to York in mid-November. The Stanley retinue was also raised for the king's cause, rather than for the rebels. The *Plumpton Correspondence* describes the array and contribution of the Stanley's, through Lord Strange:

"People in this country be so trobled, in such comandment as they have in the Kyngs name and otherwyse, marvellously, that they know not what to doe. My lord Strange forth from Lathum upon munday next with x m 1 [ten thousand] men, whether we cannot say[26]".

Whilst the size of the Stanley retinue is almost certainly exaggerated, the Stanley's were backing the king. The reasons for this are not proven. There had been tensions relating to lands between the Duke of Buckingham, the Stanley's, and other local landholders. This alone may explain the decision to back the king, rather than any sense of loyalty. Aiding in the suppression of the rebellion made sense, it ought to, and did, result in grants being made to those who supported King Richard III, with Lord Stanley being granted Kimbleton almost immediately after the Duke of Buckingham's execution on 2 November 1483. Additional grants were made to Lords Stanley and Strange the following year[27].

Once again, the question of motivation comes into play with regards decisions made by Lord Stanley. In this case, should the rebellion fail, Lord Stanley stood to gain. Should the rebellion succeed, whether Lord Stanley participated on either side, he stood to possibly lose regional influence. That line of thought, however, is complicated by the role of Lady Margaret Beaufort in the uprising. Messengers from Margaret had travelled to discuss matters with her son, Henry Tudor. Tudor had made an aborted attempt at landing in support of the revolt. In short, Lord Stanley's wife had aided the rebels.

This presents a difficult situation politically. Though married, the couple had separate households. And through those households had worked on behalf of opposing sides in the revolts of 1483. The Stanley's were a major power in the country, particularly the north west. For the King to punish Margaret for her role could result in losses for the Stanley family, whom the king had already rewarded for their input into suppressing the rebellion.

The solution is an example of the need for good lordship at any level. Richard III's Parliament recognised that Margaret Countess of Richmond should be attained. However, the king willed parliament to grant her lands to the keeping of Lord Stanley for his lifetime with reversion to the crown upon the Lord's death. The explanation in the parliamentary roll makes it clear that this is due to Lord Stanley's good service:

"Nevertheless, our said sovereign lord, of his special grace, mindful of the good and faithful service which Thomas, Lord Stanley, has given and intends to give our said sovereign lord, and for the sincere love and trust which the king has in him[28]"

Amid the turmoil of 1483 which included Lord Stanley's arrest, then rewards, was also his involvement in Richard III's coronation, as mace bearer, in July 1483. Additionally, Lord Stanley was installed as a Knight of the Garter, in place of Lord Hastings whom he had just been arrested alongside. The pace of events and levels of mistrust amongst the various political powers in summer and autumn of 1483 had led to rapid decisions being made, to some men being executed, and others like Lord Stanley being viewed with suspicion but allowed to continue in their roles with perhaps an eye on preventing further unrest. As well as freeing Lord Stanley, Richard III offered patronage. A garter stall was a high honour, bearing the mace at a coronation is equally privileged. This appeasement of Thomas Stanley may have contributed to his decision to side with Richard III when the revolts erupted, though opportunism and a calculated assessment of the likelihood of the rebellion's success would also be factors. What is clear is that the approach of the crown to Lord Stanley was subject to change rather quickly. It had been in 1459, 1471, and again now as Richard III sought to establish himself on the throne. That of course is a two-way process in which monarch and noble both consider a number of factors. Loyalty is one of those, but it was not the sole consideration of either party.

If it was not already clear to Richard III that Henry Tudor intended to invade and fight for the throne, the fact was made apparent on Christmas Day 1484. The Earl of Richmond made a declaration that he would marry Elizabeth of York. With that, the invasion was inevitable. And this made Lord Stanley and his family once again subject to scrutiny and suspicion. Could the king trust this mighty lord? Was the Stanley affinity already plotting with the king's enemies? Writing several decades after the events of 1485 but possibly based on things that Thomas

Stanley revealed to him, Polydor Virgil summarised the attitude of Lord Stanley and King Richard III towards each other as the likelihood of invasion grew:

"...others favoryd secretly the parteners of the conspyracy. Amongest these principally was Thomas Stanley, William his brother, Gylbert Talbot, and others innumerable, whose inward mynde though Richerd was ignorant of, yeat he trustyd never one of them all, and Thomas Stanley least ofall others, because he had in maryage Henryes mother, as the matter ytself made manyfest shew ; for whan he at that time wold have gone into his countrie, for his pleasure as he sayd, but indede that he might be ready to receaveerle Henry as a frind at his cooming, the king forbad him, and wold not suffer him to depart before he had left George lord Strange his soone as a pledge in the court.[29]"

Virgil's account is most certainly accurate in respect of Lord Strange being held by Richard III as security for Lord Stanley's behaviours in the face of an invader. So too is it clear that Richard III had cause for suspicion. Lord Stanley's wife, the Countess of Richmond, had already plotted once, was known to have corresponded with her son Henry Tudor, and it was clear that Lord Stanley would stand to gain considerably should he support a successful overthrowing of King Richard III. Suspicion however is not enough to say that a betrayal has taken place. The king permitted Thomas Stanley to return to his estates with Lord Strange acting as a guarantee. This was not unusual;

hostages had been used throughout the Hundreds Year War to prevent any underhand actions during negotiations.

Both parties communicated with Lord Stanley following the landing of Henry Tudor at Milford Haven. Neither party received assurances from Thomas, Lord Stanley, that he would enter the field of battle on their side. This, presumably, did not surprise King Richard III. Thomas Stanley had avoided participating in battles from 1459 onwards. He had not fought in any of the major engagements but had participated in some sieges once the ascendancy of the Yorkists was clear. He had proven to be an opportunist, developing an ability to work with one side, then another. It had happened as power shifted in 1461. Again, as Edward IV fled in 1470. Once more when the readeption came to an end in 1471. As recently as November 1483 Lord Stanley had made use of his family's retinues, along with his brother Sir William and son Lord Strange, on behalf of King Richard III against rebels who included Henry Tudor. He had also been rewarded for that participation and recognised in parliament as having been a good and faithful servant.

To whom then did Lord Stanley owe his allegiance as Henry Tudor's force marched through Wales and into England? To King Richard III as his monarch? Having participated in Richard's coronation, received patronage and honours, and seen the king opt not to attain his wife, there is clearly a strong case that he ought to remain loyal. On the other hand, the relationship between Thomas and Richard had been full of tension from

1471 onwards. Richard had threatened the Stanley holding of Hornby and the Bosworth campaign was a little over two years after Richard as Lord Protector had Lord Stanley arrested. Loyalty is a two-way thing and at times Lord Stanley had grounds to be suspicious of Richard.

Ought he be loyal to Henry Tudor based on the invader being his son-in-law? Family ties clearly are important. However, that alone is not enough to warrant loyalty. In the medieval mind patronage, extended networks, and respect for good governance all played a part in earning and retaining loyalty and Henry Tudor had yet to do any of these in England.

However, the extended network does apply itself to supporting Henry in some ways. Lord Stanley had been Steward of Edward IV's household for a period. He had enjoyed patronage from Edward IV and may have felt that his loyalty lay with the dowager queen, who had discussed Henry Tudor's invasion with the countess of Richmond.

The narrative of the days leading up to and of the Battle of Bosworth is well known. The Stanleys' met with Henry Tudor but did not commit to his cause. They had shadowed his force as it marched out of Wales into the Midlands. Lord Stanley then provided the reason of him having Sweating Sickness as grounds not to join with King Richard III prior to forming up for the battle. On the day, his force stayed out of the fighting, with Lord Stanley opting not to commit his men to either side during the battle itself.

Tudor sources suggest that Thomas Stanley had moved into the affinity of Henry Tudor in the days before the Battle of Bosworth. Polydor Virgil noted that:

"The third day before, Thomas Stanley had bene at the same place, gardyd with few lesseley came to than fyvc thowsand men well armyd, who, understanding of Henryes approche, went before, without delay, to a village caulyd Aderstone, meaning ther to tary till Henry showld draw nere.This he dyd to avoid suspition, fearing yf before they showld coome to hand strokes he showld overtly shew himself to standand hold with erle Henry, least that king Richerd, who as yeat did not utterly mistrust his loyaltie, might kill his soone George, whom, as we have before sayd, he held in custody as a pledge[30]".

Philippe de Commines writing shortly after the battle but based on a variety of reports, also suggested that Lord Stanley had joined with the Earl of Richmond prior to the battle:

"an English gentleman, called the Lord Stanley, who had married the Earl of Richmond's mother, joined the earl with 26,000 men[31]".

Commines may have been confused with regards which member of the Stanley family took to the field as Sir William did join the battle. Thomas, Lord Stanley, did not and neither of the Stanley brothers had 26,000 men under their command.

However, some in the affinity of Lord Stanley did fight for Henry Tudor. Sir John Savage held a command in the Earl of

Richmond's army[32]. Passage through Shrewsbury en route into the Midlands has been linked to Stanley input.

The actual battlefield itself suggests that there may have been collusion between Lord Stanley and his son-in-law before the onset of the battle. Though sources suggest that Lord Stanley refused an on the day request to join either army, thus becoming the 'Third Army', it has been argued that the location of the Stanley retinues worked very much in the favour of Henry Tudor by preventing King Richard from having the manoeuvrability that his forces may have wished for and by forcing the king's force into a position that also detracted from their numerical advantage[33].

This is viewed by some historians as a betrayal of King Richard III. Though no commitment had been given by Lord Stanley that he would attend the battle and fight for the last of the Yorkist kings, he had not used his powerful retinue to slow or halt the invaders advance and may have deliberately hindered Richard's tactical options. The basis of Lord Strange being detained with King Richard III though was to act as a guarantee that Lord Stanley would not fight alongside his son-in-law. In that respect, he broke no promises.

Had Lord Stanley betrayed his duty to the court, parliament, or people living under his lordship? There's a matter of interpretation with regards the effective running of parliament as a duty of any noble. There had been a major revolt against Richard's rule which resulted in the displacement of many of the gentry and an element of disillusionment in some quarters. For those who hold the view that King Richard III was a tyrant and usurper, the lack of intervention by Lord Stanley may be justified on that very basis: and it is notable that there is only clear evidence of five nobles having taken to the field on battle in Richard's army, suggesting that there was an ambivalence towards his rule. Conversely, much of the work done in Richard's brief reign was good governance. He demonstrated mercy, including to Lord Stanley and the Countess of Richmond and so was deserving of loyalty in return. On that basis, Lord Stanley's lack of intervention against the invading army and failure to join the king on the field of battle would be acts of betrayal.

Thomas, Lord Stanley, was created Earl of Derby by his son-in-law. By the end of the Wars of the Roses he had held positions of note under Henry VI, Edward IV, Edward V, Richard III, and Henry VII. He adapted to political change and had the skills, networks, and retinue to escape any serious punishments despite twice having been accused or suspected of treason. His goals were often very clearly the bettering of his own and his kins' lot. That is visible particularly through the dispute with the Harrington family. When faced with tough choices he consistently waited, observed, avoided conflict as far as possible, then sought to exploit any opportunities that arose from events. This was no different to other nobles, though most noble families did participate in far more battles or sieges than Lord Stanley. The question of betrayal is therefore unusual with regards Thomas Stanley. His methods and political approach were well known, he had used them since 1459. In a medieval setting the nobility all sought opportunities to extend their personal wealth and status. Was doing this once more at Bosworth an act of betrayal? In the eyes of those around Richard III it undoubtedly would have been. Assurances had been made by Lord Strange, and following the battle there was a curious line in the will of Sir William Catesby. One of Richard III's closest advisors and friends, Catesby noted of Lord Stanley:

"...pray for my soul as ye have not for my body, as I trusted in you.[34]"

Chapter Eight. Sir Andrew Trollope

Andrew Trollope was a career soldier who fought in the latter stages of the Hundred Years War, and in the Wars of the Roses until his death in the Battle of Towton. Trollope was not from a noble family. He had no complex family history that bound him to one or other of the branches of the Plantagenet family. Yet he had a significant role in the events of 1459-1461. As a man-at-arms at Ludford in 1459 he led other men from the Calais garrison and defected from the Yorkists to Lancastrians overnight. Trollope went on to advise the Duke of Somerset in the attempts to seize Calais, was one of the masterminds of the Lancastrian strategy that worked to great effect in the Battle of Wakefield. He was knighted on the field of battle after his actions played a significant part in the victory won by the Lancastrians in the Second battle of St. Albans.

On the face of it, Trollope was a man who followed his paymaster, the Earl of Warwick, from Calais to Ludlow, then switched sides immediately prior to a probable battle. In simple terms, this looks like a classic case of betrayal. His decision was not quite as straightforward as this appears though.

Andrew Trollope had served in France since the late 1420s. His service included a period as a mounted man-at-arms under Thomas Burgh before holding a position under Sir John Fastalf at Fresnay-le-Vicomte. His time with Sir John included participation in the rescue of Caen and it appears that Andrew was in the pay of Sir John for much of the 1430s[1].

The 1440s illustrate that Andrew Trollope was a highly regarded and competent soldier. In 1440 he was one of the men chosen to participate in the Picardy chevauchee of John Beaufort, Earl of Somerset. By 1442 he had been appointed Lieutenant of the Castle of Fresnay, with Sir Richard Woodville as his immediate commander. He held the same role under Osbert Mundeford, treasurer of Normandy. This professional relationship resulted in Andrew Trollope meeting Elizabeth Mundeford, Osbert's sister, whom Andrew married.

In 1447 Trollope was then given the barony of La Ferté Macé in May 1447 for life. It was a short-lived land grant as it soon fell to the French. However, that he was granted lands at a time when English controlled areas in France were diminishing shows that Trollope was highly thought of by the authorities.

Trollope retained roles in Normandy until he surrendered the castle of Fresnay to the French as England was ousted from northern France except Calais. His affinity to Osbert Mundeford, who had a senior role in Calais, saw him move to the port where by 1455 he held the role of master porter.

As conflict began in England, Andrew Trollope's career as a soldier, his marriage, and his albeit brief grant of baronial lands in France, all stemmed from the patronage of Lancastrians, or the crown. From 1455 onwards the situation changes slightly.

The Earl of Warwick was granted the Captaincy of Calais. This position had been awarded by the crown though, and the loyalty of the garrison at Calais had been tested beyond regular complaints over late pay.

In 1459, the Earl of Warwick chose to take 600 men from the Calais garrison to England. They were to act as a major part of the Yorkist force which was being assembled because of the deteriorating situation in England and likelihood of conflict.

The military situation in 1459 was complicated. The Queen and her affinity had armed themselves and were mustering their armies. So too were the Yorkists, including the Earl of Warwick. It did not necessarily mean that there would be a battle, or prolonged war. Often the show of force by both parties would be enough to bring about arbitration, or legal recourse. It had happened several times in England. 1452 had seen the standoff at Dartford, the Duke of York as Protector had stopped clashes in the south west by simply arriving with a large force of men, the Loveday Parade of 1458 had similarly had large bands of armed men in the vicinity of London in support of the various nobles. None had resulted in bloodshed. The responsibility of the nobility to act as good landlords extended to good governance and maintaining law and order. Conflict was damaging at all levels, so was to be avoided.

Conflict did break out though. Queen Margaret instructed Lord Audley to intercept the Earl of Salisbury, resulting in the Battle of Blore Heath on 23 September 1459. The passage of time between the Battle of Blore Heath and the defection of Andrew Trollope is significant. During this period there was a quite public show of diplomacy and political manoeuvring by the court and Yorkist lords. The Earl of Warwick had already departed Calais with Andrew Trollope and the other men of the garrison. They marched through London and on to Warwick, shadowed by the Duke of Somerset[2]. This is unsurprising, the Yorkist lords were meeting at Ludlow and so it was only natural that the Earl of Warwick would be in transit at the same time as his father's force was intercepted at Blore Heath.

The weeks that followed Blore Heath were politically and militarily quiet. The first move was made by the crown, issuing summons to a Parliament to be held at Coventry on 21 November. None of the Yorkist lords received a summons, but they all found out very quickly about the intended parliament. The implication was clear. Lords who were not summoned to a Parliament were typically about to be attainted or impeached. Alongside this was a pardon delivered to the Yorkist lords by the bishop of Salisbury. The mode of delivering the offer of a pardon was symbolic, and the offer of a pardon was pointed: the men had not been proven to have done anything requiring a pardon.

It is at this point, however, that the wider political situation was placed firmly into the public arena. The Duke of York and Earls of Salisbury and Warwick responded to the offer of a pardon in Worcester Cathedral, taking an oath swearing that they were loyal to the king and only working, *'for the prosperity and augmentation of [the king's] high estate*[3]*'*. Further to this, the motives of the Yorkist lords at this time are noted as being subject to debate[4] and the movements of the Lancastrian forces would be known to members of the Earl of Warwick's retinue as a matter of necessity.

It seems implausible that Trollope would not have known of the political situation, or the shadowing of the Earl of Warwick by the Duke of Somerset once the oath had been made. Yet the point at which Andrew Trollope realises that he and the other men of the Calais garrison are being led to fight against the King is not entirely clear from contemporary writers. Robert Fabyan notes that,

"the erle of Warwyke with a stronge bade of men, amonge the whiche was Andrewe Trollop, and many other of the beste souldyours of Calays. The duke thus kepynge his felde vpon that one party, and the kynge with his people vpon that other, vpon the nyght precedinge the day that both hootes shuld haue met, the fornamed Andrewe Trollope, wi all the chefe sowdiours of Calaies, secretly departed from the dukes hoost and went vnto the kynges, where they were ioyously receyue.[5]*"*

Gregory's Chronicle, however, contradicts this:

"Also alle that seson the Erle of Warwyke with sowdyers of Calysse were comynge unto the Duke of Yorke, and he come ovyrwharte Colsylle besyde Covyntre, and the Duke of Somerset

whythe hys men rode a-longe thoroughe the towne, and yet non of hem mette whythe othyr as hyt happyd, or by lyckely hode they wold have made a newe fraye. Ande the same day Androwe Throllope consayvyd that the Erle of Warwyke was goyng unto the Duke of Yorke and not unto the kynge, and utterly for-soke hym and come unto the kynge and was pardonyd; and that made the duke fulle sore a-frayde when he wyste that sum olde soudyers went from hym unto the kynge[6]"

In this account we have Andrew Trollope determining that the Earl of Warwick intended to face the king, rather than join him, whilst passing Coleshill near Coventry. Further, he transferred to the King's affinity on the same day. That is not at Ludford, which is roughly 60 miles to the west of Coleshill and at least two days march for a force with baggage and ordnance.

Whatever decision was made by Trollope, the consequence was apparent to the Yorkist lords very quickly. Fabyan notes that the Duke of York at once called a '*couceyll for a remedye taken they concludyd to flee, and to leue the feelde standyng as they had ben present & styll abydyn.*[7]'

Andrew Trollope had chosen to leave the service of the Earl of Warwick and join that of the king. It was a decision that contributed to the Yorkist decision to take flight, leaving Ludford Bridge in the night. Was this decision by Trollope, taken whilst marching under the banner of a lord who had been quite openly opposing the Court Party of the Queen, and by association the king, one of betrayal in the face of the enemy?

There are several issues to consider when assessing the motives of Andrew Trollope. First, he was not likely to attain personal betterment through large grants, titles, or other high level acts of patronage. He was a man-at-arms, some way down the pecking order when it came to such things. So, his motivation was something other than personal power.

Edward Hall notes of the men of the Calais garrison that:

"Andrewe Trolop and other the Calicians, whiche wer men of great knowledge and muche experience, and had liued by the kynges wages, more then a few yeres.[8]"

These professional soldiers had a longstanding relationship with the crown. It was the King whom they had sworn to serve, and from the King that they had earned their living. Yes, the Earl of Warwick had a role in the payment of their wages, but this was from grants and duties awarded for that purpose by the king's parliaments[9].

Thomas Walsingham notes that the party, led by Trollope, went straight to the king as a great fellowship.

'...but in the nyght Andrewe Trollop and all the olde souldyours of Calays with a grete felawshyp sodeynly departed... and wente strayte unto the kynges felde where they were receyved joiously...[10]"

There was no arguing, no division amongst those in the Calais garrison, no hesitation. Trollope appears to have had no problem whatsoever in transferring the allegiance of the men of the garrison from one faction to the other. And whilst Trollope was a respected soldier, he was not a man who had held senior commands so would not necessarily have the projection of a personality such as would be required to quickly win over some 600 men.

Another factor in the decision is not so much the history that Andrew Trollope had with the crown, but rather, his relationship with those who served it. The Duke of Somerset, a senior commander in the field for the Lancastrians, was a nephew of John Beaufort, under whom Andrew Trollope had served in Picardy. Sir Richard Woodville, another man under whom Andrew Trollope had served, was at this point firmly tied to the House of Lancaster through his marriage and lines of patronage. Andrew's wife, Elizabeth, was sister to a staunch Lancastrian whom Trollope had served under in France. Was it these links of affinity that led to Trollope deserting the Earl of Warwick?

There were, then, strong ties between Trollope, the crown, and those at the centre of the Lancastrian affinity. These may well be the reason for his choosing to change sides once in England. If they are, is he really betraying anybody? If, as was suggested at the time, Trollope and his men did not know of the intention to face the royal army on a field of battle, then he has changed sides to that of those to whom he owes loyalty at the earliest possible moment? Which would hardly be a betrayal on his part and more a lack of clarity or judgement from the Earl of Warwick: who had stated in Worcester that he was loyal to the king.

The chivalric ideals of loyalty to the king, his patrons, the wider affinity around the crown party are all quite admirable and as outlined, there is much to suggest that these were leading factors in the decision making process. They aren't the only considerations though. Money was possibly an issue. To what extent is hard to determine but there is evidence of financial matters that could have caused a rift between the Earl of Warwick and one of his most experienced soldiers.

The financial matter is in the form of an annuity awarded to Andrew Trollope from the lordship of Sandegate. A figure of 40 shillings and one penny had been *'disallowed by the earl of Warwick*[11]*'* There was also a matter relating to the earnings of that lordship. Trollope paid rent for the castle and land but appears to have been denied the income that would be derived from it. David Grummitt in his book *The Calais Garrison: War and Military Service in England, 1436-1558* raises the suggestion that these financial matters may have been part of a strategy from the king, or Duke of Somerset, to entice Trollope back into their affinity. There is no firm evidence to suggest that such a measure was attempted by the Lancastrian elite, though efforts to win over the more experienced and position holding men of the Calais garrison would have made sense when considering the speed at which the Lancastrian affinity was preparing itself for possible conflict in England.

Finally, on motive for changing sides, the *Croyland Chronicle* suggests that there were several considerations.

"The king's party, however, waxed stronger and stronger every day in consequence of endless multitudes of the nobles and common people, who now flocked together to his support; and the more especially, after Andrew Trollop and his paid followers, from Calais, who had been summoned by the earl of Warwick, their captain, from the parts beyond sea, as though to aid the king, had deserted the duke of York. For finding that, contrary to their expectations, they had really been brought over to act against the king, they left the duke and sided with the king, whose provisions and pay they had been in the habit of receiving[12]"

.

The *Croyland Chronicle* suggests that the matter of not wishing to fight against the king was a consideration and that the garrison had not expected to be asked to serve against the monarch. So too was the issue of pay a factor. The issue that this source notes that is lacking in most accounts is the simple pragmatic reason for any soldier choosing to change sides: likelihood of victory. The royal army is noted as becoming stronger and stronger every day. The Yorkist force was unlikely to grow. The Earls of Salisbury and Warwick had brought retinues a considerable distance to Ludlow. Additional men from those sources were unlikely. To a seasoned veteran such as Andrew Trollope the outcome of a clash on these terms would be quite clear. Fight at the heart of the Yorkist vanguard and the chances of survival are diminished. Survive and the odds remain in favour of having been on the losing side. Where would this leave a professional soldier who had been in the pay of the crown?

October 1459 was then a moment in time when there were lots of issues surrounding the choices that Andrew Trollope made. He may have felt bound by duty to serve the king. Or felt an affinity to the Beaufort and Woodville's that he was unwilling to break in battle. Money may have played on his mind, or indeed the prospects of either side should battle take place.

Did Trollope betray the Earl of Warwick and the Yorkists? The Yorkist claims of 1459 and for the Yorkists based in Calais in 1460 were that they were loyal to King Henry VI. On that basis, it is quite understandable that any soldier would question why they were suddenly being asked to face the king in battle. Countering this is the clear evidence that the divide between the two factions had reached breaking point. Had it not been at the point where war was expected, the garrison of Calais, along with other Yorkist forces, would not have been summoned to Ludlow. A man such as Andrew Trollope would have known that this was the case. Why then did he not act at an earlier time?

Though Trollope was not a noble with a large command, he was a man with authority for a smaller retinue, and with other experienced soldiers was an adjutant of sorts within the Calais system. He therefore did have a responsibility to the men of the garrison. Though it appears that there was little questioning of the decision to switch to the king's force, was he in any way betraying the men who followed him? For some, the decision would result in their deaths, as it did for Andrew Trollope himself, fighting against the Yorkists. With little on record about the views of these men, it is impossible to state whether the entirety of the force agreed with the decision, or whether it was a matter in which they were effectively given no choice. These soldiers were also placed in the enviable position of returning to Calais as part of the besieging force, requiring them to take up arms against men who had until recently been part of the same military unit and with whom they would have bonds of trust and friendship. For some, this would include having to contemplate a potentially long siege against the port, with wives and children of these besieging soldiers inside the walls of Calais.

The aftermath of the rout at Ludford shows that Trollope was quickly assimilated into the Lancastrian ranks. The Burgundian chronicler Wavrin claims that as the Yorkists escaped from Ludford, Trollope was at the head of the chase to capture them before they could take to the seas and safety.

"It so happened that as they were falling back, Andrew Trollope and his band were the first to set upon them. And there was a very great discomfiture, for the two brothers of my lord of Warwick were taken prisoners there.[13]"

Other accounts do not support this version of events. John and Thomas Neville had already been captured by the Lancastrians, having fallen into their hands after the Battle of Blore Heath[14]. However, Wavrin is right to indicate that Trollope was soon at the heart of Lancastrian action. And it was aimed very quickly at his last Captain, the Earl of Warwick.

One of the first actions taken by the Lancastrian regime post Ludford was to strip the Earl of Warwick of the Captaincy of Calais and appoint the Duke of Somerset to the role. The Earl of Warwick had fled Ludford and his whereabouts were unknown. Somerset called upon Andrew Trollope to advise him on all matters pertaining to Calais. They would know that Lord Fauconberg had been left in command of the garrison and that he himself would be loyal to the Earl of Warwick. The loyalty of the garrison itself would be best known to men like Andrew Trollope.

What Andrew Trollope and the Duke of Somerset had not counted on was the Earl of Warwick, along with the Earls of March and Salisbury, arriving at Calais before them. Furthermore, they had secured the loyalty of most of those of the Calais garrison who had not accompanied the Earl and Trollope, and they also had the support of the merchants of the Calais Staple. The Lancastrians would have to fight their way into Calais.

Trollope's local knowledge and soldiering experience enabled the Lancastrian force to take control of the castle of Guines.

Trollope was appointed as Bailiff of the castle at Guines on 24 March 1460. From here there were regular skirmishes as the Lancastrians probed for weaknesses in the port's defences. Reinforcements were arranged by the Queen, which was to sail under the command of Sir Richard Woodville, who had been appointed as Warden of the Cinque Ports for the purpose of defending against the Yorkists. Whilst holding Guines was attainable, the objective of taking Calais was not. The fleet that Sir Richard Woodville was assembling at Sandwich was attacked by a flotilla commanded by John Dynham which resulted in the capture of Sir Richard, his wife, Jacquetta, Duchess of Bedford, and several ships. This limited the forces available in the Pale of Calais and after a failed attempt to force their way into Calais at Newnham Bridge on 23 April 1460, the Duke of Somerset was forced to negotiate terms with the Earl of Warwick.

Andrew Trollope's role in the attempts to take Calais demonstrate that he was very quickly integrated into the Lancastrian military structure and that he was proving his loyalty to the crown from the off. The attempts to take Calais also made it clear that the Earl of Warwick did not enjoy the loyalty of all the men of the Calais garrison.

One example was that of Osbert Mundeford. Trollope's father-in-law was instructed to lead a force of 500 men to Guines from England to aid the Duke of Somerset. In a raid mirroring that which captured Sir Richard Woodville, Mundeford, a veteran of the Calais garrison, was attacked by John Dynham in the harbour of Sandwich. Unlike the more illustrious Woodville, Mundeford received no mercy when he arrived at Calais, being beheaded at the Tower of Rysebank[15].

The loyalty of men inside the garrison was also questioned at times. As late as August 1462 correspondence noted the probability of dissent within the garrison, mirroring the issues that may have motivated Andrew Trollope to change sides in 1459. A letter from John Russ to John Paston notes this, saying that *'it was told me secretly there were CC. in Caleyse sworn contrary to the Kyngs well, and for defaute of their wages[16]'.*

Whilst the examples of other men of the Calais garrison having remained in the affinity of the Lancastrians, or being dissatisfied with the Yorkist administration, are not necessarily reflective of Trollope's own views, they provide a context from which his own actions can be considered. With respects to Calais, it is the case that there is evidence of divided loyalties, as explored in the chapter on Calais in this book.

When the attempts to seize Calais were abandoned, Andrew Trollope made his way to England with the Duke of Somerset. Acting as a senior advisor to the Duke, Trollope was instrumental in organising the Lancastrian forces that were being massed in Yorkshire as a response to the Act of Accord. Those plans came to fruition when the Duke of York headed north to tackle the threat posed by this force.

At Wakefield, on 30 December 1460, the Lancastrian army defeated that of the Duke of York. The Duke, and Earls of Rutland and Salisbury were all killed either in the fighting, or shortly afterwards. Andrew Trollope was one of the masterminds of the Lancastrian strategy at the battle, which was a decisive victory. The nature of the victory and the deaths of the Earls of Rutland and Salisbury do pose questions relating to betrayal.

Firstly, there is a suggestion that the Yorkists were duped through false use of livery. Whilst it may be commonplace in modern warfare to adopt 'dirty' approaches to battle, it was very much against the codes of chivalry to which the nobles and knights were supposed to adhere.

The first issue surrounds the approach of John Neville, son of the Earl of Westmoreland, to the Duke of York for a commission of array. Stow records that,

"Then the Lorde Neuill, brother to the Earle of Westmerlande, vnder a co/lour of Friendshippe, came to the Duke of Yorke, requy/ring of hym a commission for hym to rayse the people for to chastice the Rebelles as he sayde."

Suggesting that the Lancastrian strategy, which may have been influenced by Trollope on issues such as this, was to try and trick the Duke of York. The strategy worked; the source continues:

"...but when he hadde raysed to the number of eighte thousande menne, hée broughte them to the Lordes of that Countrey, that is to saye, the Earle of Northumberlande, Lorde Clifforde, and the Duke of Somerset, that were aduersaries to the Duke of Yorke, and on the laste of December they fell on the sayde Duke Richarde, killed hym and his Sonne the Earle of Rutland, and many other knights and Esquiers."

The Battle of Wakefield is one for which the sources provide very different versions of what happened. Some suggest that the Duke was lured out of Sandal Castle by the ruse of men approaching wearing the livery of the Earl of Warwick. There are also suggestions that a Christmas truce had been agreed between the two sides was broken by the Lancastrians. Deceit and breaches of truces were very much against the codes of chivalry which nobles and professional soldiers were used to and expected to adhere to. For men who had served in the latter stages of the Hundred Years War breaking these chivalric conventions is something that would not be expected[17].

These breaches of the Code of Chivalry are a betrayal of societal norms and expectations of a 'fair fight'. Subterfuge on this scale, Neville is said to have had up to 8000 men with him when he arrived at Wakefield, is not the doing of one man or commander. Arraying that many men, coordinating their arrival with other matters such as luring the Duke of York into the open, all require careful planning. Whilst the idea could well have come from any man of influence at Wakefield, the plan would have been known to Andrew Trollope in his role as advisor to the Duke of Somerset and commander in the field. He may have switched to the side of the Queen and Duke of Somerset as a matter of honour, at Wakefield he was possibly complicit in acts that in the context of the day would be viewed as being incredibly dishonourable: indeed, the executing of the Earls of Rutland and Salisbury rather than following normal practice led to reprisals at the Battle of Towton in March 1461 by Edward IV in the form of a no-mercy command in respect of any captured Lancastrian knights or nobles. As such it can be argued that he had betrayed his responsibilities as a soldier and commander through his role in these actions.

From Wakefield the Queen's army marched south. They faced opposition at St. Albans on 17 February 1461, in the form of a series of sturdy defences constructed by the Earl of Warwick and his brother, John. Andrew Trollope is credited with securing victory in this battle. He led a mounted assault that broke through a gap in the lines and drove back the Yorkists. Most accounts suggest that the Yorkists were already withdrawing when Trollope made this move. However, some also suggest that the flanking move conducted by Trollope was enabled by betrayal of the Earl of Warwick's plans by Sir Henry Lovelace.

The story of Lovelace's betrayal of the Earl of Warwick is one that has several versions. Each agrees that he was a man of Kent. Some suggest that he had been in the employment of the Earl as a Captain. Others suggest a variety of forenames:

Richard, John, and Henry all appear across a wide selection of books on the Wars of the Roses. They also all agree that the seeds of the betrayal were sown on the battlefield at Wakefield.

An English Chronicle notes that Lovelace had struck a deal at Wakefield. When captured he escaped with his life by promising to never take up arms against the Northmen again:

"And at the laste, thorow the witbdrawyng of the Kentisshmen with thayre capteyne, called Lovelace, that was in the vaunt-warde, the whych Lovelace fauored the Northe party, for as moche as he was take by the Northurnmen at Wakefeld whan the duk of York was slayne, and made to theym an othe for to saue his lyfe, that he wold neuer be agayns theym.[18]*"*

Lovelace seemingly then made his way south, joining with the Earl of Warwick in time to face the advancing Lancastrian force at St. Albans. When battle is raging, Lovelace then makes good on his promise to aid rather than face the northerners.

"...thorow the witbdrawyng of the Kentisshmen with thayre capteyne, called Lovelace, that was in the vaunt-warde,—the whych Lovelace fauored the Northe party.[19]*"*

This account suggests that Lovelace deliberately withdrew his men from the defensive line held by the Yorkists. If true, it could explain how Andrew Trollope was able to execute such a bold mounted move whilst many of the Earl of Warwick's men were still in position. A premeditated battlefield betrayal had seemingly been executed. Accounts of Lovelace's betrayal of the Earl of Warwick's plans are very inconsistent though. Some eye-witness accounts make no reference to him. Others are written by Yorkist sympathisers for whom attributing the failure at St. Albans to betrayal would serve a political purpose.

As a strategist for the Lancastrian army, such plans would have been made with Andrew Trollope's input. If this account is true, it suggests that the timing of Trollope's defection in 1459 may also have been calculated to inflict the most damage to the Yorkists, rather than being based on honour, or a last minute realisation that the king was in the field.

Trollope's actions in the Second Battle of St. Albans were sufficient for him to be knighted by King Henry VI in the immediate aftermath of the Lancastrian victory. This poses the question of why then? There had been men knighted after Wakefield. There had been opportunity for patronage or honours as a reward for his defection in 1459, or by proxy in 1460. Yes. Second St. Albans was important in that it freed King Henry VI from Yorkist hands, but forcing the Yorkists into flight in 1459, and dealing decisively with Richard Duke of York and Earl of Salisbury, were both enough to warrant other men, with lesser roles, being knighted or rewarded.

Whatever the reasons for the timing, Andrew Trollope is reported as being incredibly self-effacing when receiving his knighthood. *Gregory's Chronicle* records the scene:

"And the Prynce made many knyghtys. The fryste that he made was Androwe Trolloppe, for he was hurte and myght not goo for a calletrappe in hys fote; and he sayde, "My lorde, I have not deservyd hit for I slowe but xv men, for I stode stylle in oo place and they come unto me, but they bode stylle with me." And then come Whytyngam, Tresham, and many moo othyr, and were made knyghtys that same tyme[20]".

Trollope may have been modest about his influence. The Yorkists, however, were far from that. When Edward was proclaimed king of England in London, a series of proclamations followed. They were intended to win over any undecided men and set out his intentions should the war be won in his favour. One proclamation offered pardons to men valued at less than 100 marks. Another offered a reward of £100 to anybody who brought about the death of any man on a list of wanted Lancastrians. Andrew Trollope was one of those listed[21]. This was undoubtedly because of his changing sides at or close to Ludford. The Earl of Warwick most probably certainly viewed the defections as a major betrayal. When forces reinforcing the Duke of Somerset were swept by winds into a situation where they needed to enter the harbour of Calais to save the ships, the men onboard who had deserted the Yorkists with Trollope were summarily executed.

The loyal service to the Queen's party and Duke of Somerset continued with the preparations to face the Yorkists in the north. Trollope was again involved as an advisor to the Duke of

Somerset. As such he no doubt had a say in the choice of ground near Saxton and Towton. He would have already been aware of the bridge at Ferrybridge and the defence qualities that it had. In the battle of Towton, Trollope once more served the Queen and Duke of Somerset loyally. He paid for this with his life, one of the many who died in the clash.

Many died on that day, most of whom remained anonymous. Contemporary records refer to the names of the nobles who fought and fell, of those who fled, or were captured during the ensuing rout. What is perhaps remarkable is that many of these accounts also mention Sir Andrew Trollope. He is mentioned by name in the Paston Letters, and in chronicles such as Gregory's, and his significance remained worthy of note by Tudor chroniclers such as Hall.

Sir Andrew Trollope died on the field of battle a true Lancastrian. He was as senior a man could be on the battlefield without holding a noble rank. His service to the crown was exemplary throughout his career to 1455 and again from the moment he defected in 1459 until his death at Towton in March 1461. The manner of his changing sides in 1459 is questionable. Was he bound to serve his commander, the Earl of Warwick? Was changing sides the honorable thing for him to do? Did he desert the Yorkist force at the earliest opportunity, or manipulate the situation for strategic gain? Were future actions of deception influenced by Trollope? And if so, are they consistent with the expectations of the day?

Chapter Nine. Towns: Calais and York

Towns and civic bodies had a great deal of interaction with the various factions during the period of the Wars of the Roses. They played an important role in the fortunes of Lancastrians, Yorkists, King Henry VII, and rebels. Though the nature of governance of a town varied over time and from place to place, there were common features: a notion of good governance, ensuring law and order, defending the realm, and enabling a vibrant economy.

Some towns held close ties to individual lords. York, for example, was closely associated with Richard Duke of Gloucester in the 1470s until his death through his role as lord of the north. Calais was similarly linked to the Earl of Warwick through his captaincy of garrison from 1456 to 1470. Yet the towns themselves were not usually beholden to one lord. They often held charters and grants direct from the crown. Local taxes could be adjusted by parliament through reductions in the fee farm and liberties to self-govern could be granted. Financing of defences or other major works could be administered through a variety of methods both through national and local means.

For towns to receive grants and liberties there had to be a good reason. This could be as simple as economic need, urgent defensive expenditure, or through a town having proven its worth to the crown. In short, the extent of civic liberties and rights granted would reflect the ongoing need for good governance at a local level, with national considerations playing a part in forming those decisions. In many ways this mirrors the way in which senior nobles would interact with their retainers and tenants.

Some English towns stand out as having national significance. London was at the heart of government, had by far the largest population[1], was the most important trading centre, and was a source of loans for the crown. Calais provided an economic and military foothold on mainland Europe, enabling duties to be collected, the collection of plate and bullion, as a military base, along with having a key role in diplomatic missions to and from continental powers. To the north York acted as a regional seat of government and was where armies mustered for campaigns against the Scots. Elsewhere many ports held value, with Bristol, Hull, Newcastle, Sandwich, Southampton, Bishops Lynn, amongst others having significant roles to play in England's economic links with the wider world. The Cinque Ports and others such as Exeter, Portsmouth, Plymouth and at times Scarborough had military significance with regards the keeping of the seas.

With towns having varied roles and rates of urbanisation, the nature of civic governance was not uniform. This is reflected in the way that the crown and parliament interacted with these towns. The number of towns that were granted incorporated status rose quite sharply. King Henry VI's reign saw 13 towns granted such status. Edward IV's reign saw 12 grants of incorporated status, and the reign of Richard III saw a further 9 grants of incorporated status granted to English towns. Alongside these were additional grants for a town council. For example, the reign of Richard III saw 24 Inspeximus Charters granted, effectively confirming rights that had been granted to urban corporations at an earlier date[2]. In addition to towns that held charters, or that had arrangements with the crown concerning their governance and tax arrangements, there were also towns such as St. Albans that were held by the church, and those such as Nottingham and Derby that were held directly by the crown[3].

The relationship between a town and the crown was not then one for which there is a standardised policy. Towns changed their status during the Wars of the Roses; for example, Scarborough was granted county status during the reign of Richard III. There were differing levels of dependency and interaction with the crown and Parliament, ranging from low level interaction relating mainly to taxation, through to Parliament intervening on a regular basis with regards the defences, or economic arrangements of an urban area, as was often the case with Calais. The relationship with the Crown and Parliament was two-way, as larger towns elected members of parliament who could defend the interests of towns and civic institutions.

What the towns had in common was the duty of care to its citizens and a broader responsibility to play its role in the defence and economic well--being of the area. In return for the effective administration of these key areas a town expected good governance from the king, his council, and Parliament. Regional magnates and the gentry would similarly be expected to play their part in ensuring that a town enjoyed an environment in which it could prosper.

On a simple level, this provided towns with the status of justices of the peace. This role is evident ~~ced~~ in the records of towns that have remained intact to this day. For example, the first entry in the *York House Books* relates to a suspected felon being brought before the Mayor of York, just one of many examples that can be found in the city records[4]. The role of maintaining law and order also includes security. This comes in several forms. In 1450 the City of London initially barred its gates to the rebels under Jack Cade. It again barred its gates in 1452, to Richard 3rd Duke of York, and again in 1461 to Queen Margaret. York also limited access to within the walls, limiting the entourage that could accompany Edward IV within the walls in 1471. On a day to day basis security was required for maintaining general law and order. The town of Canterbury barred entry to the rebel forces led by Jack Cade in 1450. In November 1461 the City of York ensured that wardens were in place and that they had clearly defined duties[5]. Crisis also affected the security requirements of a town, for example in 1476 Calais responded to the diplomatic crisis that followed the death of Charles the Bold by increasing security in Calais and throughout the pale[6]. So too did the civic bodies have a requirement to work with the crown to limit unrest. This included civic bodies playing a role in limiting espionage, through devices such as limiting the ability of aliens [foreigners] to enter a town[7], or through ensuring that proclamations were made in relation to issues such as sedition[8].

These requirements placed a financial burden on towns. Those with a more prominent military role regularly had to fund repairs to town walls and defences or purchasing weapons. Examples of this in practice include the town of Southampton conducting a survey of the town's defences[9]; the City of York repairing its walls[10]; or the ongoing funding of the garrison and defences at Calais which had a fundamentally different role to any other English town.[11].

Towns also held an important role in the economy as they were the centres of commerce, sites of markets, and home to the warehouses, docks and hubs on the medieval road network that enabled trade. In larger towns, such as London, the guilds had a great deal of influence. In general, a town would be governed by a Council with bailiffs appointed to fulfil required tasks. Council members and Mayors were often guild members, resulting in economic interests being at the forefront of political thinking. This led to petitions to Parliament from the guilds with support from the elected representatives in towns[12]. It also led to the civic authorities and magnates needing to establish good lines of communication, as it was mutually beneficial and ensured good governance and lordship within and around towns. An example of this is the two-way patronage that existed in the 1470s between the city of York and Richard Duke of Gloucester. The Duke used his influence to address things on a local level that improved things for the commons of York, for example through intervention on matters relating to fishgarths in 1476[13]. This type of intervention saw the town sending gifts to the duke, illustrating the appreciation of good lordship, and his exercising of influence on the town's behalf[14]. The expectation of good lordship also resulted in magnates using their influence to defend the rights of their own manors, holdings, or responsibilities within towns. This on occasion reduced the capacity of the town to gain revenues but reflected the benefits that some manors and their inhabitants had. This affected towns that interacted with people who lived in lands held by the Duchy of Lancaster as the right of the tenants of the Duchy to be exempt from tolls was asserted in November 1476[15].

Towns therefore had a mixture of roles within the national picture. As with nobles, they had responsibilities and rights. They also expected things of the crown, and the responsibility of the crown was asserted at times. John Fortescue in his work *'Governance'* noted the king's *'ordinary charge'* to maintain Calais, and that of Keeping the Seas [from Calais] along with a general maintenance of the navy[16]. It was therefore a relationship that placed rights and responsibilities upon the crown, parliament, civic authorities, and organisations such as guilds. As with good lordship, these needed to be maintained to ensure peace and prosperity. Should this relationship break down, there is then scope for one party, or the other, to have a legitimate grievance against the other. Similarly, it is also possible for one of the parties involved in this exchange of rights and responsibilities to let down other parties, or to betray them.

Calais

The port and town of Calais became an English possession in 1347, following a successful siege by Edward III. It quickly became an integral part of the English plans for the execution of the Hundred Years War, and for England's economic policies in relation to continental Europe. War and the economy shaped the way in which Calais developed. As England's major foothold in northern France, Calais had immediate strategic importance, and this was recognised from its early days as an English held town through garrisoning and the development of the port and towns defences. Similarly, the economic potential of Calais was realised at an early stage and before the end of the 14th century policies and practices were put in place that would shape the relationship of Calais with the crown throughout the era of the Wars of the Roses.

The governance of Calais as England headed towards the Wars of the Roses was based around that connection with the crown, and the significant role that the port and its surrounding area had militarily and economically.

The military aspects of rule in Calais were undertaken initially by a Captain, appointed by the crown. The Captain of Calais appointed a lieutenant to act on his behalf whilst absent, a marshal, and several captains of the garrison. This garrison varied in size over the second half of the 15th century. In 1451 the indenture with Edmund Beaufort, Duke of Somerset, in his role as Captain of Calais was for a garrison of 30 mounted knights, 30 mounted archers, 200 men-at-arms, 40 crossbowmen, 25 carpenters, and 15 masons. The Calais accounts show that the indenture was not enacted precisely, listing the Captain, Lieutenant, Marshall, and 257 men-at-arms who were not mounted[17]. This garrison was supplemented by men garrisoning the fortifications at Hammes and Guines, along with 'crews' of men who were hired by members of the garrison. In 1451 the crews are noted as accounting for a further 300 men[18]. This was by far the largest permanent garrison that the English maintained at this time, as Berwick on the Anglo-Scottish border had a garrison of no more than one hundred men.

The size of the garrison rose and fell according to need and finance. In 1466 the muster roll listed 527 men. Significantly,

193 of these were personally retained by John, Lord Wenlock, a man close to the Earl of Warwick[19].

The Captain of Calais was also Governor of the Pale of Calais. This meant that he had oversight of the garrison, which when servants and other military aged men are added would average around 700 men, and oversight of civic and economic interests. From 1471 the role was changed, with a king's Lieutenant being appointed who had rights not dissimilar to those held earlier by the Lieutenants of France, or Ireland.

Merchants of the Calais Staple controlled the commercial life of Calais[20]. The Company of Staplers had its origins in the early 14th century, overseeing the export of wool to 'staples' in St. Omer, and Antwerp. These safe havens for English merchants had been replaced by the Calais Staple in 1363. The Staple at Calais had a monopoly on export of English wool to the Low Countries from English ports[21]. It also maintained its own mint for producing coins and was subject to a range of restrictions on trade, for example at times requiring payment in plate or bullion rather than credit. The English merchants operating within the Calais Staple, known as Staplers, had a series of benefits for maintaining these systems. Acts of Retainer provided the Staplers with exemptions in exchange for their administration of the system for the benefit of the crown and Calais itself[22].

The relationship with the crown was in theory quite straightforward. Calais had been won by the crown and was an

English resource that would benefit the crown, through its beneficial position between France and Flanders. The Captain of Calais was a crown appointee, answerable to the monarch. Captains were granted almost complete autonomy in managing Calais and the Pale, and the crown was committed to providing funds through parliamentary grants for the maintenance of the garrison and the defences of the region. In practice, the financing of Calais had been fraught with problems in the early 15th century. Throughout the 15th century Magnates and Clerics had loaned the crown funds to cover the wages of the garrison. These loans were secured against future customs duties. However, many people including officials in Calais were due income from these duties which led to delays in payments of crown debts and problems in securing additional funds. This resulted in the garrison seizing wool and taking the profits as pay in 1433, and mutinies in 1442 and 1454.

In 1465 the Earl of Warwick set out the requirements for his lieutenant and captains with respect to the governance of Calais in his absence:

"capitaignes counsillours and officers of the seid towne be of gode due & diligent oubeissaunce & attendance to the lieutenant of the seid towne by the seid capitaine deputed ... shewyng hem of true and lovyng & faithfull affeccion to him bi their advise counsell and assistence[23]."

In keeping with wider expectations, good service in Calais would be expected to be met with reward. For men of rank this could be additional patronage, or grants. For professional soldiers it could be promotion, elevation into the household of the captain, grants of land or annuities, or opportunities for advancement of their family through appointments or introductions. This is an integral part of the system, it requires good lordship on the part of the captain, and the crown and parliament need to play their part in enabling the professional soldiers and Staplers benefitting from patronage.

Here, perhaps, is one of the reasons why Calais and the Staple became a problem for the crown at times during the wars of the roses. Until the 1466 Act of Retainer, there was no formal structure to the financing of the garrison, or its maintenance of security for the Staplers[24]. This in turn meant that the magnate who had been appointed to command Calais as Captain and Governor of the Pale was in a position where financing the payment of the garrison was a significant issue. Indeed, when the Earl of Warwick was appointed as Captain of Calais, the garrison refused him entry until assurances were given that he would pay the men wages that were overdue. This required credit from the Staplers, and assurances from Parliament and the Earl[25]. As the Captaincy was transferred, the garrison simply placed the matter in the hands of their new Captain. To whom did these men now owe their allegiance? To their new Captain who had facilitated their being paid, to the Staplers who had provided the funds through loans, or to the crown that had failed to ensure regular pay but to whom they ultimately were employed by? It lent itself to the scenario of retainers being used within the garrison, and crews being tied to the nobility serving within the garrison. For these men, the bond of patronage and kinship was first and foremost to their lord, not necessarily to the crown, as pay, family prospects, and a history of affinity are naturally going to override other considerations at times.

This issue comes to the fore on several occasions in the Wars of the Roses. Men of the garrison are bound to defend the realm; it is their primary function as professional soldiers. Many had served in France prior to the English being defeated by the French in Normandy. These established members of the Calais garrison had served the crown, had been commanded by the Dukes of Somerset and York, and had signed up to the service of the King. This was at odds with newer members of the garrison, to whom allegiance was as likely to be based on affinity to the lord who had employed them.

This led to the scenario at Ludford Bridge in 1459, discussed in the chapter on Andrew Trollope. This contingent remained loyal to the crown and whilst willing to travel with the Earl of Warwick to assist in restoring order in England, were unwilling to do that against an army that flew the royal standard. That defection of the soldiers under Andrew Trollope led to Calais becoming prized territory. With the Earls of March, Salisbury, and Warwick taking refuge in Calais with the support of many, but not all, of the garrison remaining in Calais and the neighbouring fortresses at Hammes and Guines. Here we see the split in loyalties. Trollope and his command chose to join with the Lancastrian faction. Those in Calais, in general, were loyal to the Earl of Warwick. In aiding in the defence of Calais when the newly appointed Captain, the duke of Somerset, attempted to gain then force entry, were the garrison and citizens of Calais betraying the crown?

The leadership of both factions asserted that they were owed loyalty and had the right to govern Calais and the Pale, with the Duke of Somerset having the legal authority that the attainted Earl of Warwick did not. Some men who had served in the Calais garrison under the Earl of Warwick who aided the Duke of Somerset's assault executed when captured. Prominent men such as Sir Thomas Kyriell were executed when falling into Lancastrian hands, in Kyriell's case as one of the knights who remained with King Henry VI as the Yorkists fled the field at the Second Battle of St. Albans. To what extent was that bloodlust, and what extent is it a consequence of Kyriell having abandoned his Lancastrian roots to fight for the Yorkists[26]? It hints at the very act of choosing to fight for the opposing side being viewed at this early stage in the conflict as being an act of betrayal by those on both sides.

The very nature of the role of Captain of Calais had led to the division of the men in the Calais garrison. Captains wanted to know that the defences and Staple were well administered. This led to them appointing people to key positions who had worked for them in England. This led to men such as Lord Wenlock and

Walter Blount, later Lord Mountjoy, accompanying the Earl of Warwick to Calais. With this, there was always a sizeable proportion of the garrison who were tied to the Captain in terms of kinship and patronage. Alongside these appointees were men who owed their livelihood and positions to longstanding family ties to the garrison, or to other English garrisons in Normandy and France. These men, such as Richard Woodville, later Earl Rivers, and Andrew Trollope who are discussed at length in dedicated chapters, owed their ranks and positions to the systems that had been in place within the garrison for generations. As a result, their loyalty was to the crown, or to earlier captains who had enabled their rise to senior positions within the garrison.

Similarly, the Staplers themselves had mixed loyalties. Not only were most of the Staplers London based merchants but they had experienced economic slumps, been forced into extending loans to pay for the maintenance of the garrison and defences and benefitted or suffered because of diplomatic policy with regards mainland continental powers, particularly France and Burgundy. They relied upon good governance, peace, and cordial relations with potential client states to prosper. Were they duty bound to support the crown if it failed in respect of these matters? As Fortescue noted, the king had a duty to ensure the safety and good governance of Calais. Whilst Fortescue's work is from the 1460s, that idea was one that was held throughout the 15th century.

The issue of loyalties was far from new. As recently as 1452 the divisive nature of politics and its relationship to Calais was made clear. When the Duke of York challenged the position of the Duke of Somerset his letters referred to the failings of the Lancastrian faction:

"namely unto the Duke of Somerset, when he had the commandance and charge thereof; the which loss hath caused and encouraged the King's enemies for to conquer and get Gascony and Guienne, and now daily they make their advance for to lay siege unto Calais; and to other places in the Marches there.[27]"

Not only was there disagreement surrounding the management of Calais and the Staple, but there was by 1459 a current and real political dilemma for the garrison and citizens of Calais to consider. It resulted in Calais becoming a Yorkist stronghold at a time when the Yorkist nobility were attainted and in exile. That the citizens and Staplers were willing to support the Yorkists is not simply due to the presence of many armed men who were loyal to the Yorkist Lords. The citizens and merchants of the region were disillusioned. The *Paston Letters* shows this with reference to the scenario as it was in February 1458, one which had deteriorated in 1459 and into 1460:

"The King's safe conduct is not holden but broken, as it is voiced here, and that will do no good to merchants till it be amended.[28]"

Robert Fabyan outlined the consequences of Calais being not only militarily allied to the Yorkists but the Staplers being disgruntled. Fabyan describes the fighting between the forces loyal to the Duke of Somerset and those within the fortifications at Calais. He notes the losses, which were more considerable for those in the attacking Lancastrian force, the execution of men who had deserted the Earl of Warwick at Ludlow, and then explains how the garrison of Calais was paid during this siege:

"...so that they watyd no men, but money to meynteyne theyr dayly charge with. For remedy whereof they shyfted with the staple of Calays for. xviii.M./i. whiche summes of money whit they had receyued.[29]*"*

The Staplers were financially supporting the Yorkists. This illustrates that the level of disenchantment within Calais and the Pale with the policies of Henry VI's government was sufficient for them to back the Yorkist lords. The Yorkist lords at this time still promoted the notion of themselves being loyal opposition who wanted nothing more than good governance and an end to maladministration and poor policy. Was this betrayal of the crown? It was certainly denying the crown the opportunity to implement its chosen Captain but if the crown is held to be corrupt and failing in its duties, are the people of Calais obliged to accept such an appointment? If the rights of the Staplers are to be maintained, the responsibilities of the crown and its parliament must also be maintained. If it is accepted that the crown has failed in this duty, could the town,

Staplers, or garrison, legitimately stand up for their rights?. Typically, the method of doing this would be via petitions to parliament and pressure applied as merchants on men of influence at court. Presented with a fait accompli appointment, the issue becomes forced, and resistance of a different nature would be required that may not be within the legal framework of the day. The counter arguments to this are that the actions of the Yorkist faction in England were a primary cause of the political problems that led to the Staplers suffering. Though the failure of diplomatic policy and breakdown in safe passage as noted in the Paston letters above, was hardly due to a Yorkist lords' policy at that time. Similarly alternative methods of resisting the will of the government were available to the Staplers and garrison. This could include disrupting the wool trade or withholding loans by the Staplers, a garrison did not have to resist with force of arms, it could revert to methods such as forcing pay through seizure of goods, though this would not necessarily prevent the imposition of an unwanted appointment of captain.

Henry Beaufort, 3rd Duke of Somerset's appointment as Captain of Calais was not solely about the governance of Calais though. It had far wider political meaning and was always likely to result in conflict. It resulted in the siege of Calais by the Lancastrians, the failure of the Duke of Somerset's forces in the Battle of Newnham Bridge[30] and led to the Yorkist Lords turning Calais into a stepping stone for their successes in 1460.

The Yorkist use of Calais as a base from which to launch their counter offensive began with a sea raid. In January 1460 a flotilla of ships left the port of Calais under the command of Sir John Dinham [Dynham]. It sailed to the Kentish port of Sandwich, where a Lancastrian fleet was anchored in the haven. The Yorkists had been alerted to the fact that the Lancastrians were preparing to send reinforcements to the Duke of Somerset. This force could swing the balance in favour of the besieging force of the Duke of Somerset. Dynham's flotilla changed that. They caught the Lancastrian fleet by surprise. In a swift raid they not only captured 32 ships, and sank others including the impressive Grace Dieu, but also took prisoner the commander of the Lancastrian force, Lord Rivers, and his son, Anthony Woodville[31].

Calais now controlled the straights of Dover. This enabled the Earl of Warwick to travel to Ireland by sea, to discuss plans with the Duke of York. He had enough ships to sail a strong force to Ireland whilst also being able to leave enough vessels at Calais to ensure that the Yorkists retained full control of the seas at that critical part of the English Channel. Upon his return from Ireland, which was partially shadowed by a fleet commanded by Henry Holland, Duke of Exeter, the Yorkists could once again utilise Calais and its military and maritime mechanisms for their political and military ends. Propaganda was distributed along the coastline of the South East. Including copies of the Kentish Memorial, a 13 point outline of their criticisms of the King's government which was a reissue of Jack Cade's manifesto of

1450. It includes two key points that make it clear that they themselves did not consider their acts, or that of the Staplers or Garrison of Calais to be a betrayal. Quite the opposite, the argument is that the crown is breaking its own oaths to the people:

"2. They say, that our Sovereign Lord is above law, and that the law was made but to his pleasure; and that he may make and break it as often as him list, without any distinction. The contrary is true. And also, that he should not have been sworn, in his coronation to keep it, which we conceive for the highest point of treason that any subject may do against his prince, to make him reign in perjury.

3. They say, how that the King should live upon his commons, so that all their bodies and goods be[en] his. The contrary is true; for then he need never to set parliament to assess any goods of them.[32]"

The king, and by virtue of that his counsellors and government, are seen as being beholden to the law of the land. It shows that financial matters, critical to the prosperity of the Calais Staple, are not the crowns to do with as they please but subject to assessment by parliament, by which they mean both the Lords and the elected MPs within the commons. As the crown is, in their view, failing to uphold these requirements, they can justify forcing changes that will bring about just and fair governance. Therefore, Calais is far from betraying the crown and the Lancastrian government in this argument, instead it is attempting to enforce things that they and the commons of England have a simple right to, good governance by competent and fair officials, nobles, and crown. Of course, this argument was one that was constructed by senior Yorkists but it one which had the backing of the Staplers and men remaining in the garrison.

The combination of maritime and military might at Calais, along with sympathies for their cause in large parts of the south east enabled the Yorkists to launch an invasion in the summer of 1460. Sailing from Calais, they landed at Sandwich, established a beachhead, and then marched to London. Leaving a force to besiege the Tower of London, the bulk of the force from Calais marched, with additional forces, to confront the army of the Queen. This resulted in the Battle of Northampton on 10 July 1460 which saw men from the Calais garrison engaging the Lancastrian army in an assault on a fortified camp. The result of the battle was an overwhelming success for the force that had departed from Calais. Their victory included taking possession of King Henry VI and once the Tower of London had fallen, the Yorkists had control of not only the king, but also the seat of government and England's most important port, that of London.

Calais played a pivotal role in this success. Without the support or compliance of the people of Calais such an invasion would not have been possible, there would have been too large a risk of Calais being taken in a counter offensive. Throughout this phase of the Wars of the Roses the argument was that the lords, and their supporters in Calais, were engaging in exercises that were aimed at establishing good governance in the name of King Henry VI. That soon changed. The Duke of York's arrival in London saw him immediately claim the throne, sparking a debate which resulted in the Act of Accord. Now the clashes between current and previous members of the Calais garrison were in support of dynastic ambitions.

These clashes saw former members of the Calais garrison such as Andrew Trollope taking a central role in defeating Yorkist armies at Wakefield [December 1460] and in the Second Battle of St. Albans [February 1461]. The division in the loyalties of these men was clear, and deadly. It culminated in the campaign led by the newly proclaimed King Edward IV and Earl of Warwick that saw the Lancastrian army heavily defeated in the Battle of Towton. This campaign too saw the importance of support from Calais. Men from the garrison, supplies from the Pale of Calais, and funding from the Staplers and their mercantile partners in London all played a role in enabling this victory. In 1461, Calais played a hugely significant role in ousting King Henry VI and establishing Edward IV as the first Yorkist king. Whether this was a betrayal, or a justified act is a matter of contemporary allegiance, or modern interpretation. It is clear though that Calais could force political change, and with it the fortunes of war and dynasties.

Following the establishment of Edward IV as King, the Captaincy of Calais remained in the hands of the Earl of Warwick. He retained a great deal of autonomy over the governing of the Pale and fortifications and continued to mould the garrison to make it an effective force that was known by and loyal to himself. The first major change in the relationship between the crown and Calais came in the 1466 Act of Retainer. As previously mentioned, this formalised the way the costs of maintaining Calais were funded. From this point on, the Staplers funded the garrison at a rate of £10022 4s 8d per annum in return for their being able to collect customs. The policy made sense in terms of ensuring ongoing funding, as it limited the risk of mutiny, allowed the Captain to fund maintenance of the fortifications, and ensured that the keeping of the seas was also funded. It also increased the autonomy of the Captain of Calais, as he now had access to resources that previously he may have had to fund from his own funds, or through lines of credit. This arrangement works well when the Captain is a loyal kinsman, as Edward IV undoubtedly viewed the Earl of Warwick in 1466 but has implications should there be a dispute between the crown and the noble who had been appointed as Captain.

That scenario soon happened. As discussed in the chapter on Richard Neville, 16th Earl of Warwick, a combination of disagreements over foreign policy, disgruntlement at the promotion of members of the Queens family, a lowering of status as Edward IV asserted himself as king, and decisions such as the King removing George Neville from positions whilst the Earl of Warwick was on an ambassadorial mission to France combined to lead the Earl to feel disenfranchised. He had a powerful ally in George, Duke of Clarence, who similarly felt that he was being unduly overlooked and maltreated. The outcome of this is discussed in other chapters but it placed Calais at the heart of matters relating to opposition to King Edward IV. The Earl of Warwick and Duke of Clarence used Calais as a base from which they could orchestrate an uprising against King Edward IV. Following the marriage of George Duke of Clarence to Isabel Neville, daughter of the Earl of Warwick, in Calais, men in the Earl's affinity rose in revolt in the north of England. Under the leadership of 'Robin of Redesdale' an army marched south. They met a force loyal to King Edward IV at Danes Moor, near Edgcote on 24 July 1469[33]. The battle was a victory for the rebels. *Hearne's Fragment* notes that the outcome was sealed by:

"...the Earl of Warwick, he sent out of London one Clapham with the sum of fifteen thousand men, what of household men and soldiers of Calais, whose coming was the winning of the field.[34]"

The battle resulted in King Edward IV being taken into the custody of the Earl, leaving him and the Duke of Clarence, in effective control of government for a short period of time. When King Edward IV regained his freedom and was able to assert his rule, he was aware of the problems caused by his, and previous kings, granting of so much power to the Captain of Calais. It had enabled himself and other Yorkist lords to dictate matters in 1460 and now enabled a successful revolt against his own rule in 1469. In April 1470, Edward attempted to address this by confirming Calais appointments through letters patent. This, in theory, ties the post holders to the crown. In practice, it didn't work, as the men were loyal to the Earl of Warwick who in July 1470 formulated the Angers Agreement with the exiled Queen Margaret and in August declared for King Henry VI and issued a fresh manifesto, criticising the maladministration of King Edward's regime[35]. Calais, however, had not remained entirely safe for the Earl of Warwick throughout this period. When the Earl and Duke of Clarence were forced to flee England in April 1470, they found that not only had the King realised that Calais would be the likely destination: the Earl's ship The Trinity was impounded at Southampton to prevent its use, but upon arrival at Calais via Honfleur, the Earl was refused entry to the port. This was either by Lord Duras, the Marshall of Calais[36], or by Lord Wenlock, who Phillipe de Commines describes as having turned the Earl away:

"There were at that time several of the earl's servants in the town, and one in the quality of his lieutenant, Lord Wenlock, who, instead of receiving him, fired his great guns upon him.[37]"

It seems from Commines' wider account that Duras remained loyal to King Edward IV and retained enough authority in Calais to make the entry of the Earl of Warwick potentially dangerous. Indeed, Commines suggests that Lord Wenlock notified the Earl that it was simply too dangerous to let him sail into the port. Soon after, when the Earl of Warwick had made his way to the French court, the garrison at Calais was found to be quite different in its attitude. Also in 1470, though not dated, is an entry by Commines that notes that he visited Calais having secured a safe conduct from Lord Wenlock. Upon his arrival he found that:

"nobody came out to meet me, as formerly; all were in the Earl of Warwick's livery.[38]"

Calais therefore once again had a garrison that had mixed loyalties. The power that the Earl of Warwick had in the 1460s to make his own appointments seems to have enabled him to establish control, through Lord Wenlock, after dissention by Lord Duras, who was a Gascon noble who had transferred to Calais following the fall of Bordeaux and was indebted to King Edward IV due to patronage and positions he had been granted. Calais played little direct role in the readeption of King Henry VI. The Earl and Duke sailed from France to the South West of England. Calais simply ensured that the seas were held by those in the affinity of the new alliance of exiled Lancastrians and those in the affinity of the Earl of Warwick and Duke of Clarence. However, Calais did potentially play a role in events that were to happen once Edward returned to England to try and reclaim his throne. Calais played host to many diplomats and the town and Pale were frequented by people who were exiled from England. As a result, it was a town in which plotting could take place, and it seems that as the Earl of Warwick was planning with the Lancastrians, the House of York was simultaneously utilising Calais to make overtures to the Duke of

Clarence with regards his future and his allegiances. Commines is once again the source of this information. He noted that:

"He [Lord Wenlock} told me farther, that it would be no hard matter to compass an accommodation, for that very day there was a lady passed by Calais into France, with letters to the Duchess of Clarence, and in them overtures of peace from King Edward; and he said truly; but as he had done with others, so the lady dissembled with him; for her business was of another kind of importance, which she accomplished at last, to the prejudice of the Earl of Warwick and all his party.[39]*"*

As the Duke of Clarence did join his brother's side when he was marching south from Ravenspur to London, it is entirely plausible that the negotiations did take place through the Duchess of Clarence whilst at Calais.

Calais' next significant input into the Wars of the Roses came not because of clashes in England, but as a result of the Earl of Warwick's pro-French Foreign Policies. In 1471 the French and Burgundians once again went to war. The Earl of Warwick committed men of the Calais Garrison to the French cause[40]. The opening of hostilities by the English readeption government against Burgundy resulted in the duke of Burgundy adopting a positive stance towards the exiled Edward IV. As a result of the Calais Garrison having engaged with Burgundian forces, Edward was soon equipped with a fleet and funds to facilitate his return to England. Through showing loyalty to the Earl of Warwick, the garrison at Calais inadvertently provided Edward IV with the means to begin his own return to the throne.

The Staplers and the merchants of London also impacted upon Foreign Policy at this time. Though the garrison engaged with troops from Burgundy, the intended full-scale assault alongside French forces never materialised. Commines attributes that to the actions and words of the wool merchants of Calais and London:

"But the great merchants of London (many of whom were then at Calais) diverted him [the Earl of Warwick] from that undertaking [invading Flanders], because it was the staple of their wools, and it is almost incredible what prodigious returns they make from thence twice every year; there their wool lies till the merchants come over, and their chief vent is into Flanders and Holland: for which reason, therefore, they were very solicitous to promote this accommodation, and stop the forces which the Earl of Warwick was sending over.[41]"

This not only shows that the mercantile class had a great deal of influence over politicians of all factions but illustrates that they would apply pressure based on economic grounds rather than through affiliation to one faction. For them the endgame is profit, they would support policies that enabled that and apply pressure where a policy, in this case a potential war, may damage it. In the same way that some nobles and men of the gentry acted simply on the grounds of what would serve them best at any given time, so too would the Staple. Their loyalty was to their business, not to a faction, though they would at times support one over the other simply because of their perceptions of economic gains to be had.

Edward landing on the Yorkshire coast on 14 March 1471 and beginning his journey south once again led to Calais having a military role in England. Thomas Neville, the bastard of Fauconberg, raised a force and equipped the Calais fleet. He then sailed from Calais for the Thames. Not knowing that the Earl of Warwick had already perished in the Battle of Barnet, he began a siege of London from the Thames and by land. The assault included a naval bombardment of the Tower's defences alongside assaults on the walls from a force that was largely recruited in the South East. The strength and professionalism of the Calais garrison and fleet made this a perilous time for the defenders of London. The siege was not lifted until Richard Duke of Gloucester returned to London from the Battle of Tewkesbury with a contingent of men large enough to force the Lancastrian Calais based force into retreat. The restoration of Edward IV was finally secured only when this fleet and accompanying army had been dealt with, which was achieved through negotiation with Thomas Neville.

Edward IV's restoration led to changes in the way that Calais was governed. It was clear from the experiences from 1458 to 1471 that Calais could prove to be a thorn in the side of the crown as much as it was an asset economically and militarily on the continent. The changes were subtle but significant. In July

1471 Edward IV appointed William Lord Hastings as Lieutenant, rather than Captain, of Calais. The letters patent confirming the appointment gave Lord Hastings many rights and privileges but there were differences from the way that previous governors of the Pale had been able to run the garrison, Staple, and surrounding Pale. Firstly, Lord Hastings was not a senior magnate tied to the crown through blood. He held lands in the midlands but many of those were lands granted to him by Edward IV, they had not all been inherited. This meant that whilst the crown was appointing a man who had proven his loyalty, there was no sizeable network of retainers upon which the newly appointed Lieutenant could draw upon for roles in Calais. The potential for a large and rebellious garrison was reduced at a stroke. Further to this, Lord Hastings chose John, Lord Howard as his deputy. Lord Howard was a member of the king's household. His appointment was also confirmed by letters patent. Again, the crown is ensuring that it has control over major appointments in Calais and this would continue throughout the remainder of the Wars of the Roses into the reign of King Henry VII[42].

Calais' role in unseating Henry VI, then Edward IV, had made it clear that the crown needed to retain an active interest in the affairs of Calais. The arrangements outlined in the 1466 Act of Retainer were quickly confirmed, with the Staplers contributing an annual amount of £10022 4s 4d towards the cost of maintaining the garrison and defences of Calais[43]. Alongside this was the policy of appointing capable men from within the King's

Household or affinity to the senior roles, and those appointed were no longer given the role based on their seniority as a noble. Instead, it was allegiance and loyalty to the crown along with competence that took precedence.

The policy was successful enough for King Edward IV to make use of Calais as a staging post for the Invasion of France in 1475. Its usefulness for the crown is easy to see here. Commines tells us that the Burgundians loaned Edward some 500 ships suited to transporting horses. In addition, Edward arrested ships from English ports for the transportation of his army, its horses, and supplies. He continues that the entire venture of moving the army across the channel took three weeks. For that to be done safely required a stronghold, which Calais was able to provide. Its loyalty is also important here. Any dissenters, or spies, could present a real threat to the undertaking. Yet the logistical aspect of the invasion ran smoothly.

The Treaty of Picquigny that ended the short-lived invasion of France brought about a period of economic prosperity for Calais and ports that traded through the Staple. This illustrates the importance of diplomatic agreements and the benefits of peace for merchants. Trade agreements favoured the Staplers, reaffirming the relationship between crown and the continental enclave. Diplomacy in and around Calais was conducted frequently. Ambassadors and envoys from many states visited the port, exchanging political views and engaging in commercial pacts. Whilst this clearly benefitted the Staple in times of peace, it left the region vulnerable when English relations with any continental power deteriorated, or at times of continental diplomatic crisis.

Peaceful coexistence on the continent was not to last for long. Following the death of Charles the Bold, Duke of Burgundy, a diplomatic crisis erupted that exposed the vulnerabilities of the Calais Staple and made it of great use to the crown. William Lord Hastings was placed in a scenario where he was attempting to maintain Calais' role as the leading mercantile port of the region. At the same time, he was having to engage in diplomacy with France and Burgundy to try and avoid England, through the Staple, becoming embroiled in a major continental war.

Achieving this was no easy task. In July 1477 Lord Hastings wrote to King Louis XI of France bemoaning the pillaging of vessels bound for Calais by ships sailing out of Boulogne. This was *'directly against and to the prejudice of the good agreements made between the king, your said cousin, and you...*[44]*'* . The matter was complicated by virtue of the fact that the looted vessel was heading for Flanders, an area in direct conflict with France at this time. In effect Lord Hastings is attempting to reassert the neutrality of England at this time, which incorporated seaborne trade to and from Calais.

Such diplomacy was required not only to try and prevent the conflict spreading into the Pale of Calais but also to ensure that the defences of the Port could be improved. Only three weeks earlier correspondence from Lord Hastings to the King of France had noted that *'there are many ships both under the sovereignty of England, and elsewhere, hired to bring and convey certain beams, wood, stone and other stuff*[45]*'*. Here, the inference is quite clear. We need to import items for the upgrading of the defence of Calais and the Pale and it is in the interests of France as well as England for this operation to happen smoothly.

It was a precarious time for Calais. In France there was a suggestion that the Calais garrison was being prepared to send a force of 500 men to aid forces facing them. At the same time, the Dowager Duchess of Burgundy had made that exact request of the English, a request that was politely declined. The political intrigue was in part fuelled by the very nature of Calais. It was cosmopolitan, having merchants and messengers from feuding and neutral parties exchanging gossip alongside factual news which in turn heightened suspicion of duplicity or of secret pacts. Previously, Calais had seen such rumours come to fruition, the memories of Calais under the Earl of Warwick looming large over any actions taken by the Lieutenant or his representatives. And at this time of great diplomatic delicacy, the stance taken by Lord Hastings, the Staplers, the garrison, and the civic administration, was steadfast in its loyalty to the crown. There was no deviation from the policy of the king, as there had been during the English crisis years of 1469-71.

This raises the question as to whether the apparent loyalty of Calais to the crown was that of the town itself, or of the man appointed to govern there. Both the Earl of Warwick and Lord

Hastings were talented diplomats. Both forged good links on the continent. Economic interests were taken seriously under the leadership of both. Yet their approach towards the same monarch was very different, as was that of those who they governed and commanded. Was this simply due to their choices? Had the reforms made by Edward IV changed the dynamic of Calais politics to such an extent that it was far more controllable? Or was it due to changing attitudes among the people of Calais, be that the wealthy merchants, lower ranked members of the garrison, and the hundreds of people associated with the military or commercial activities within the town?

That Calais remained a source of potential trouble for the crown is clear. Upon the death of Edward IV, Lord Hastings remained a senior figure not only within Calais but also within the royal household and government. His men contributed towards ensuring the safe arrival of Edward V in London. And then, Lord Hastings was arrested by Richard Duke of Gloucester, who was acting as Protector and Constable, tried for treason, and executed. If the then Duke of Gloucester did believe that Lord Hastings was either guilty of treason, or simply a threat to plans he had to take the throne, then the role of Calais may well have been at the forefront of the Duke's mind. Were there to be another armed struggle, control of the garrison and its loyalty was hugely important. Lord Hastings himself had, when faced with the prospect of the Woodville's dominating Edward V's reign, threatened to return to Calais where he did have command, and would have enjoyed support from many within the military establishment of the south east. Clearly, Lord Hastings was willing to utilise Calais as a means of demonstrating his strength[46].

In the event, when Lord Hastings was executed the response of the Calais garrison appears to have been muted. There is no evidence of a mutiny, nor of any major concerns[47]. This suggests that the change in policy enacted by Edward IV had paid dividends.

Calais was to play further roles in the fortunes of the warring parties. Lord Hasting's retainers were noted as quickly becoming assimilated into the network under the Duke of Buckingham. This had implications when he and others rebelled. Following these revolts many of those who had been implicated took themselves into exile, often via Calais. This led to men who may previously have been within opposing factions finding themselves with a common purpose: the removal of Richard III. Allied with French support and Henry Tudors existing entourage, the negotiations that took place made an invasion viable.

Whilst members of the royal household retained positions in Calais and the Pale during the reign of Richard III, it soon became clear that not all these men remained loyal to him. The most striking example is that of James Blount. In 1484, Blount was constable of Hammes Castle in the Pale of Calais. James was thought to be loyal and trustworthy, his brother Sir John being nominally in command of the Pale. As a result of the rebellions in England the prized prisoner John Vere, Earl of Oxford was sent from England to continue their imprisonment in the supposed safety of Calais. They were subsequently held in Hammes Castle. As rumours of an invasion in support of Henry Tudor's claim mounted, the order was sent by Richard III for the pair to be returned to England where they could be guarded in a royal castle. As the order was being taken to Calais, James Blount allowed the pair to escape. Whether or not he had already become disillusioned or needed persuasion is unclear but the highest ranking Lancastrian prisoner held by Richard III's regime was now at large and able to join with Henry Tudor in advance of the invasion.

The response of the Calais Garrison to the treachery at Hammes Castle was an assault in January 1485, led by John Dynham. Whilst no siege is assured of success the superiority of the force from the main Calais garrison ought to have been overwhelming. Yet it was not. The Earl of Oxford and Thomas Brandon were able to lead an attack that broke the siege lines enough for the Hammes Garrison to leave the castle and join the forces of Henry Tudor. Calais had once again demonstrated that it's garrison and officials were not always loyal to the crown.

Calais held a unique position within the administration of England's affairs. Her leadership was, in theory, a Crown appointee, yet the structures in place did not always ensure that the garrison remained loyal. This was in part due to the ability of the Governors of the port and pale of Calais being able to entrust their own men with positions, in part due to the Stapler's changing attitudes to economic and diplomatic policies, and at times due to the civic administration failing in its duty to prevent sedition, or espionage. At times within the period the Pale of Calais housed exiles, whom the authorities either had the inability to control, or as seen with the example of James Blount, an inclination to support opponents of the crown. Betrayal certainly took place within the confines of the town and Pale, these tended to be instigated by individuals such as James Blount, or via having amassed large personal control over the military resources within Calais as was the case with the Earl of Warwick.

York

York holds the unusual distinction of having been the Lancastrian base from which campaigns in 1460 and 1461 were launched, and the town with which the last Yorkist king, Richard III is perhaps most closely associated with. As such it was apparently loyal to both the Houses of Lancaster and York at different stages of the Wars of the Roses. Furthermore, the civic authorities within York welcomed Henry Tudor upon his becoming king and, despite having been a Yorkist seat of power just years earlier, played a part in opposing the invading Yorkist force of 1487. Is it possible for a civic body, with some officials remaining in place across several reigns, to be apparently so supportive of all factions at various times without them betraying their responsibilities to a monarch, their oaths of allegiance, or their duty of care to the citizens of the town?

York was to all intents and purposes a capital of the north in the second half of the fifteenth century. It's location on the river Ouse had made it an important economic centre centuries earlier, as it could act as a port from which imports and exports, or military vessels, could embark and disembark. The size of the walls and presence of a castle made it a formidable military base, from which campaigns could be launched. These combined to attract all manner of merchant to York, which had a large market containing goods from across the region and from overseas[48]. It was also a significant Ecclesiastical location; York only being rivalled in the north by Durham in terms of seniority within the church.

Drawing in merchants from near and far, being ideally situated as a military base and housing one of the most important diocesan seats in the country meant that York had close ties to the crown and senior magnates in the region. Consequently, the civic organisation of the city of York incorporated regional administrative functions. Yorkshire is a large county and was unique in that its administration was divided into three ridings. The county court at which matters of importance were heard was based in York. This ensured regular communication between local magnates and the civic authorities. Those magnates also had a greater deal of autonomy over their lands than nobles of similar rank would be able to attain in most other parts of England.[49] To complicate matters, not all the lands in the north east answered directly to the king's appointed representatives, such as his sheriff, but to officials in honours who were appointed from the households of the relevant magnate[50]. Thus, York was a conduit through which regional justice would pass, with some being directly managed within the town and other matters of note being communicated to the crown through York.

Similar arrangements were in place for matters relating to the regional economy. This is illustrated through commissions into the maintenance of waterways. In 1475 a commission on the matter included citizens of York alongside gentry from the Vale of York and legal advisors[51]. In effect, the city of York is acting in much the same way as a magnate would, by appointing officials and representatives to explore matters. This again required close ties with regional magnates, which at times may be complicated by animosity between the region's main lords. Indeed, this matter ultimately required the assistance of the Duke of Gloucester who intervened and ensured that the waterways were cleared for safe passage of merchant vessels. That the civic authorities took a lead in coordinating matters that impacted on the regional economy at this time is unsurprising. When Europe went into an economic depression and bullion crisis in the 1440s it affected the merchants of York at an early stage and quite severely[52]. It also faced regional competition on a larger scale than ever before as the West Riding was increasing productivity of wool and they exported via the river Aire rather than from York. Additionally, York and the surrounding area suffered crisis levels of mortality due to the plague on several occasions in the fifteenth century[53]. These testing times for York also affected the wealth of the regional landholders such as the Duchy of Lancaster, Duke of York, and Earls of Northumberland and Warwick. To increase the likelihood of prosperity York, the region, and the magnates, there needed to be a combined and concerted effort with regards the agrarian economy. The shrinking of regional exports is evident in the Custom Rolls of Hull. By the end of King Edward IV's reign wool exports from York merchants passing through Hull had fallen from £10000 to £2500 and the value of all trade through Hull decreased by 58%[54].

The localised economic problems were compounded by two other factors. First, the church was a source of loans for York merchants. This exacerbated the woes of the merchant class in York as much of the churches income in the area was derived from the woollen trade. As profit fell, so did the availability of loans. Secondly, the economic problems in York and the ridings lasted longer and cut deeper than elsewhere in England. This had the result of the city and local magnates seeing their incomes falling at a time when their counterparts, particularly in the south east, were enjoying an economic recovery [55]. These combined to become contributory factors in local feuds as men of power sought farmland simply to increase their share of a depleted market.

For the civic authorities within York there was also the fact that some properties within the walls were owned by regional magnates and members of the knightly and gentry classes. As such they had to weigh up potential conflicts of duty to all their citizens against those of influential people who may have different political or economic priorities.

The authorities within York then had a series of responsibilities and priorities with regards governance of the town as England entered the Wars of the Roses. As with Calais the considerations were dominated by Economic and Military matters, and York also hosted diplomatic meetings. This meant that the authorities within York had a degree of responsibility for maintaining safe passage for merchants to and from the market or quay. Here we can include river management as this was vital to the prosperity of the town. Law and order were key issues. This was particularly relevant when the risk of conflict was heightened, and this came not only from feuding lords, but it was also suggested by a Venetian ambassador that there was a potential threat from the Scots[56]. Authorities also had a responsibility to liaise closely with other bodies and people who for whom York was important. The most visible of these within medieval York was the church, but it extends to bodies such as the Duchy of Lancaster, regional nobles and the gentry, the guilds that existed in York at the time, and to the Crown.

With regards the crown York had a responsibility in respect of the threat from Scotland. York was ideally situated to respond to any major assault on the north. It could act as a mustering point; provide provisions; had links to the sea to enable heavier weaponry or baggage to be shipped; and in the Great North Road linked York to London had the best north-south route in the country for marching armies. This meant that the city always had to be prepared for such an eventuality. Further responsibilities to the crown came through York hosting diplomatic conferences and hosting major events such as the investiture of Edward of Middleham as Prince of Wales. All require a great deal of planning which was to be undertaken and implemented by local officials.

In return, York expected patronage from the crown, and support from magnates. This could come in the form of grants for specific things such as improvements to defences, or reductions in the fee farm. The relationship with magnates being two way the authorities expected that their interests be promoted at council and to the king. Likewise, in times of warfare the responsibilities of regional magnates included assisting in the defence of York, as is illustrated in correspondence to and from the Earl of Northumberland in 1487 as the invasion force of the pretender Lambert Simnel approached[57].

York as the Wars of the Roses first broke out in 1455 had a staunchly Lancastrian belt of manors to her south and west.

These areas, bordering the river Aire and extending some distance on both banks, included the Royal Castle at Pontefract, and lands held by men such as Barons Clifford and Welles. To the east and north the picture was less clear. This was the southern part of the region dominated by the Percy and Neville families. Their manors were sometimes found surrounded by those of the other family. And some of these manors, and those further south, had been subject to territorial disputes. Those disputes had been violent with a battle or skirmish being fought between the two sides close to York at Stamford Bridge. As these clashes intensified York played a role in Councils intervention. When Thomas Percy, Lord Egremont, was captured he was taken via Middleham Castle to York where he was indicted for the sum of £10000 before being transferred to Newgate Gaol in London[58].

The events of 1455 had no direct impact on York itself but tension in the region was heightened. The deteriorating political situation in London was to have an effect though. When the Yorkists moved a force south to Ludlow in 1459 there remained a sizeable number of retainers in North Yorkshire. In the summer of 1460 these men and their forces then began a campaign of disruption across Yorkshire. As a result, Henry Percy was granted a commission of Oyer and Terminer to tackle the culprits. Further to this was an instruction to remove Neville retainers, using force if necessary, from Castles at Pontefract, Wrestle, and Penrith. This placed York in a state of readiness. There would be repercussions across the region which would almost certainly result in prisoners of note being taken to York for trial and imprisonment. The disruptions and Earl of Northumberland's attempts to deal with the problem coincided with the Yorkist landing at Sandwich.

Events in the south had an immediate impact on York. With the Yorkists taking control of London and then the King at the battle of Northampton, the Lancastrian faction needed a strong base from which to organise their response. York was the obvious choice. The Earl of Northumberland had a well-rehearsed system of mustering men at short notice. The Lancastrian lands along the Aire Valley were close enough to send fighting aged men quickly. And York could make use of the Ouse to ship ordnance and other heavy goods from loyal ports.

This amassing of manpower in Yorkshire alarmed the Duke of York enough for himself, his son Edmund, Earl of Rutland, and the Earl of Salisbury to march north to face the threat. The result was the Battle of Wakefield which was an overwhelming success for the Lancastrian army. Now the significance and symbolism of York itself was to come to the fore. The heads of the leading Yorkists were taken to York and displayed on the walls for all to see. As a posthumous humiliation the Duke of York is said to have had a paper crown placed on his head and a banner stated 'let York overlook York[59]' attached to his remains.

York was now de facto capital of the Lancastrian regime. Margaret of Anjou, and shortly afterwards senior commanders such as the Duke of Somerset along with many barons and their retainers had made their way to York. Within the walls the leaders planned their next moves, outside the walls an army that is likely to have been the largest of the Wars of the Roses was encamped. The logistics of feeding and equipping such a large force would have been a joint affair, with the officials of the nobles liaising with local officials. This would ensure that the equipment, weapons, and provisions required for the forthcoming campaign most efficiently: and for that to happen, local knowledge and oversight of movements in and around York was necessary. Clearly with such a large force massed in the area there was minimal room for dissent within the walls of York, but it is notable that nothing remains in the records that suggests that there was sedition or passive resistance to the Lancastrian cause from York's mayor, aldermen, or citizens[60]. In part any thoughts of dissention would be put aside simply from the financial gains to be had from business conducted with the army, nonetheless, the evidence suggests that as the heads of the Duke of York and earls of Rutland and Salisbury were being ceremonially mocked and placed upon the walls of York, that the inhabitants of all classes were loyal to King Henry VI and his Queen.

The campaign that followed is one of the most intense and deadly to have ever taken place on English soil. The Lancastrian army left York in early January, heading for London and what they hoped would be a second victory that would bring about a swift and decisive victory. On the march to London the Lancastrians secured an indecisive victory. The victory resulted in King Henry VI being left on the battlefield by the Yorkists as they fled back to London. From St. Albans the army marched on London, where they found the gates barred to them. Unwilling to attempt an assault on London, the Lancastrian army marched back up the Great North Road and once again made York their base. The Yorkists followed the Lancastrians once they had regrouped and arranged for additional forces to join them on their march north. The Yorkists then secured victories in a skirmish at Worksop, followed in March 1461 with a series of battles in short succession at Ferrybridge, Dintingdale, and Towton. Victory at Towton was hugely significant for the Yorkists. Losses for the Lancastrian army were such that there was no effective fighting force remaining for a defence at York[61]. With that, the Lancastrian leadership was forced to flee as soon as news of their catastrophic defeat reached them in York.

Several things stand out across the campaigning from the Lancastrian victory at Wakefield to their defeat at Towton. Firstly, the nature of the advance caused some dismay. The *Croyland Chronicler* described the advance as a whirlwind from the north. Though the stories of a rampaging army are exaggerated, rumour of looting had an effect. The mayor and aldermen of London, albeit with many Yorkists within the walls of London, opted to refuse the Queen entry to the city for fear of looting. This army had supply problems at York but did not loot. York was held in high esteem by the Lancastrian elite and discipline in the area was different to that elsewhere. Secondly, when news of the Yorkist victory reached York, nobody tried to stop the royal party from leaving. In the previous defeat at Northampton, an attempt had been made to intercept Queen Margaret. At York, she was allowed free passage even with it being quite clear that the reward from Edward IV would be great should she and the king be handed over as prisoners. Is this loyalty to the Lancastrian cause on the part of York, or simple inability to prevent their departure? Is the lack of looting around York due to the bond between the town and Lancastrian regime, or due to other factors?

As York had served the Lancastrian regime so well, it may be expected that it would remain loyal to the defeated King Henry VI. This was not the case. The Paston Letters tell us that King Edward IV:

"uppon the Munday next after Palmesunday, he was ressevd in to York with gret solempnyte and processyons. And the Mair and Comons of the said cite mad ther menys to have grace be Lord Montagu and Lord Barenars, whiche be for the Kyngs coming in to the said cite desyred hym of grace for the said cite, whiche graunted hem grace[62]".

In effect the city asks for and receives the victor's goodwill. Pragmatism perhaps, but it is also due to the realities of regional politics. Whilst York had been home to the Lancastrian army, it also had a history of links with the Neville family. An urban setting would not only attempt to ensure that it evaded a siege but had a duty to its citizens to keep the peace and enable prosperity. Whatever the true death toll in the battle of Towton, it would have been very clear that for now at least, the Yorkists would be the dominant force in England.

The following years saw York act as a hub for military and diplomatic activity. As attempts were made to oust the Lancastrians from the far north east, York hosted the king, was the venue for the diplomatic meeting that brought about a truce with Scotland, and remained a key part of King Edward IV's northern defences should the Lancastrians gain enough support for an advance. York was also considered as a site for a Parliament. Sessions were summoned for February 1463, which was transferred to Leicester and again in February 1464 where the session was prorogued twice before eventually being relocated to Westminster.

Following the Yorkist victory at Hexham several notable prisoners were taken to York for trial, execution, and public display. The regional importance of York is clear here. It is the seat of government in the region, dispenses justice, and did still have ties to people who had continued to resist Yorkist rule further to the north east. York would therefore continue to be used to remind the commons what the fate of captured rebels would be.

The next test of loyalty for York occurred in 1469. A revolt in North Yorkshire broke out. Led by a 'Robin of Redesdale' it was coordinated by men who remained loyal to the Earl of Warwick. Designed to cause a disruption in the north that would distract the king and make the Earl of Warwick and Duke of Clarence's plans in the south easier, this force marched on York.

The *Warkworth Chronicle* notes that some 20,000 men led by Sir William Conyers, under the pseudonym Robin of Redesdale, rose in revolt. *Rapin's Acta Regia* puts the number at 15,000[63]. Whilst the number of men may well be exaggerated, it was clearly a considerable army and, through Neville retainers, was one with many contacts within the walls of York. Yet York chose to remain loyal to the crown. Intriguingly, the countermeasures were led by John Neville, Lord Montagu, then Earl of Northumberland. Instead of becoming complicit in plots against the king, the Earl of Warwick's brother and authorities in York sought to simply protect the town from the rebel force.

A combination of the rebel force and actions to the south of York led to King Edward IV being taken into the custody of the Earl of Warwick and Duke of Clarence. For a period, there was an attempt to rule in the king's name. It was short lived, for several reasons. Firstly, the uprisings that had been instigated by the Earl of Warwick and Duke of Clarence led to other outbreaks of unrest which proved difficult to suppress. Secondly, the king retained enough support amongst the nobility for the attempt to rule in his name to face significant political opposition. The third factor was that the king escaped from his captivity. This escape was undertaken through York, with the *Warkworth Chronicle* telling us that Edward:

"Escapes and afterwards to York; city; and there by fair speech and promise, the King (es)caped out of the Bishop's hands, and came unto London[64]".

The King had therefore enough support and loyalty from people in York to be able to facilitate his free passage onwards to London to address the situation that he had been placed in by his brother and cousin's actions.

The following year a further rebellion had broken out, in Lincolnshire. Again, this involved agitation from men acting on behalf of the Duke of Clarence and Earl of Warwick. Following his success at Losecote Field, King Edward appears to have travelled to York. This, presumably, is to be on hand should there be a repeat of the uprisings in North Yorkshire. Again, the king has placed his faith in York and utilised it as a safe site from which to coordinate his response to any further military threat: which came in the south west, and then from the Marquis of Montagu changing sides whilst in the close vicinity of Edward IV.

King Edward and his closest advisors were forced to flee, to Burgundy, because of these changes to his military situation. It was not until the following year that he was able to return to England, with his party landing on the Yorkshire Coast. Once more, Edward IV chose to make for York. However, on this occasion, he did not receive the immediate support that he had enjoyed previously. Instead, he needed to assure the authorities within York that he was merely claiming his rights to the dukedom of York. This enabled Edward and part of his entourage to enter the walls of York.

Soon after, when at Nottingham, Edward once again proclaimed himself King. It was a move that seemingly was not greeted enthusiastically by everybody of note within York. Within *Grafton's Chronicle* it is noted that:

"This proclamation cast a great shame and dolour into the hearts of the Citizens of York, for that they might apparently perceive, that they were seduced and for their goodwill nnhonestly (if it might be said) deluded and mocked[65]".

Nonetheless, shortly after the victories at Barnet and Tewkesbury the Earl of Northumberland informed the king, from York, that the north was at peace. The Arrivall notes of this:

"The citie of Yorke, and othar good townes, and contryes, lowly submittinge them, and [promysinge] than to the Kynge theyr dwe obedyence. And so, by the xiiij. day of May, it was knowne clerly, by suche as were sent unto the Kynge from th'Erle of Northombarland, from the citie of Yorke, and othar dyvars places in the northe, that there was no rebellyon in all the northe begon, but that it was so passyfied that it ne myght ne shwld anoy the Kynge, in any wyse.[66]"

The role of the Earl of Northumberland, by now Henry Percy who had been restored to the Earldom, is perhaps critical in determining the response of York to Edward IV's return and victory. Edward IV had made the political decision to return the Earldom to the Percy family. Whilst this resulted in the defection of the Marquis of Montagu, it gained an important ally. Regionally the Percy landholdings were of significance, as was his families relationship with the authorities in York. That is perhaps best demonstrated by his remaining in the north and ensuring that the region remained at peace whilst the fight for the throne took place in the south. It also explains the reluctance of the people of York to admit Edward IV. The Earl of Northumberland commanded much respect and many men. So too did the man who had been granted the Earldom when the Percy family were out of favour and the Marquis of Montagu had been relatively close to York when Edward had asked for admittance.

The second reign of King Edward IV brought about major changes in the dynamics of politics across Yorkshire and Northumberland. Edward granted his brother Richard, Duke of Gloucester, large tracts of lands in the region that had been held by the now deceased Earl of Warwick. Richard had spent a large part of his upbringing in the Neville household, and so was familiar with the networks that were in place within the region. Coupled with the return of a supportive Henry Percy as Earl of Northumberland, it led to a period in which many of the previous problems in the region were no longer an issue.

Both the Duke of Gloucester and Earl of Northumberland had regular input into affairs concerning York. Good lordship was extended from manors into towns such as York and Scarborough. As Richard extended his landholdings within this region, it led to further ties with York and a scenario where it was in the interests of the major magnates and town authorities to work together.

Examples of the relationship between York and major magnates in this period are plentiful within the *York House Books*. Correspondence related to a wide range of issues, from the local economy, through rights of tenants, to upkeep of the walls at York. It did not entirely result in permanent goodwill though. In 1476 the Duke of Gloucester needed to attend York with a retinue to maintain the peace. Later, in 1482 a case was sent for trial in York, by the Duke of Gloucester, relating to a fracas between a member of the duke's extended household and a prominent citizen of York. Law and order, with a variety of causes, remained an issue for the city of York throughout this period, and into following reigns.

That York remained viewed as being loyal is clear though. It was from York that the main campaigns against Scotland in 1480-82 were planned. And upon the accession of Richard to the crown, the relationship of the crown to the city of York and surrounding areas was quickly formalised. A Council of the North was established and based in York. A decision was made to employ men from across the region as crown retainers for specific purposes, usually relating to administration, or justice. In simple terms, as King, Richard set about creating a system in and around York that was designed with the purpose of ensuring ongoing that the area was prosperous and peaceful.

The relationship that York had with Richard as Duke of Gloucester and as king is of note in relation to the subject of betrayals. The period of Edward V's reign was one in which there was potential for unrest. Leading magnates and members of the royal household were suspicious of one another, and some made moves to secure the child king as soon as news reached them of his accession. Whether or not they intended to utilise the minority of the king for their own gain is a matter for elsewhere, that these moves were viewed as plots is of note in relation to York and Richard in his relatively short-term acting as a protector of England.

The death of King Edward IV was noted in city records on 7 April 1483 [Before he had died]. Following this several formalities were carried out, such as selecting men to represent York at the parliament that had been called, and making the cities preparations for the expected coronation of King Edward V. These preparations lasted as late as 13 June 1483[67], when decisions were made about expenses for members of parliament in respect of their travel to and time in London were made. It was at this time that affairs in London had been changing at speed, and the mayor and aldermen of York were soon called upon by the Duke of Gloucester to aid him against threats in the south[68].

The pace of change from discussing expenses to making military provisions was rapid. Just 48 hours after discussing travel expenses for the coronation, the city recorded horsemen being sent defensibly arrayed to support the Duke of Gloucester. A day later, on 16 June, arrangements were discussed for soldiers to be sent to London. Pay and equipment were discussed on 17 June, and by 21 June the soldiers had been mustered and Parliament had been cancelled[69].

The response to Richard Duke of Gloucester's requests for military assistance in the south were then incredibly quick. Decisions were made based on information in his correspondence and so were based on the trust that the mayor and aldermen of York had in the integrity of the duke of Gloucester. This is of note. The dignitaries of York would know that Earl Rivers, a Woodville, had been arrested and imprisoned at Pontefract. They may also know some of the context behind that arrest. They would not, however, know that Queen Elizabeth had seen it necessary to enter Sanctuary, nor that William, Lord Hastings, had been arrested and executed whilst Richard's letter was in transit. In short, York did not know that the legitimacy of the marriage of Edward IV and Elizabeth Woodville was about to be questioned in public: it has been suggested that this matter had been raised to Richard prior to his asking York for military assistance[70].

York, in effect, was acting based on its trust in Richard. He had supported the city through good lordship, they had benefitted, they saw no reason to question the request. It was therefore a series of decisions made based on trust, integrity, and loyalty to the duke. This loyalty continued once news of the illegitimacy of Edward V and subsequent accession of Richard III reached the city. Unlike Calais, where a question as to how the events could be justified in relation to the garrison's oath to protect King Edward V, there is no such questioning recorded for the city of York. Indeed, the entries in the York records for the period immediately after Richard became king are largely concerned with arrangements for gifts to Prince Edward at Middleham, and for the visit of King Richard III. It is not until September of 1483 that other items other than attendance lists appear in the records. York as an urban community simply welcomed Richard's accession, made quick arrangements to send gifts, and were thorough in their preparation for his visit[71].

This loyalty to Richard continues when he was faced with the revolts commonly termed Buckingham's rebellion. The city was once again asked to send men to aid Richard, and a proclamation regarding the treachery of the duke of Buckingham was read[72]. The ongoing workings of crown to civic authorities continued throughout the reign of Richard III. As rumours spread about the king's intention to marry Elizabeth of York, a letter regarding sedition was received and acted upon by the local authorities. Similarly, as the likelihood of an invasion in support of Henry Tudor became expected imminently, the city placed itself at the ready to defend the realm.

The response of York to the potential, then actual, invasion in 1485 is of interest. In July 1485 the mayor commanded that:

"evere man of any craft within this citie forsaid being ffranchest be redie defensibly areyed to attend upon the mayre of this citie and his brether for saveguard of the same to the kings behove or otherways at his commandment.[73]*"*

This command for readiness was made on 8 July 1485. On 19 August, some 42 days later, the city sent 80 men to support King Richard III. For a city with a population estimated to in the region of 10,000 this figure seems decidedly small, especially given the urgency of King Richard's need and the amount of time that the authorities had to plan for mustering a force. The city knew that men would need to be sent, so why only 80?

There are several plausible reasons for this. Despite the size of York, it, like other towns, had a limited number of men who were equipped for war. 80 is therefore a reasonable number, especially considering other factors. York like many other English towns suffered an outbreak of the plague in August 1485[74]. When plague hit a town or city provisions to limit its spread reduced the movement of people around the town, reducing communication. Men who had been identified for mustering may have been affected by the plague, so finding 80 men may have been the limit of the city's capabilities. Likewise, York held other military responsibilities. Any invasion by Henry Tudor may be accompanied by uprisings in the north, or by invasions from Scotland. In either of those instances York would need to be defensible, and men of military age would need to be retained for that purpose. The numbers sent in 1485 were lower than that sent in 1483 when the matter at hand was a possible uprising rather than an actual invasion. Did the city of York let King Richard III down? Were they indifferent to the outcome in 1485? Had the bond between the King and city of York deteriorated?

The men who did set off to aid Richard did not arrive in time for the battle. Whilst marching does take time, the outcome of the battle was recorded in York just a day after it had been fought. Such a message would be relayed far faster than 80 soldiers could travel but it suggests a lack of haste from the contingent.

York's response to the victory of Henry Tudor was different to the simple request for the good grace it asked to be shared with Edward IV when he had triumphed at Towton. Indeed, in 1485 the response was mixed. On 23 August a letter was dispatched to the Earl of Northumberland. It cites a great treason by the Duke of Norfolk as the reason for King Richard being killed in battle. Further, it notes that Richard had *'mercifully reigned'* and his ending was *'pitiously slain and murdred to the great hevynesse of this citie'*[75].

Based on this immediate reaction, the city of York had remained true to Richard III. They had little need to openly express sorrow following his death in battle. That there was to be regime change must have been very apparent to the city even at this early stage after the battle. Yet instead of orchestrating any further resistance to Henry Tudor, the City of York and the nobles of the region who had not fought for Richard at Bosworth, did nothing of the sort. In early October proclamations were read out in King Henry VII's name[76]. The city armed itself to repel an expected Scottish invasion on 15 October[77], thus not taking the opportunity to allow or attempt any attack on the new regime. On 25 October the mayor and aldermen took the oath of allegiance to the new king[78]. Additionally, in an undated letter sent by the city of York to King Henry VII, the city expressed its longstanding loyal service to the house of Lancaster, to the king's uncle King Henry VI and cites the military support offered to the Lancastrian cause at St. Albans, Wakefield and Towton. King Edward's rule, they said, left many impoverished and they bemoan the *'extreme miserie'* that Edward's rule had brought about.

The city is being quick to ingratiate itself to the new king. It is also quick to distance itself from Richard III, including *'povertie was soo evidently knowne to be true unto the duc of Gloucestre, in his days being continually amonges your said subgiettes and expertly proving the same.'*

As with any urban area, the priorities for a civic body are the prosperity and health of the town. The mayor, council members and aldermen were merchants. Power was held by the guilds. Their interests were in making money and bettering themselves, which necessitated their individual priorities being invested into a broader civic picture. This lends itself to seeking as peaceful an existence as is achievable, something that is especially difficult in a civil war, even more so when so much of the conflict was caused by local rifts and fought in local battles by regional magnates who supported all sides. In the same way that some nobles sought to avoid active involvement in warfare, whilst picking up the beneficial pieces of the aftermath, so too did successive mayors, aldermen, and leaders of guilds within York and other towns. They acted in their own interests and for the City of York, those interests were best served by remaining a seat of regional power no matter who held the crown. That is quite clearly illustrated in the speed at which they asked Edward IV for favour, the passive approach to Edward's return in the spring of 1471, the cities nonplussed response to Edward V being declared illegitimate, and finally in it making its longstanding loyalty to Henry Tudors relatives known. Does this mean that the town has betrayed anybody? It may have been perceived that way at times by various parties, but the responsibilities of the mayor and aldermen are to both the crown and to the people of York. Similarly, the crown had responsibilities towards York and other towns, including law and order, good governance, and ideally peace. Where any of those break down, a town will be faced with a dilemma in relation to where its loyalties lay. And they lacked the resources to challenge a poor monarch or major magnate so were often bound to accept things that they collectively may not have desired to happen.

Bibliography

Attred, Lorraine. *York House Books 1461-1490. Volume One.* (Stroud, Alan Sutton for Richard III & Yorkist History Trust, 1991).

Attred, Lorraine. *York House Books 1461-1490. Volume Two.* (Stroud, Alan Sutton for Richard III & Yorkist History Trust, 1991).

Bentley, S. *Excerpta Historica.* (London, Samuel Bentley, 1831).

Bicheno, Hugh. *Blood Royal: The Wars of Lancaster and York, 1462–1485.* (Ebook, Head of Zeus, 2016).

Brie, Friedrich. *The Brut or, The chronicles of England.* (London, Early English Text Society, 1906-08).

Bruce, John. *Historie of the arrivall of Edward IV. in England and the finall recouerye of his kingdomes from Henry VI.* (London, Camden Society, 1838).

Burgess, L. A.. *The Southampton Terrier of 1454.* (London, Her Majesty's Stationery Office, 1976).

Carpenter, Christine. *The Wars of the Roses. Politics and the constitution of England, c. 1437-1509.* (Cambridge, Cambridge University Press, 1997).

Childs, Dr. Wendy R. *The Customs Accounts of Hull 1453-1490.* (Yorkshire Archaeological Society, 1986).

Clark, K.L. *The Nevills of Middleham: England's most powerful family in the Wars of the Roses*. (Stroud, The History Press, 2017).

Cox, D C, J R Edwards, R C Hill, Ann J Kettle, R Perren, Trevor Rowley, and P A Stamper. *Domesday Book: 1300-1540." A History of the County of Shropshire: Volume 4, Agriculture.* Edited by G C Baugh, and C R Elrington. (London: Victoria County History, 1989).

Cunningham, Sean. *Richard III A Royal Enigma*. (London, The National Archives, 2003).

Davies, John Silvester. *An English chronicle of the reigns of Richard II, Henry IV, Henry V, and Henry VI written before the year 1471; with an appendix, containing the 18th and 19th years of Richard II and the Parliament at Bury St. Edmund's, 25th Henry VI and supplementary additions from the Cotton. ms. chronicle called "Eulogium."* (London. Camden Society, 1856)

Dockray, Keith. *Edward IV from contemporary chronicles, letters and records.* (Stroud, Fonthill Media, 2015)

Dockray, Keith. *Henry Vi, Margaret of Anjou and the Wars of the Roses from contemporary chronicles, letters and records.* (Stroud, Fonthill Media, 2016)

Ellis, Henry, Sir. Grafton, Richard. *The chronicle of John Hardyng.* (London, F. C. and J. Rivington, 1912).

Ellis, Henry. *Original letters, illustrative of English history including numerous royal letters; from autographs in the British Museum, and one or two other collections.* (London, Printed for Harding and Lepard, 1827).

Evans, Graham. The Battle of Edgcote - 1469: Re-evaluating the evidence. (Northampton, Northamptonshire Battlefields Society, 2019)

Fabyan, Robert. Ellis, Henry. *The new chronicles of England and France, in two parts : by Robert Fabyan. Named by himself The concordance of histories.* (London. F.C. & J. Rivington, 1811).

Farrar, William. *The court rolls of the honor of Clitheroe in the county of Lancaster.* p. 14. (Manchester, Elliot and Co, 1897).

Flenley, Ralph. *Bale's Chronicle*. In, *Six Town Chronicles*. (Oxford, Clarendon Press, 1911).

Gairdner, James. *The Paston Letters, Volume 1*. (London, Chatto and Windus, 1904)

Gairdner, James. *The Paston Letters, Volume 2*. (London, Chatto and Windus, 1904)

Gairdner, James. *The Paston Letters, Volume 3*. (London, Chatto and Windus, 1904)

Gairdner, James. *The Paston Letters, Volume 4*. (London, Chatto and Windus, 1904)

Gairdner, James. *The Paston Letters, Volume 5*. (London, Chatto and Windus, 1904)

Gairdner, James. *'A Short English Chronicle: London under Henry VI (1422-71)'*, in *Three Fifteenth-Century Chronicles with Historical Memoranda by John Stowe.* (London, via *British History Online*, 1880)

Gairdner, James *'Gregory's Chronicle: 1451-1460'*, in *The Historical Collections of a Citizen of London in the Fifteenth Century*. (London, via *British History Online*, 1876)

Garmon, John (ed). *York And Lancaster 1399-1485.* Third Edition. (London, G Bell and Son, 1920).

Giles, John Allen. The Chronicles of the White Rose of York: A Series of Historical Fragments, Proclamations, Letters, and Other Contemporary Documents Relating to the Reign of King Edward the Fourth ; with Notes and Illustrations, and a Copious Index (Great Britain, James Bohn, 1845)

Gillingham, John. *The Wars of the Roses.* (Londong, Weidenfeld and Nicolson, 1981).

Grummitt, David. *The Calais Garrison: War and Military Service in England, 1436-1558.* (Woodbridge, Boydell Press, 2008).

Hall, Edward. *Chronicle: The history of England. Henry IV and the succeeding monarchs*. London, J Johnson etc, 1809.

Halliwell, James Orchard. *Warkworth's Chronicle of the first thirteen years of the reign of King Edward the Fourth.* (London, Camden Society, 1839)

Hammond, P. W. Richard III, Loyalty, Lordship and Law. (London, Richard III and Yorkist History Trust, 1986).

Hicks, Michael. *False, Fleeting, Perjur'd Clarence*. (Gloucester. Alan Sutton, 1980)

Hicks, Michael . *Warwick the Kingmaker.* (Oxford, Blackwell Publisher, 1998)

Hinds, Allen B. 'Milan: 1467', in *Calendar of State Papers and Manuscripts in the Archives and Collections of Milan 1385-1618.* (London, via British History Online, 1912).

Ingram, Mike. *Bosworth 1485.* (Stroud, Spellmount, 2015)

Johnson, P A. *Duke Richard of York, 1411-1460.* (Oxford, Clarendon Press, 1988)

Johnson, Lauren. *Shadow King, the life, and death of Henry VI.* (London, Head of Zeus, 2020)

Kekewith, Margaret. Richmond, Colin. Sutton, Anne. Visser-Fuchs, Livia. Watts, John. *The Politics of Fifteenth Century England: John Vale's Book*. (Stroud, Alan Sutton Publishing, 1995).

Kingsford, Charles Lethbridge. *Chronicles of London*. (Oxford, Clarendon Press, 1905).

Kingsford, Charles Lethbridge. *The Stonor letters and papers, 1290-1483*. (London, Royal Historical Society, 1919).

Kleineke, Hannes, Steer, Christian. *Harlaxton Medieval Studies Volume XXIII. The Yorkist Age*. (Donington, Shaun Tyas, 2013).

Lewis, Matthew. *The Wars of the Roses. The key players in the struggle for supremacy*. (Stroud, Amberley Publishing, 2016)

Meek, Edward L. *The Calais Letterbook of William Lord Hastings (1477) and Late Medieval Crisis Diplomacy 1477-83.* (Donington, Richard III and Yorkist History Trust and Shaun Tyas 2017).

Moorhouse, Dan, *On this day in the Wars of the Roses.* (Leeds, Dan Moorhouse, 2021)

Murray Kendall, Paul. *Warwick the Kingmaker and the Wars of the Roses.* (Cardinal Books, 1973)

Nicolas, Nicholas Harris, Sir; Tyrrell, Edward. *A Chronicle of London*. (London, Longman, 1827).

Nichols, J.D (ed) *Chronicle of the Rebellion in Lincolnshire 1470.* (London, Camden Society, 1847).

Oman, Charles. *Warwick the Kingmaker*. (London, New York, Macmillan, 1891).

Oman, Charles. *A History of England.* (London, Edward Arnold, 1904).

Plumpton, Edward, Sir; Stapleton, Thomas. *Plumpton correspondence. A series of letters, chiefly domestick, written in the reigns of Edward IV. Richard III. Henry VII. and Henry VIII.* (London, Camden Society, 1839).

Pollard, A.J. *North-Eastern England during the Wars of the Roses. Lay Society, War, and Politics 1450-1500.* (Oxford, Clarendon Press, 1990)

Riley, Henry. *Ingulph's chronicle of the abbey of Croyland with the continuations by Peter of Blois and anonymous writers.* (London, H.G. Bohn, 1854)

Rose, Susan. *Calais: An English Town in France.* (Woodbridge, The Boydell Press, 2008).

Ross, Charles. *Richard III.* (Berkeley, University of California Press, 1981)

Ross, Charles. *Edward IV.* (London, Yale, 1998).

Rymer, Thomas. *'Rymer's Foedera with Syllabus.* (London, Thomas Rymer, 1739-1745),

Scoble, Andrew, R. *Memoirs of Phillipe de Commines.* (London, George Bell and Sons, 1877).

Stevenson, J. *Letters and Papers Illustrative of the Wars of the English in France During the Reign of Henry the Sixth of England, Rolls Series, no. 22, vol. II pt.1& 2* (London, 1864).

Thomas, I.D and Thornley A.H. *The Great Chronicle of London.* (London, G.W. Jones, 1938).

Thompson, Edith. *The Wars of York and Lancaster, 1450-1485: Extracts from Blakman, Gascoigne ... the Rolls of Parliament, the Paston and Other Letters, and Various Contemporary Chronicles and Songs.* (Great Britain, D Nuut, 1892).

Virgil, Polydor. Ellis, Henry. *Historie of England.* (London, Camden Society, 1844)

Walsingham, T. *Historia Anglicana, vol. ii.* (London, Longman, 1864)

Footnotes. Chapter One: Introduction

[1] Ellis, Henry, 1777-1869, ed. *Original letters, illustrative of English history including numerous royal letters; from autographs in the British Museum, and one or two other collections*. (London, Printed for Harding and Lepard, 1827). pp. 162-166.
[2] Flenley, Ralph [ed]. *Bale's Chronicle*. In, *Six Town Chronicles*. (Oxford, Clarendon Press, 1911). p.150
[3] The feuds were not restricted to the South West and North East. A longer list of ongoing feuds and violent clashes of the 15th century can be found here: https://thewarsoftheroses.co.uk/regional-feuds-and-violence-of-the-15th-century/
[4] Davies (ed). *An English Chronicle*. (London. Camden Society, 1846) pp. 79-80.
[5] This is point two from the Kentish Memorial, a manifesto that was posted in Canterbury in 1460. The full manifesto can be found online at https://thewarsoftheroses.co.uk/kentish-memorial-1460/
[6] Lee, J. *'Ye shall disturbe noe mans right': Oath-taking and oath-breaking in late medieval and early modern Bristol.* Urban History (2007). p.34, pp. 27-38. https://doi.org/10.1017/S0963926807004312
[7] Warkworth's Chronicle, quoted in Giles, John Allen, ed. *The Chronicles of the White Rose of York: A Series of Historical Fragments, Proclamations, Letters, and Other Contemporary Documents Relating to the Reign of King Edward the Fourth ; with Notes and Illustrations, and a Copious Index* (Great Britain, James Bohn, 1845). p. 116

Footnotes. Chapter Two: George Duke of Clarence

[1] Shakespeare, William. *King Richard III* (Arden Shakespeare: Second Series) Act 1, Scene 4

[2] Chris Given-Wilson, Paul Brand, Seymour Phillips, Mark Ormrod, Geoffrey Martin, Anne Curry and Rosemary Horrox, eds. *'Edward IV: June 1467'*, in *Parliament Rolls of Medieval England*, (Woodbridge, 2005), *British History Online* http://www.british-history.ac.uk/no-series/parliament-rolls-medieval/june-1467 [accessed 15 April 2022].

[3] Johnson P.A, *Duke Richard of York 1411-1460*. (Oxford Historical Monographs. Clarendon Press, Oxford, 1988). pp.21-24

[4] Hicks, Michael. *George, duke of Clarence (1449–1478), prince.* (Oxford Dictionary of National Biography. Oxford University Press). Date of access 17 Apr. 2022, <https://www.oxforddnb.com/view/10.1093/ref:odnb/9780198614128.001.0001/odnb-9780198614128-e-10542>

[5] Rymer, Thomas, ed. *Rymer's Foedera with Syllabus: 1466*, in *Rymer's Foedera Volume 11* (London, 1739-1745), pp. 558-576. *British History Online* http://www.british-history.ac.uk/rymer-foedera/vol11/pp558-576 [accessed 17 April 2022].

[6] This is expanded upon in Hicks, Michael. *False, Fleeting, Perjur'd Clarence*. (Gloucester. Alan Sutton, 1980) pp.42-43.

[7] Hicks, Michael. *Warwick the Kingmaker.* (Oxford, Blackwell Publisher, 1998) pp264-5 and Murray Kendall, Paul. *Warwick the Kingmaker and the Wars of the Roses.* (Cardinal Books, 1973) Chapter 4 outlines the potential for such a meeting during the earl's authorised visit to France.

[8] Ellis, Henry, Sir, ed; Grafton, Richard, ed. *The chronicle of John Hardyng.* (London, F. C., and J. Rivington, 1912). p. 441

[9] Halliwell, James Orchard, ed. *Warkworth's Chronicle of the first*

thirteen years of the reign of King Edward the Fourth. (London, Camden Society, 1839). p.6

[10] Gairdner, James, ed. *The Paston Letters*, Volume 5. (London, Chatto and Windus, 1904) p.35]

[11] Manifesto issued at Calais on 12 July 1469. Giles, John Allen, ed. *The Chronicles of the White Rose of York*. pp 219-224

[12] The Earl of Warwick's statement of 1459 can be found here https://thewarsoftheroses.co.uk/justifications-of-yorkist-actions-1459-by-the-earl-of-warwick/

[13] Giles, John Allen, ed. *The Chronicles of the White Rose of York*. p.219

[14] The manifesto lists those that the rebels claimed to be advising the king with 'their mischievous assent and opinion'. These are: Lord Rivers, the Duchess of Bedford, The Queen, the sons of Elizabeth Woodville, Sir William Herbert, Earl of Pembroke; and Humphrey Stafford, Earl of Devonshire ; the Lord Audley, and Sir John Fogg, and others, 'so that he [the king] may not live honourably and maintain his estate and charges ordinary, within this land'..

[15] The pardons issued in relation to the uprising include Warwick's deputy warden of the West March, his deputy constable of Carlisle Castle and many who held land from the Earl in Richmondshire. Those killed at Edgcote included the son of the Steward of Middleham Castle and the Earl's brother-in-law, Lord Fitzhugh.

[16] See Evans, Graham. *The Battle of Edgcote – 1469: Re-evaluating the Evidence.* (Northampton, Graham Evans and the Northamptonshire Battlefields Society, 2019)

[17] Allen B Hinds, ed. *'Milan: 1469'*, in *Calendar of State Papers and Manuscripts in the Archives and Collections of Milan 1385-1618*, (London, 1912), pp. 128-134. *British History Online* http://www.british-history.ac.uk/cal-state-papers/milan/1385-1618/pp128-134 [accessed 19 April 2022].

[18] Halliwell, James Orchard, ed. *Warkworth's Chronicle*. p.7.

[19] Riley, Henry. *Ingulph's chronicle of the abbey of Croyland with the*

continuations by Peter of Blois and anonymous writers. (London, H.G. Bohn, 1854).
[20] Paul Murray Kendall, p250/251. A discussion of the options available to the Duke of Clarence and Earl of Warwick concludes that the negotiation with King Edward IV was, *'a hideous expedient of despair, and Warwick was too responsible and too self-confident to plunge England into chaos'*.
[21] Thomas, I.D and Thornley A.H, eds. *The Great Chronicle of London.* (London, G.W. Jones, 1938). p.208.
[22] Riley, Henry. *Ingulph's chronicle of the abbey of Croyland.* p.459
[23] Halliwell, James Orchard, ed. *Warkworth's Chronicle*. p.8
[24] Nichols, J.D (ed) *Chronicle of the Rebellion in Lincolnshire 1470.* (London, Camden Society, 1847). pp.10-11..
[25] Nichols, J.D (ed) Chronicle of the Rebellion in Lincolnshire 1470. pp. 22-23
[26] Bird, H.B, and Ledward, K.H. *"Close Rolls, Edward IV: March 1470." Calendar of Close Rolls, Edward IV: Volume 2, 1468-1476.* (London: Her Majesty's Stationery Office, 1953). pp 133-138. *British History Online*. Web. 22 April 2022. http://www.british-history.ac.uk/cal-close-rolls/edw4/vol2/pp133-138.
[27] Ibid
[28] Ibid
[29] Kingsford, Charles Lethbridge (ed). *The Stonor letters and papers, 1290-1483*. (London, Royal Historical Society, 1919). pp.115-116
[30] Scoble, Andrew, R (ed). *Memoirs of Phillipe de Commines.* (London, George Bell and Sons, 1877). p. 189.
[31] Ibid.
[32] Gairdner, James, ed. *The Paston Letters*, Volume 5. p.80
[33] Halliwell, James Orchard, ed. Warkworth's Chronicle. p.10.
[34] Bruce, John, (ed). *Historie of the arrivall of Edward IV. in England and the finall recouerye of his kingdomes from Henry VI.* (London, Camden Society, 1838). p.10

[35] Ibid
[36] Ibid
[37] Bruce, John, (ed). *Historie of the arrivall of Edward IV. in England and the finall recouerye of his kingdomes from Henry VI.* (London, Camden Society, 1838). pp. 10-11.
[38] Kingsford, Charles Lethbridge (ed). *Chronicles of London*. (Oxford, Clarendon Press, 1905). p. 184.
[39] Ellis, Henry (ed). *The Chronicle of John Hardyng*. London, 1812. p. 453
[40] Halliwell, James Orchard, ed. *Warkworth's Chronicle*, p. 14.
[41] Bruce, John, (ed). *Historie of the arrivall of Edward IV*. p. 11.
[42] Hicks, Michael. *False, Fleeting, Perjur'd Clarence*. p. 123
[43] Hicks, Michael. *False, Fleeting, Perjur'd Clarence*. p. 135
[44] Riley, Henry ed. *Croyland Chronicle*. p. 478
[45] Riley, Henry ed. *Croyland Chronicle.* p. 479
[46] Hall, Edward. *Chronicle: The history of England. Henry IV and the succeeding monarchs*. London, J Johnson etc, 1809.
[47] Chris Given-Wilson, Paul Brand, Seymour Phillips, Mark Ormrod, Geoffrey Martin, Anne Curry and Rosemary Horrox eds. 'Edward IV: January 1478', in *Parliament Rolls of Medieval England*, ed. (Woodbridge, 2005), *British History Online* http://www.british-history.ac.uk/no-series/parliament-rolls-medieval/january-1478 [accessed 12 May 2021].
[48] Ibid
[49] Ibid, citing *TNA* C49/40/1.
[50] Ibid

Footnotes. Chapter Three: Richard Neville, 16th Earl of Warwick

[1] The term Kingmaker originates with Scottish intellectual John Mair who in 1521 described Richard Neville as being a 'regum creator'. Its first English usage was in a poem by Samuel Daniel's. Written in the reign of Elizabeth I he included the line 'That brave Kingmaker, Warwick' in his poem *The History of the Civil War*. The term was also used by Shakespeare in his play *Henry VI Part 3*. The latter popularised the term and it has been used widely by historians and writers of fiction since then.

[2] The Earl of Salisbury was made to resign the position of Chancellor. He did this on Friday 7th March. The Earl was humiliated in the process, the Calendar for Close Rolls recording that: "Richard earl of Salisbury the chancellor laid upon a stool before the king one great seal of silver in a black leathern bag and two others, one of gold and one of silver severally in two bags of white leather, all previously in the said chancellor's keeping under his seal, and after an interval of about half an hour... king caused the three bags to be opened, the seals drawn out and each thoroughly examined" In C T Flower ed. 'Close Rolls, Henry VI: June 1455', in *Calendar of Close Rolls, Henry VI: Volume 6, 1454-1461*, (London, 1947), pp. 69-75. *British History Online* http://www.british-history.ac.uk/cal-close-rolls/hen6/vol6/pp69-75 [accessed 16 May 2022].

[3] The Percy-Neville feud had erupted because of the disparity in recent appointments, financial struggles, agricultural crises and, in 1453, the granting of a former Percy manor to the Neville's at a time where Lord Egremont may have been expecting a reversion to his family and his own grant of the manor of Wressle.

[4] Gairdner, James ed. *'A Short English Chronicle: London under Henry VI (1422-71)'*, in *Three Fifteenth-Century Chronicles with Historical Memoranda by John Stowe*, (London, 1880), pp. 58-78. *British History Online* http://www.british-history.ac.uk/camden-record-soc/vol28/pp58-78 [accessed 16 May 2022].

[5] Gairdner, James ed. *'A Short English Chronicle: London under Henry*

VI (1422-71)', in *Three Fifteenth-Century Chronicles with Historical Memoranda by John Stowe*, (London, 1880), pp. 58-78. *British History Online*), pp. 58-78. *British History Online* http://www.british-history.ac.uk/camden-record-soc/vol28/pp58-78 [accessed 18 May 2022].

[6] Oman, Charles. *Warwick the Kingmaker*. (London, New York, Macmillan, 1891). p. 70.

[7] The Paston Letters confirm the Queen's order for men to muster at Leicester. Margaret Paston wrote to her husband on 29 April 1459 that: *"The intent of the wrytyng was, that they sshuwlde be wyth the Kyngg at Leycester the x. day of May, wyth as many personys defensebylly arayid as they myte acordyng to her degre, and that they schwld bryng wyth hem for her expensys for ij. Monythis."* Gairdner, James, ed. *The Paston Letters*, Volume 3. (London, Chatto and Windus, 1904)

[8] Gairdner, James ed. *'A Short English Chronicle: London under Henry VI (1422-71)*'pp. 58-78. *British History Online* http://www.british-history.ac.uk/camden-record-soc/vol28/pp58-78 [accessed 20 May 2022].

[9] *Harleian MSS 543* cited in Giles, John Allen, ed. *The Chronicles of the White Rose of York*, p. plxviii.

[10] Scoble, Andrew, R (ed). *Memoirs of Phillipe de Commines*. pp.86-87

[11] Garmon, John (ed). *York And Lancaster 1399-1485*. Third Edition. (London, G Bell and Son, 1920). p. 77.

[12] Gairdner, James, ed. *The Paston Letters*, Volume 3. Letter 410, p.222.

[13] Gairdner, James ed. *'A Short English Chronicle: London under Henry VI (1422-71)'*, in *Three Fifteenth-Century Chronicles with Historical Memoranda by John Stowe*. pp. 58-78. *British History Online* http://www.british-history.ac.uk/camden-record-soc/vol28/pp58-78 [accessed 23 May 2022].

[14] Scoble, Andrew, R (ed). *Memoirs of Phillipe de Commines*. p. 300

[15] Davies, John Silvester. *An English chronicle*. pp. 82-3. https://quod.lib.umich.edu/c/cme/ACV5981.0001.001/1:2.4.37?rgn=div3;view=fulltext

[16] Kekewith, Margaret. Richmond, Colin. Sutton, Anne. Visser-Fuchs, Livia. Watts, John. *The Politics of Fifteenth Century England: John Vale's Book*. (Stroud, Alan Sutton Publishing, 1995). pp.198-200

[17] Chris Given-Wilson, Paul Brand, Seymour Phillips, Mark Ormrod, Geoffrey Martin, Anne Curry and Rosemary Horrox 'Henry VI: October 1460', in *Parliament Rolls of Medieval England*. (Woodbridge, 2005), *British History Online* http://www.british-history.ac.uk/no-series/parliament-rolls-medieval/october-1460 [accessed 24 May 2022].

[18] Jones, M. *Edward IV, the earl of Warwick and the Yorkist Claim to the Throne*. Historical Research.1997 Vol. 70; Iss. 173

[19] Chris Given-Wilson, Paul Brand, Seymour Phillips, Mark Ormrod, Geoffrey Martin, Anne Curry and Rosemary Horrox 'Edward IV: November 1461', in *Parliament Rolls of Medieval England*. (Woodbridge, 2005), *British History Online* http://www.british-history.ac.uk/no-series/parliament-rolls-medieval/november-1461 [accessed 24 May 2022].

[20] Chris Given-Wilson, Paul Brand, Seymour Phillips, Mark Ormrod, Geoffrey Martin, Anne Curry and Rosemary Horrox 'Edward IV: June 1467', in *Parliament Rolls of Medieval England*. (Woodbridge, 2005), *British History Online* http://www.british-history.ac.uk/no-series/parliament-rolls-medieval/june-1467 [accessed 24 May 2022].

[21] Gairdner, James *'Gregory's Chronicle: 1451-1460'*, in *The Historical Collections of a Citizen of London in the Fifteenth Century*. (London, 1876), pp. 196-210. *British History Online* http://www.british-history.ac.uk/camden-record-soc/vol17/pp196-210 [accessed 24 May 2022].

[22] Pollard, A.J. *North-Eastern England during the Wars of the Roses. Lay Society, War, and Politics 1450-1500*. (Oxford, Clarendon Press,

1990) p.270

[23] Brie, Friedrich. *The Brut or, The chronicles of England.* (London, Early English Text Society, 1906-08). p.532

[24] Rymer, Thomas. *'Rymer's Foedera with Syllabus: January-June 1464'*, in *Rymer's Foedera Volume 11*, ed. Thomas Rymer (London, 1739-1745), pp. 512-531. *British History Online* http://www.british-history.ac.uk/rymer-foedera/vol11/pp512-531 [accessed 25 May 2022].

[25] Murray Kendall, Paul. *Warwick the Kingmaker and the Wars of the Roses.* p.174

[26] Moorhouse, Dan, *On this day in the Wars of the Roses.* (Leeds, Dan Moorhouse, 2021). p.169.

[27] Hinds, Allen B. 'Milan: 1467', in *Calendar of State Papers and Manuscripts in the Archives and Collections of Milan 1385-1618.* (London, via British History Online, 1912). pp. 117-122. http://www.british-history.ac.uk/cal-state-papers/milan/1385-1618/pp117-122

[28] Ibid

[29] Ibid

[30] Clark, K.L. *The Nevills of Middleham: England's most powerful family in the Wars of the Roses*. (Stroud, The History Press, 2017). p.298

[31] Scoble, Andrew, R (ed). *Memoirs of Phillipe de Commines.* p.183

[32] *Hearne's Fragment* quoted in Giles, John Allen. *The Chronicles of the White Rose of York*, pp.23-24

[33] *Stowe's Transcripts* quoted in the Giles, John Allen. *The Chronicles of the White Rose of York*, p.235. The contents of the letter and accompanying Robin of Redesdale Manifesto are covered in more depth in the Chapter on George, Duke of Clarence.

[34] For details of the Battle of Edgcote see the Northamptonshire Battlefields Society website at https://northantsbattles.com/edgecote-1469/

[35] Halliwell, James Orchard. *Warkworth's Chronicle. p.* 53

[36] Payling, S.J. *Edward IV and the politics of consolidation in the early 1460's.* Within: Kleineke, Hannes, Steer, Christian. *Harlaxton Medieval Studies Volume XXIII. The Yorkist Age*. (Donington, Shaun Tyas, 2013). p. 81

[37] The Confession of Sir Robert Welles can be found in Bentley, S. *Excerpta Historica*. (London, Samuel Bentley, 1831). p. 282

[38] The Confession of Sir Robert Welles can be found in Excerpta Historica, ed Bentley, S. Page 282, or in modernised English in English Historical Documents, Volume IV, ed A.R. Myers. Page 282.

[39] Bentley, S. *Excerpta Historica.* p. 294

[40] The Battle is also referred to as The Battle of Empingham and by variations of spelling, Losecote/Losecoat/Lose Coat.

[41] Nichols, J.D (ed) *Chronicle of the Rebellion in Lincolnshire 1470.* p.10

[42] Gairdner, James. *The Paston Letters,* Volume 5. pp.68-69

[43] Bentley, S. *Excerpta Historica.* p284

[44] *Hearne's Fragment*, Chapter 18. (https://thewarsoftheroses.co.uk/hearnes-fragment-full-text/)

[45] Fabyan, Robert. Ellis, Henry. *The new chronicles of England and France, in two parts : by Robert Fabyan. Named by himself The concordance of histories.* (London. F.C. & J. Rivington, 1811). p. 658.

[46] Ellis, Henry. *Original letters, illustrative of English history.* pp. 135-139.

[47] Halliwell, James Orchard. *Warkworth's Chronicle.* pp. 9-10, outlines some of the other agreements made at Angers.

[48] Giles, John Allen. *The Chronicles of the White Rose of York.* p. 233.

[49] Scoble, Andrew, R. *Memoirs of Phillipe de Commines.* p. 193

[50] Bruce, John. *Historie of the arrivall of Edward IV.* p. 1

[51] Within the era of the Wars of the Roses the use or show of force against the King had been attempted unsuccessfully in 1452 and 1459, and successfully in 1455 and 1460. Prior to these wars change to governance was a consequence of force on numerous occasions, most famously resulting in Magna Carta but also the development of

parliament because of Simon de Montfort's show of force, and the actions of the Lords Appellant during the reign of Richard II.

[52] Bruce, John. *Historie of the arrivall of Edward IV*. p. 12

[53] Bruce, John. *Historie of the arrivall of Edward IV*. p. 9

[54] Bruce, John. *Historie of the arrivall of Edward IV*. p. 12

[55] Scoble, Andrew, R. *Memoirs of Phillipe de Commines*. p. 202

Footnotes. Chapter Four: Henry Beaufort, 2nd Duke of Somerset

[1] Richmond, Colin. *"Beaufort, Edmund, first duke of Somerset (c. 1406–1455), magnate and soldier."* Oxford Dictionary of National Biography. 04. Oxford University Press. Date of access 28 Jun. 2022, <https://www.oxforddnb.com/view/10.1093/ref:odnb/9780198614128.001.0001/odnb-9780198614128-e-1855>

[2] Fabyan, Robert. Ellis, Henry. *The new chronicles of England and France*. p.626

[3] Fabyan, Robert. Ellis, Henry. *The new chronicles of England and France*. p.627

[4] Gairdner, James. *The Paston Letters*, Volume 2. (London, Chatto and Windus, 1904) p.290 contains the Duke of Norfolk's Petition.

[5] The Duke of Somerset was released on bail on 5 February 1455. Flower, CT. *'Close Rolls, Henry VI: February 1455'*, in *Calendar of Close Rolls, Henry VI: Volume 6, 1454-1461*, ed. (London, 1947), p. 9. *British History Online* http://www.british-history.ac.uk/cal-close-rolls/hen6/vol6/p9 [accessed 28 June 2022].

[6] Gairdner, James. *The Paston Letters*, Volume 3. pp.23-24 contains the *Memorial to Henry VI.*

[7] Gairdner, James. *The Paston Letters*, Volume 3. pp.107-109

[8] Gairdner, James. *The Paston Letters*, Volume 3. p.126

[9] Flower, CT. *'Close Rolls, Henry VI: March 1458'*, in *Calendar of Close Rolls, Henry VI: Volume 6, 1454-1461*. (London, 1947), pp. 292-295. *British History Online* http://www.british-history.ac.uk/cal-close-rolls/hen6/vol6/pp292-295 [accessed 30 June 2022].
[10] Flenley, Ralph [ed]. Bale's Chronicle. In, Six Town Chronicles. Oxford, Clarendon Press, 1911.
[11] Moorhouse, Dan. *On this Day in the Wars of the Roses*, 2021. p. 113.
[12] Amin, Nathen. *The House of Beaufort: The Bastard Line that captured the crown*. Amberley, 2017. p. 246.
[13] Davies, Rev. John Silvester (ed). *An English Chronicle*. p. 84.
[14] Davies, Rev. John Silvester (ed). *An English Chronicle*. p. 85.
[15] Gairdner, James. *The Paston Letters, Volume 3.*
[16] Flenley, Ralph. *Bale's Chronicle*. In, *Six Town Chronicles*. p.152.
[17] Kleineke, Hannes. *A New Dawn? The accession of Edward IV on 4 March 1461. History of Parliament Commons 1461-1504 project.* (https://thehistoryofparliament.wordpress.com/2021/03/04/a-new-dawn-the-accession-of-edward-iv-on-4-march-1461/ Accessed 02/07/2002).
[18] Contemporary and near contemporary accounts provide a wide range of casualty figures. As such they should not be taken as being reliable. Modern interpretations suggest that whilst the battle was clearly large, casualty figures were most probably far lower than suggested in Hearne's Fragment.
[19] Hearne's Fragment, Chapter 3 (https://thewarsoftheroses.co.uk/hearnes-fragment-full-text/)
[20] Gairdner, James. *The Paston Letters*, Volume 3. pp.306-307
[21] Gairdner, James. *The Paston Letters*, Volume 3. Pp.311-312
[22] Bird, W H B. Ledward, K H. *'Close Rolls, Edward IV: 1461'*, in *Calendar of Close Rolls, Edward IV: Volume 1, 1461-1468.* (London, 1949). pp. 7-16. British History Online http://www.british-history.ac.uk/cal-close-rolls/edw4/vol1/pp7-16 [accessed 4 July 2022].
[23] Bird, W H B. Ledward, K H. *'Close Rolls, Edward IV: 1461'*, in *Calendar*

of Close Rolls, Edward IV: Volume 1, 1461-1468. (London, 1949). pp. 26-31. British History Online http://www.british-history.ac.uk/cal-close-rolls/edw4/vol1/pp26-31 [accessed 4 July 2022].
[24] Gairdner, James. *The Paston Letters*, Volume 4. (London, Chatto and Windus, 1904). pp. 35-36
[25] Gairdner, James. *The Paston Letters*, Volume 4. pp. 58-59
[26] *Hearne's Fragment*, Chapter 8. (https://thewarsoftheroses.co.uk/hearnes-fragment-full-text/)
[27] Halliwell, James Orchard. *Warkworth's Chronicle. p. 3.*
[28] Bicheno, Hugh. *Blood Royal: The Wars of Lancaster and York, 1462–1485.* (Ebook, Head of Zeus, 2016). Chapter 2: Warwick..
[29] Gairdner, James. *The Paston Letters*, Volume 4. pp. 95-97.

Footnotes. Chapter Five: Henry Percy, 4th Earl of Northumberland

[1] Bruce, John. *Historie of the arrivall of Edward IV.* p. 32.
[2] Riley, Henry. *Ingulph's chronicle of the abbey of Croyland. p.* 502.
[3] Bean, J. M. W. "*Percy, Henry, first earl of Northumberland (1341–1408), magnate and* rebel." Oxford Dictionary of National Biography. Oxford University Press. Date of access 8 Jul. 2022, <https://www.oxforddnb.com/view/10.1093/ref:odnb/9780198614128.001.0001/odnb-9780198614128-e-21932>
[4] Ellis, Henry, Sir. Grafton, Richard. *The chronicle of John Hardyng*. p. 361.
[5] Pollard, A.J. *North-Eastern England during the Wars of the Roses.* p. 247.
[6] An assassination attempt was made on the life of the Earl of Warwick on 9 November 1458. It was presumed to have been ordered by a lord in the Queens affinity. Davies, John Silveste. *An English Chronicle*. p.

78.
[7] Pollard, A.J. *North-Eastern England during the Wars of the Roses.* p. 269-70..
[8] Cox, D C, J R Edwards, R C Hill, Ann J Kettle, R Perren, Trevor Rowley, and P A Stamper. *Domesday Book: 1300-1540." A History of the County of Shropshire: Volume 4, Agriculture.* Edited by G C Baugh, and C R Elrington. (London: Victoria County History, 1989). pp. 72-118. British History Online. Web. 9 July 2022. http://www.british-history.ac.uk/vch/salop/vol4/pp72-118.
[9] Gairdner, James. *The Paston Letters, Volume 3.* p. 269
[10] Henry, Lord Percy was attended to by four servants whilst in custody of the crown.
[11] Bird, W H B and Ledward, K H. *"Close Rolls, Edward IV: 1468-1470." Calendar of Close Rolls, Edward IV: Volume 2, 1468-1476.* (London: Her Majesty's Stationery Office, 1953). p. 94-103. *British History Online*. Web. 10 July 2022. http://www.british-history.ac.uk/cal-close-rolls/edw4/vol2/pp94-103.
[12] Gairdner, James. *The Paston Letters,* Volume 5. p. 71
[13] The Lincolnshire revolt was all but over at this point, the battle of Losecote Field having taken place on 12 March 1470. However, Henry Percy was reinstated just days after the submission of the Earl of Warwick's chief allies to the king and whilst proclamations were being made on the king's orders by the sheriff throughout Yorkshire with regards to the legality of arrays. The Earl of Warwick and Duke of Clarence were both at large at this time and had travelled north, so further unrest was a risk.
[14] Gairdner, James. *The Paston Letters,* Volume 5. p. 81
[15] Pollard, A. J. *Lord Fitz Hugh's Rising in 1470.* (Historical Research, Volume 52, November 1979). p. 173.
[16] Horrox, Rosemary. *Preparations for Edward IV's Return from Exile.* (The Ricardian Vol VI No. 79 December 1982. Richard III Society). pp. 124-127.

[17] Halliwell, James Orchard. *Warkworth's Chronicle*. pp. 13-14.
[18] Bruce, John. *Historie of the arrivall of Edward IV*. pp. 6-7.
[19] Weiss, Michael. *A Power in the North? The Percies in the Fifteenth Century.* (The Historical Journal, Vol. 19, No. 2, June, 1976). pp. 501-509
[20] Bruce, John. *Historie of the arrivall of Edward IV*. p. 32
[21] Ellis, Steven G. Oxford Dictionary of National Biography. *Percy, Henry, fourth earl of Northumberland.* (Oxford University Press, 2006). https://www.oxforddnb.com/view/10.1093/ref:odnb/9780198614128.001.0001/odnb-9780198614128-e-21935 Accessed 19/07/2022.
[22] He bore the curtana, a blunt sword that symbolises the mercy of the king.
[23] Pollard, A.J. *North-Eastern England during the Wars of the Roses.* p. 359.
[24] Oman, Charles. *A History of England*. (London, Edward Arnold, 1904). p. 271
[25] Riley, Henry. *Ingulph's chronicle of the abbey of Croyland.* p. 502.
[26] Riley, Henry. *Ingulph's chronicle of the abbey of Croyland.* p. 504.
[27] Riley, Henry. *Ingulph's chronicle of the abbey of Croyland. p.* 514.
[28] Attred, Lorraine. *York House Books 1461-1490. Volume Two.* (Stroud, Alan Sutton for Richard III & Yorkist History Trust, 1991). p. 544.
[29] Attred, Lorraine. *York House Books 1461-1490. Volume Two.* pp. 561-571.
[30] Plumpton, Edward, Sir; Stapleton, Thomas. *Plumpton correspondence. A series of letters, chiefly domestick, written in the reigns of Edward IV. Richard III. Henry VII. and Henry VIII.* (London, Camden Society, 1839). p. 61.
[31] John Skelton's poem is cited on: Ellis, Steven G. *"Percy, Henry, fourth earl of Northumberland (c. 1449–1489), magnate."* (Oxford Dictionary of National Biography. Oxford University Press). Date of

access 8 Aug. 2022,
<https://www.oxforddnb.com/view/10.1093/ref:odnb/9780198614128.001.0001/odnb-9780198614128-e-21935>

Footnotes. Chapter Six: Richard Woodville, 1st Earl Rivers

[1]There are clear ties to the households of John, Duke of Lancaster and to his son, Henry IV, and the then Prince Henry. This may have resulted in Richard being raised in the household, if not he was certainly close to it. This is noted in Pidgeon, L. *The Wydeviles. 1066-1503. A Re-assessment.* (Southampton, Phd Thesis, University of Southampton, 2011). p. 108. https://eprints.soton.ac.uk/367325/1/Thesis%2520revision%25201.pdf and the suggestion of a household link is included in Hicks, Michael. Oxford Dictionary of National Biography. *"Woodville [Wydeville], Richard, first Earl Rivers (d. 1469), magnate."* (Oxford. Oxford University Press). Date of access 13 Sep. 2022, <https://www.oxforddnb.com/view/10.1093/ref:odnb/9780198614128.001.0001/odnb-9780198614128-e-29939>

[2] Gairdner, James. *The Paston Letters, Volume 3*. p. 204.

[3]See Pidgeon, L. The Wydeviles. 1066-1503. A Re-assessment. Sections 2.2 and 3.1 provide details. The work of Thomas is further covered on the history of Parliament blog at https://www.historyofparliamentonline.org/volume/1386-1421/member/wydeville-thomas-1364-1435

[4] Calendar of Patent Rolls, 1413-1416. Membrane 15, page 53. https://babel.hathitrust.org/cgi/pt?id=mdp.39015031079596&view=1up&seq=65&skin=2021

[5] Richard Woodville Snr was based in Normandy or France with few

breaks between 1417 and 1435. Details of his service can be access via https://www.medievalsoldier.org/database/

[6]Chris Given-Wilson, Paul Brand, Seymour Phillips, Mark Ormrod, Geoffrey Martin, Anne Curry and Rosemary Horrox. *'Henry VI: October 1435'*, in *Parliament Rolls of Medieval England*, ed. (Woodbridge, 2005), *British History Online* http://www.british-history.ac.uk/no-series/parliament-rolls-medieval/october-1435 [accessed 13 September 2022].

[7]Hicks, Michael. Oxford Dictionary of National Biography. *"Woodville [Wydeville], Richard, first Earl Rivers (d. 1469), magnate."* (Oxford, Oxford University Press). Date of access 13 Sep. 2022, <https://www.oxforddnb.com/view/10.1093/ref:odnb/9780198614128.001.0001/odnb-9780198614128-e-29939>

[8]The case between Humphrey, duke of Gloucester and Henry Beaufort, bishop of Winchester, 1426. British Library Cotton MS Julius B II, folios 72r-81v, printed in Kingsford, Charles Lethbridge. *Chronicles of London.*

[9]Nicolas, Nicholas Harris, Sir; Tyrrell, Edward. *A Chronicle of London.* (London, Longman, 1827). p. 114. Hall, Edward. *Chronicle: The history of England.* p. 138.

[10] Stevenson, J. *Letters and Papers Illustrative of the Wars of the English in France During the Reign of Henry the Sixth of England, Rolls Series, no. 22, vol. II pt.1& 2* (London, 1864). pp. 433-7

[11] *Calendar of Patent Rolls 1436-1441*. p. 53. Available at https://catalog.hathitrust.org/Record/009029274

[12] *Calendar of Patent Rolls 1429-1436*. p. 359. Available at https://catalog.hathitrust.org/Record/009029274

[13] *Calendar of Patent Rolls 1436-1441*. p. 72.

[14]Chris Given-Wilson, Paul Brand, Seymour Phillips, Mark Ormrod, Geoffrey Martin, Anne Curry and Rosemary Horrox. *'Henry VI: November 1450'*, in *Parliament Rolls of Medieval England.* (Woodbridge, 2005), *British History Online* http://www.british-

history.ac.uk/no-series/parliament-rolls-medieval/november-1450 [accessed 26 September 2022].

[15] See Appendix 11 of the Parliamentary Roll for November 1450.¶Letter of Hans Winter to the Grand Master the of the Teutonic Order, Ludwig von Erlingshausen, written in London on 15 November 1450. https://www.british-history.ac.uk/no-series/parliament-rolls-medieval/november-1450

[16]*Calendar of the patent rolls 1446-1452*. pp. 456-457. Available at https://catalog.hathitrust.org/Record/009029274

[17]*Calendar of the patent rolls 1446-1452*. pp. 512-3.

[18] *Calendar of patent rolls 1452-1461*. p. 457.

[19] *Calendar of patent rolls 1452-1461. p.* 555.

[20] *Calendar of patent rolls 1452-1461* .p. 555

[21] Gairdner, James. *The Paston Letters, Volume 3*. p. 203.

[22] Davies, John Silvester. *An English Chronicle. p.* 84.

[23] Gairdner, James. *The Paston Letters, Volume 3. p.* 204.

[24] Pidgeon, Lynda J. *The Wydeviles 1066-1503 A Re-assessment.* p. 172.

[25] Pidgeon, Lynda J. *The Wydeviles 1066-1503 A Re-assessment.* p. 175

[26] Hinds, Allen B. *'Milan: 1461'*, in *Calendar of State Papers and Manuscripts in the Archives and Collections of Milan 1385-1618*. (London, 1912), pp. 37-106. *British History Online* http://www.british-history.ac.uk/cal-state-papers/milan/1385-1618/pp37-106 [accessed 26 September 2022].

[27] Hinds, Allen B. *'Milan: 1461'*, in *Calendar of State Papers and Manuscripts in the Archives and Collections of Milan 1385-1618*, (London, 1912), pp. 37-106. *British History Online* http://www.british-history.ac.uk/cal-state-papers/milan/1385-1618/pp37-106

[28]*Calendar of the patent rolls. 1461-1467. p* 35.

[29] *Calendar of the patent rolls. 1461-1467. pp.* 169-70.

[30] *Calendar of the patent rolls. 1461-1467. pp.* 212-13

[31] *Calendar of the patent rolls. 1461-1467*. p. 227

[32] *Calendar of the patent rolls. 1461-1467*. p. 279.

[33] Hicks, Michael. *"Woodville [Wydeville], Richard, first Earl Rivers (d. 1469), magnate."* Oxford Dictionary of National Biography. (Oxford, Oxford University Press). Date of access 27 Sep. 2022, <https://www.oxforddnb.com/view/10.1093/ref:odnb/9780198614128.001.0001/odnb-9780198614128-e-29939>
[34] *Hearne's Fragment*, Chapter 10. https://thewarsoftheroses.co.uk/hearnes-fragment-full-text/
[35] *Calendar of the patent rolls. 1461-1467*. p. 431.
[36] Scoble, Andrew, R. *Memoirs of Phillipe de Commines.* p. 184.

Footnotes. Chapter Seven: Thomas Stanley, 1st Earl of Derby

[1] Gairdner, James. *The Paston Letters, Volume 1.* (London, Chatto and Windus, 1904). p. 80.
[2] Sir Thomas was one of a number of men who arrived after the battle had taken place. Others included the duke of Norfolk, Earl of Oxford, Earl of Shrewsbury, and Lord Cromwell. A list of those involved is given in the Gairdner, James. *The Paston Letters, Volume 1*. p. 30.
[3] Chris Given-Wilson, Paul Brand, Seymour Phillips, Mark Ormrod, Geoffrey Martin, Anne Curry and Rosemary Horrox *'Henry VI: July 1455'*, in *Parliament Rolls of Medieval England*. (Woodbridge, 2005), *British History Online* http://www.british-history.ac.uk/no-series/parliament-rolls-medieval/july-1455 [accessed 9 November 2022].
[4] Giles, John Allen. *The Chronicles of the White Rose of York. p.* lviii.
[5] Chris Given-Wilson, Paul Brand, Seymour Phillips, Mark Ormrod, Geoffrey Martin, Anne Curry and Rosemary Horrox. *'Henry VI: November 1459'*, in *Parliament Rolls of Medieval England.* (Woodbridge, 2005), *British History Online* http://www.british-

history.ac.uk/no-series/parliament-rolls-medieval/november-1459 [accessed 5 December 2022].

[6] Chris Given-Wilson, Paul Brand, Seymour Phillips, Mark Ormrod, Geoffrey Martin, Anne Curry and Rosemary Horrox. *'Henry VI: November 1459'*, in *Parliament Rolls of Medieval England.* (Woodbridge, 2005), *British History Online* http://www.british-history.ac.uk/no-series/parliament-rolls-medieval/november-1459 [accessed 5 December 2022].

[7] Bennett, Michael J. Oxford Dictionary of National Biography. *"Stanley, Thomas, first earl of Derby (c. 1433–1504), magnate."* (Oxford, Oxford University Press). Date of access 5 Dec. 2022, <https://www.oxforddnb.com/view/10.1093/ref:odnb/9780198614128.001.0001/odnb-9780198614128-e-26279>

[8] Ingram, Mike. *How a King was defeated in the Battle of Northampton.* (Northampton, NE Enquirer). https://nenequirer.com/2017/06/27/how-a-king-was-defeated-at-the-battle-of-northampton/

[9] Giles, John Allen. *The Chronicles of the White Rose of York*. p. lxxvii

[10] Bennett, Michael J. *"Stanley, Thomas, first earl of Derby (c. 1433–1504), magnate."* Oxford Dictionary of National Biography. (Oxford, Oxford University Press). Date of access 6 Dec. 2022, <https://www.oxforddnb.com/view/10.1093/ref:odnb/9780198614128.001.0001/odnb-9780198614128-e-26279>

[11] Chris Given-Wilson, Paul Brand, Seymour Phillips, Mark Ormrod, Geoffrey Martin, Anne Curry, and Rosemary Horrox. *"Edward IV: November 1461." Parliament Rolls of Medieval England*. (Woodbridge, Boydell, 2005). *British History Online*. Web. 6 December 2022. http://www.british-history.ac.uk/no-series/parliament-rolls-medieval/november-1461.

[12] Richard III Society. *Rebellions and Uprisings.* https://richardiii.net/richard-iii-his-world/the-war-of-the-

roses/rebellions-and-uprisings/

[13] Thomas, Lord Stanley was Steward of Blackburnshire in 1465. Farrar, William. *The court rolls of the honor of Clitheroe in the county of Lancaster*. p. 14. (Manchester, Elliot and Co, 1897). In addition, Sir William Stanley had just been awarded Skipton Castle and its rights. The Tempest family who captured King Henry VI held lands in both areas.

[14] Bennett, Michael J. Oxford Dictionary of National Biography. *"Stanley, Thomas, first earl of Derby (c. 1433–1504), magnate."* (Oxford, Oxford University Press). Date of access 6 Dec. 2022, <https://www.oxforddnb.com/view/10.1093/ref:odnb/9780198614128.001.0001/odnb-9780198614128-e-26279>

[15] Ellis, Henry, Sir. Grafton, Richard. *The chronicle of John Hardyng.*

[16] Gairdner, James. *The Paston Letters, Volume 2*. p. 142

[17] History of Parliament Blog. Moreton, *Charles Dr. Bristol and the Readeption Parliament of Henry VI.* https://thehistoryofparliament.wordpress.com/2021/01/28/bristol-and-the-readeption-parliament-of-henry-vi/

[18] Giles, John Allen. *The Chronicles of the White Rose of York*. p. 117.

[19] Rymer, Thomas. *'Rymer's Foedera with Syllabus. Volume II*. p. 700

[20] Myers, A.R. *An Official Progress through Lancashire and Cheshire, 1476*. [https://www.hslc.org.uk/wp-content/uploads/2017/05/115-2-Myers.pdf] Instruction to seize, page 24. Instructions pertaining to the Castle, p. 13.

[21] Hall, Edward. *Chronicle: The history of England. Henry IV and the succeeding monarchs*. p. 308.

[22] *Myers, A.R. An Official Progress through Lancashire and Cheshire, 1476*. p. 5.

[23] Duchy Correspondence cited in Myers, page 7.

[24] For a more detailed appraisal of the Council meeting see Lewis, Matthew. *The Infamous Council Meeting*, 13 June 1483.

[https://mattlewisauthor.wordpress.com/2017/06/13/the-infamous-council-meeting-13-june-1483/]

[25] Virgil, Polydor. Ellis, Henry. *Historie of England*. (London, Camden Society, 1844). p. 182

[26] Plumpton, Edward, Sir; Stapleton, Thomas. *Plumpton correspondence* p. 44.

[27] Grant: The King to Sir Thomas Stanley, Knight, Lord Stanley, and George Stanley, Knight, Lord Leatrange, his son. 7 September 1484. Held by and available online through Lancashire Archives. [https://archivecat.lancashire.gov.uk/calmview/Record.aspx?src=CalmView.Catalog&id=DDK/1/20&pos=1&fbclid=IwAR0NCvr6hqFJ-clLnHZxZUl4ojzYHuLLRDMICNoos3jv8Lz08-m2QMCvbBI]

[28] Chris Given-Wilson, Paul Brand, Seymour Phillips, Mark Ormrod, Geoffrey Martin, Anne Curry, and Rosemary Horrox. *"Richard III: January 1484." Parliament Rolls of Medieval England*. (Woodbridge, Boydell, 2005). *British History Online*. Web. 4 January 2023. http://www.british-history.ac.uk/no-series/parliament-rolls-medieval/january-1484.

[29] Virgil, Polydor. Ellis, Henry. *Historie of England*. p. 212.

[30] Virgil, Polydor. Ellis, Henry. *Historie of England*. p. 218.

[31] Scoble, Andrew, R. *Memoirs of Phillipe de Commines*. p. 396.

[32] Lewis CP. Thacker A T. *"Later medieval Chester 1230-1550: City and crown, 1350-1550." A History of the County of Chester: Volume 5 Part 1, the City of Chester: General History and Topography*. (London, Victoria County History, 2003). pp. 55-58. *British History Online*. Web. 4 January 2023. http://www.british-history.ac.uk/vch/ches/vol5/pt1/pp55-58.

[33] Ingram, Mike. Richard III Society Website. [https://richardiii.net/richard-iii-his-world/the-war-of-the-roses/the-battles/the-battle-of-bosworth/]

[34] William Catesby's Will can be found in Cunningham, Sean. *Richard III A Royal Enigma*. (London, The National Archives, 2003). p. 76.

Footnotes. Chapter Eight: Sir Andrew Trollope

[1] The rescue of Caen was in 1433. He then appears in a muster roll for 1436 that is held on the Medieval Soldier Database, https://www.medievalsoldier.org/database/. It is probable that Trollope was further employed in ensuring the security of Normandy as the Duchy saw resistance in the mid 1430s, see Evans, M. R. (1992) *Brigandage and resistance in Lancastrian Normandy: a study of the remission evidence*. Reading Medieval Studies, XVIII. pp. 103-134. ISSN 0950-3129 Available at https://centaur.reading.ac.uk/84359/.

[2] Johnson, P A. *Duke Richard of York, 1411-1460.* (Oxford, Clarendon Press, 1988). p. 186

[3] *Whethamstead's Chronicle* cited in Johnson, P A. Duke Richard of York, 1411-1460.p. 187-188.

[4] Johnson, P A. *Duke Richard of York, 1411-1460.* p. 188.

[5] Fabyan, Robert. Ellis, Henry. *The new chronicles of England and France*. p. 634.

[6] Gairdner, James *'Gregory's Chronicle: 1451-1460'* pp. 196-210.

[7] Fabyan, Robert. Ellis, Henry. *The new chronicles of England and France*. pp. 634-635.

[8] Hall, Edward. *Chronicle: The history of England.* p. 241.

[9] Payment of the Calais Garrison was far from straightforward. Nobles who held the Captaincy often used their own wealth to pay the men with grants being late to materialise.

[10] Walsingham, T., *Historia Anglicana, vol. ii.* (London, Longman, 1864)

[11] Note from the treasurer's accounts. Quoted in: Grummitt, David. *The Calais Garrison: War and Military Service in England, 1436-1558.* (Woodbridge, Boydell Press, 2008). p. 107.

[12] Riley, Henry. *Ingulph's chronicle of the abbey of Croyland.* p. 464.

[13] Wavrin, Jean quoted in Thompson, Edith. *The Wars of York and Lancaster, 1450-1485: Extracts from Blakman, Gascoigne ... the Rolls of Parliament, the Paston and Other Letters, and Various Contemporary Chronicles and Songs.* (Great Britain, D Nuut, 1892). p. 60.
[14] For example, the capture of Thomas and John Neville is noted in Gregory's chronicle at the end of the account of the battle of Blore Heath. *'Gregory's Chronicle: 1451-1460'.* pp. 196-210.
[15] Gairdner, James. *A Short English Chronicle*. p. 406.
[16] Gairdner, James. *The Paston Letters, Volume 4*. p. 58.
[17] Oxford Bibliographies provides an overview of chivalry in the Middle Ages, https://www.oxfordbibliographies.com/view/document/obo-9780199791279/obo-9780199791279-0032.xml
[18] Davies, John Silvester. *An English chronicle.* p. 108.
[19] Davies, John Silvester. *An English chronicle. p.* 108.
[20] Gairdner, James. 'Gregory's Chronicle: 1461-1469'. pp. 210-239.
[21] Ross, Charles. *Edward IV.* (London, Yale, 1998). p. 35. Gillingham, John. The Wars of the Roses. (Londong, Weidenfeld and Nicolson, 1981). p. 191.

Footnotes. Chapter Nine: Towns: Calais and York

[1] Population figures for the late medieval period are difficult to state accurately. Studies of population in the period make use of the 1377 Poll Tax returns, records from the early 16th century, and datasets based on Inquisitions Post Mortem. In general terms the population is believed to have lowered in the first half of the 15th century, rising in the second half. In 1377 London had a population of 23314, York 7248, Bristol 6345, Coventry 4817, Norwich 3952. Only 8 towns in England had a recorded population above 3000. The majority of the population

lived in a rural environment. The overall population of England in the 15th century is estimated rather than being a precise figure. Studies range in their figures but suggest that during the Wars of the Roses the population as a whole was between 2 million and 3 million.

[2] Sutton, Anne F. *Peace, Love and Unity.* Within Kleineke, Hannes, Steer, Christian. *Harlaxton Medieval Studies Volume XXIII. The Yorkist Age*. p. 124.

[3] Sutton, Anne F. *Peace, Love and Unity.* Within Kleineke, Hannes, Steer, Christian. *Harlaxton Medieval Studies Volume XXIII. The Yorkist Age*. p. 123.

[4] Attred, Lorraine. *York House Books 1461-1490. Volume One.* p. 3.

[5] Attred, Lorraine. *York House Books 1461-1490. Volume Two.* p. 689.

[6] Meek, Edward L. *The Calais Letterbook of William Lord Hastings (1477) and Late Medieval Crisis Diplomacy 1477-83.* (Donington, Richard III and Yorkist History Trust and Shaun Tyas 2017). p. 111.

[7] Attred, Lorraine. *York House Books 1461-1490. Volume One.* p. 109.

[8] Attred, Lorraine. *York House Books 1461-1490. Volume One.* p. 359.

[9] Burgess, L. A. *The Southampton Terrier of 1454.* (London, Her Majesty's Stationery Office, 1976).

[10] Attred, Lorraine. *York House Books 1461-1490. Volume Two.* p. 690.

[11] Funding of the garrison at Calais had been a crown matter from 1347 onwards. Arrangements changed in the 1470s with the Staplers taking on the financial burden in return for beneficial taxation. Under the crowns control a variety of mechanisms had been used, loans from magnates and clergy, allocation of duties collected a specific ports for the keeping of the seas and Calais defences, for example the port of Hull's revenues were for a period directed to Richard Neville, Earl of Warwick. At other times Parliamentary grants were made directly and more urgent planning, such as in 1477, required a combination of Stapler and Government investment to facilitate improved defences: see The Calais Letterbook of William Lord Hasting, letter 9a, page 103, for an example of this level of urgency.

[12] For example, the first parliament of Edward IV's reign, in November 1461, included a petition that was aimed at addressing losses incurred due to privileges enjoyed by Hanseatic merchants and a second petition urging talks with the Duke of Burgundy about mercantile matters. Copies of the petitions are included in the appendix of the parliamentary roll held online at https://www.british-history.ac.uk/no-series/parliament-rolls-medieval/november-1461

[13] Attred, Lorraine. *York House Books 1461-1490. Volume One.* p. 10.

[14] For example, in 1481 York sent Richard duke of Gloucester and others were sent a gift of money and a selection of fish, sweet wines and red wine. Attred, Lorraine. *York House Books 1461-1490. Volume Two.* p. 233. Also, see Pollard p. 335

[15] This had implications for York which had many interactions with lands held by the Duchy of Lancaster. The right of Duchy tenants to be toll free within York was asserted on 9 and 19th November 1476. Attred, Lorraine. *York House Books 1461-1490. Volume One.* p. 63.

[16] Kekewith, Margaret. Richmond, Colin. Sutton, Anne. Visser-Fuchs, Livia. Watts, John. *The Politics of Fifteenth Century England: John Vale's Book.* p. 62.

[17] Grummitt, David. *The Calais Garrison: War and Military Service in England, 1436-1558.* p. 45.

[18] Grummitt, David. *The Calais Garrison: War and Military Service in England, 1436-1558.* p. 57.

[19] Grummitt, David. *The Calais Garrison: War and Military Service in England, 1436-1558.* p. 49.

[20] Rose, Susan. *Calais: An English Town in France.* (Woodbridge, The Boydell Press, 2008). p. 40.

[21] There were some exceptions to the monopoly. Exports to Italy and the Iberian states were direct, though in the case of Italy, exports were sometimes transported overland from Calais.

[22] In 1450 the Stapler's paid a duty on goods that they sold to foreign merchants. They were also expected to assist the Captain of Calais

through extending him lines of credit for the maintenance of the garrison and defences. In the 1470s that arrangement was altered with the Staple being required to pay a set amount per annum. This minimised the risks involved in parliament having to try and raise capital quickly in times of crisis.

[23] Ordinance cited in Grummitt, David. *The Calais Garrison: War and Military Service in England, 1436-1558.* p. 64.

[24] The 1466 Act of Retainer introduced new methods of checking exports to Calais and introduced new responsibilities for both the Crown and the Staplers. Its purpose was to minimise non payment of duties. An overview of the contents of the Act and its implications can be found on British History Online at https://www.british-history.ac.uk/london-record-soc/vol27/xi-xlvii

[25] Baker, Patrick S. *"Sanctuary and Fortress: Calais' Role in the Yorkist Triumph." Medieval Warfare*, vol. 5, no. 3, 2015, pp. 15–17. *JSTOR*, https://www.jstor.org/stable/48578450. Accessed 21 Jan. 2023.

[26] Sir Thomas Kyriell had served Henry V and Henry VI. First serving in the 1415 Agincourt campaign he went on to act as captain of several castles in Lancastrian Normandy, before holding a command in the ill-fated Battle of Formigny. He had also played a role in repelling the French at Sandwich in 1457 and was one of the senior captains of the garrison in Calais. Like men such as Richard Woodville and Andrew Trollope his service was largely for the Lancastrian regime, so whilst his summary execution is bloodlust on the part of the young Prince Edward, his fate may well have been sealed by virtue of the fact that the Lancastrian army at St Albans in 1461 contained those men who had joined the Lancastrian forces at Ludford Bridge in 1459.

[27] Richard 3rd Duke of York's letter to the citizens of Shrewsbury in 1452 is quoted in Giles, John Allen. *The Chronicles of the White Rose of York*. p. XI.

[28] Gairdner, James. *The Paston Letters, Volume 3*. p. 126.

[29] Fabyan, Robert. Ellis, Henry. *The new chronicles of England and*

France. p. 634.

[30] Santiuste, David. *Edward IV and the Wars of the Roses. Pen and Sword Military. Chapter Two.* Via Erenow [https://erenow.net/postclassical/edwardivandthewarsoftheroses/5.php]

[31] For further details of the raid on Sandwich see https://thewarsoftheroses.co.uk/raid-on-sandwich-15-january-1460/

[32] *Kentish Memorial*, 1460. The full manifesto can be found at https://thewarsoftheroses.co.uk/kentish-memorial-1460/

[33] The date of the battle is sometimes given as 26 July 1469. Northamptonshire Battlefield Society have researched the matter extensively and have determined that it took place two days earlier, on 24 July 1469. For further details see: https://northantsbattles.com/edgecote-1469/

[34] *Hearne's Fragment, Chapter 16.* https://thewarsoftheroses.co.uk/hearnes-fragment-full-text/

[35] The Angers Agreement is a shortened name for 'The Manner and guiding of the Earl of Warwick at Angers' the text of which can be read here https://thewarsoftheroses.co.uk/angers-agreement/. The declaration for King Henry VI was made at Calais in August 1470, that can be read here https://thewarsoftheroses.co.uk/proclamation-for-king-henry-vi-issued-august-1470-by-the-earl-of-warwick/

[36] Rose, Susan. *Calais: An English Town in France.* p. 89.

[37] Scoble, Andrew, R. *Memoirs of Phillipe de Commines.* p. 184.

[38] Scoble, Andrew, R. *Memoirs of Phillipe de Commines.* p. 196.

[39] Scoble, Andrew, R. *Memoirs of Phillipe de Commines.* p. 188.

[40] Grummitt, David. *The Calais Garrison: War and Military Service in England, 1436-1558.* p. 13.

[41] Scoble, Andrew, R. *Memoirs of Phillipe de Commines.* p. 198.

[42] Appointments to key positions within Calais, the Pale and other fortifications within the region are outlined in Grummitt, David. *The Calais Garrison: War and Military Service in England, 1436-1558.* pp.

68-70.

[43] Grummitt, David. *The Calais Garrison: War and Military Service in England, 1436-1558.* p. 142.

[44] Meek, Edward L. *The Calais Letterbook of William Lord Hastings (1477). p.* 107.

[45] Meek, Edward L. *The Calais Letterbook of William Lord Hastings (1477). p.* 105.

[46] Grummitt, David. *William, Lord Hastings, the Calais Garrison and the Politics of Yorkist England*. Ricardian Online [http://www.thericardian.online/downloads/Ricardian/12-153/03.pdf] p. 269

[47] Ibid, page 270

[48] Pollard, A.J. *North-Eastern England during the Wars of the Roses*. pp. 40-43.

[49] Kleineke, Hannes, Steer, Christian. *Harlaxton Medieval Studies Volume XXIII. The Yorkist Age*. p. 95.

[50] Pollard, A.J. *North-Eastern England during the Wars of the Roses*. p.145.

[51] Pollard, A.J. *North-Eastern England during the Wars of the Roses*. p. 167.

[52] Pollard, A.J. *North-Eastern England during the Wars of the Roses*. p. 71.

[53] Pollard, A.J. *North-Eastern England during the Wars of the Roses*. p. 48. Plague deaths were particularly high in 1466, 1471 and 1479.

[54] Childs, Dr. Wendy R. *The Customs Accounts of Hull 1453-1490.* (Yorkshire Archaeological Society, 1986). Also see Pollard, A.J. *North-Eastern England during the Wars of the Roses*. pp. 71-74.

[55] Pollard, A.J. *North-Eastern England during the Wars of the Roses*. p. 79.

[56] In 1496 the venetian ambassador noted that York seemed as though it was on the border with Scotland, so deep were raids into English territory at that time. The threat of a Scottish invasion never went

away in the 15th century, it simply become or less likely.

[57] Attred, Lorraine. *York House Books 1461-1490. Volume One.* p. 570.

[58] Pollard, A.J. *North-Eastern England during the Wars of the Roses*. p. 260.

[59] Whilst the 'Let York overlook York' banner is legend that may or not have happened, the placing of the paper crown is noted in Polydor Virgil's account.

[60] The records for 1460 and 1461 have not survived in their entirety so it is possible that evidence has been lost. However, there is no mention of dissention in other contemporary sources such as the Chronicles, many of which were Yorkist leaning and presumably would have noted that people within York were Yorkists. Nor do the Paston Letters make any reference to any pro-Yorkist or anti-Lancastrian feeling.

[61] Chroniclers suggest that the numbers killed were in the region of 28000. Modern historians suggest that the likely number of fatalities would be far smaller than this. See the Towton Battlefield Archaeology Project Website for an example of the way that some modern historians are trying to establish a more accurate death toll: http://towtonbattle.free.fr/index.php/re-interpretation/

[62] Gairdner, James. *The Paston Letters, Volume 3*. pp. 266-268.

[63] Both quotes are found in Giles, John Allen. *The Chronicles of the White Rose of York.* p. 110.

[64] Giles, John Allen. *The Chronicles of the White Rose of York.* p. 112.

[65] Giles, John Allen. *The Chronicles of the White Rose of York.* p. 122.

[66] Bruce, John. *Historie of the arrivall of Edward IV*. p. 32.

[67] Attred, Lorraine. *York House Books 1461-1490. Volume One.* p. 283.

[68] Richard Duke of Gloucester's letter to York was dispatched from London on 10 June 1483. It stated: *"Right trusty and well-beloved ... we heartily pray you to come unto us in London as speedily as possible after the sight of this letter with as many well-armed men as possible, to aid and assist us against the Queen, her blood and other adherents*

and affinity who intend to murder and utterly destroy us and our cousin, the Duke of Buckingham and the old royal blood of this realm".

[69] Attred, Lorraine. *York House Books 1461-1490. Volume One.* pp. 284-286.

[70] Sir Clement Markham was the first to make this assertion.

[71] There is only one entry, other than attendance lists, on any subject other than King Richard or Prince Edward in the York records from late June 1483 to Mid-September 1483. The exception was a gift of Venison to York from the Earl of Northumberland, which in itself may have been intended for the reception of King Richard III. These records are in Attred, Lorraine. *York House Books 1461-1490. Volume One.* pp. 286-293.

[72] Attred, Lorraine. *York House Books 1461-1490. Volume One.* pp. 414-415.

[73] Attred, Lorraine. *York House Books 1461-1490. Volume One.* p. 366.

[74] Measures against pestilence (plague) were recorded in the city records on 16 August 1485. Attred, Lorraine. *York House Books 1461-1490. Volume One.* p. 367.

[75] Attred, Lorraine. *York House Books 1461-1490. Volume One.* pp. 368-369.

[76] Attred, Lorraine. *York House Books 1461-1490. Volume One.* p. 371.

[77] Attred, Lorraine. *York House Books 1461-1490. Volume One.* p. 381.

[78] Attred, Lorraine. *York House Books 1461-1490. Volume One.* p. 379.

Index

Printed in Great Britain
by Amazon

25049989R00205